Chisholm
Family Heritage

The Richard Henry "R.H." & Hardina Taylor Chisholm Family

ZENNA CHISHOLM SNOWDEN

Dana S. Chisholm (ed.)

TRAIL MEDIA

Chisholm Family Heritage
Copyright © 2018 Dana S. Chisholm

Trail Media, Publishing
ChisholmTrailMedia.com
ChisholmFamilyFoundation.org
https://www.facebook.com/trailmediaLLC
https://www.facebook.com/ChisholmFamilyFoundation
https://www.facebook.com/groups/ChisholmFamily
www.facebook.com/groups/ClintonTexas

Printed in the United States of America
All rights reserved
ISBN-13: 978-0692675380 (Trail Media)
ISBN-10: 0692675388

Cover art:
Danielle Keltner of Dannie Ann Photography & Designs
dannieannphotodesigns.com/

Interior design:
Dana S. Chisholm
Facebook.com/DanaS.ChisholmAuthor

CONTENTS

DEDICATION

*I am thankful for my courageous men and women ancestors whom I have learned
to love and respect through my research of them.*
Zenna Chisholm Snowden

For Our Children

The Richard Henry "R.H." Chisholm (b.1799) and Hardina Taylor Chisholm (b. 1812) family
has a long and rich heritage rooted in Texas and American history. The stories passed down include
tales of blood feuds, cattle trails, Texas Revolution, and rich military records of service from Indian
Wars, Civil War, WWII heroes and prisoner of war through Vietnam and Enduring Freedom today.
Chisholm's set off for the Gold Rush and blazing trails in the Grand Canyon, founding of the town
of Clinton, TX in the early 1800's, cowboys and families of faith…the Chisholm family heritage is
indeed rich.

With trail blazers, war heroes, pioneers, politicians and warm homes where everyone is welcome
faith, family and country are central to the Chisholm family heritage.

One relative, Zenna Chisholm Snowden (9/15/1921 – 2/6/2014), worked tirelessly researching
the Chisholm family tree – before internet searches, social media heritage sites, or heritage tourism,
she did it the hard old fashion way - and shared her research with the family as her gift of love in
time, talents, and treasures. She was in her 80's and learning the computer and new software – a
pioneer just like the ancestors she was getting to know. She passed away at 92 years old in 2014. This
book contains the Chisholm Family Heritage of the R.H. and Hardina Taylor Chisholm family for
nine generations based on the research of Zenna Chisholm Snowden. She would have loved to have
seen it in print for the entire family to enjoy. With the added work of Chisholm family members
Sharon and David Wakefield, Allie Holden, Christen Morris, Clarence Chambers, Raquel Lindaas,
Wayne Taylor, and Dana S. Chisholm, we hope to pass these stories to generations to come.

*What you leave behind is not what is engraved in stone monuments,
but what is woven into the lives of others.*
Pericles 523 bce
Left on Zenna's Memorial page by Michele Goza

ZENNA CHISHOLM SNOWDEN

ACKNOWLEDGEMENTS

On a family trip through Arizona, me (Dana Chisholm) a young mom of two boys about four and eight years old, with my brother and his wife and sister and her husband and kids and our parents, we stopped for a visit with extended family. I had been doing some research into our family history. In the 1990's and into the new millennium heritage website didn't really exist, certainly weren't popular and prolific. Research had to be done by visiting courthouses and libraries, talking to family, finding old journals or the family Bible.

"There's someone here you need to meet." My dad said. "She knows all the old stories." It was Zenna. The entire family and extended relations there that day pulled up chairs and we sat in a circle listening to Zenna and her stories. I grabbed paper and started writing as fast as I could. I couldn't keep everything she was saying straight in my head unless I wrote it down and could see it.

"You mean the husband and wife were also step-brother and sister? Because the two kids married, then one each of their parents died and the surviving parents married each other?" the questions were endless and a relationship was born.

My branch of the family all lived in San Diego. My moms side of the family all lived in Bakersfield. But, my dad's side of the family, the Chisholm side, were scattered around California and Arizona and our history stretched back to Texas, although at that time I had no idea. At that time just glimpses and stories. Zenna said she was working on documenting all her findings. She had reached out and started working with the Mormon Church who kept extensive records for religious purposes. They were the best and only resource with the data we all needed. She invested in the program they offered for family research. Zenna was relentless and determined.

We emailed back and forth – me always asking questions, clarifying, adding more detail to my own understanding of our family tree. Zenna was always patient with my questions, and I promised her I would someday write a book – maybe many books! The stories were too unbelievable some of them! They could be fiction or at least a really amazing plot line. Zenna always encouraged me in my writing. But, a single mom raising two young boys, life always got in the way. Life never got in Zenna's way. She was steadfast.

Zenna was lighthearted and loved the Lord, and also relentless in her pursuit of history. She was in her 70's and 80's making trips, going to courthouses, making connections with experts, patiently answering questions of the younger generations always bugging her (like me) and learning the computer right into her 90's. If ever the word "amazing" could be used to describe a strong woman it was Zenna. She completed her work and was not stingy with it. She put everything on CD's and mailed the discs to any family member who was interested. All we had to do was download the Mormon Church special program that she had loaded on the disc's and then we would have access to all she had accumulated. It was extensive.

For years Zenna checked in on me and we talked about making a trip back to Clinton, Texas – the town RH Chisholm had founded. Zenna had made trips, but as time marched forward, more and more Zenna said her health wouldn't allow her to make the trip again. My mom passed away in 2013, Zenna checked in on me. And Zenna called me the night before her own surgery – making sure I had all the information I needed, and where all her data was. Zenna passed away in 2014 and in 2015 I decided to finally make the trip we had always talked about. I went to the RH Chisholm land in Texas and lived there a month, soaking it all in, asking more questions, collecting more data, reading Zenna's book and seeing for myself – "boots on the ground" all that Zenna had written.

In April 2016 we had a family reunion in old Clinton, TX and a small group of extended family walked our heritage, stood where they stood. I met the other heritage hunters in the family. Sharon and David Wakefield live in Northern California and made the trip out to Texas to walk the trails. Sharon shared her father the WWII POW with us in his writing and stories and in her own beautiful writing that Zenna included in her research. Sharon works tirelessly preserving our heritage, helping collect every collectors book on the Chisholm family that exists and compiling it in old Clinton, TX so everyone will have access to them one day. Sharon exemplifies the Chisholm's of today carried forward from lost pioneer days having lived through the major water battles in California and the life and loss of the family farm. Her stories are books waiting to be published all their own.

Allie Holden – in the short time I was able to spend with her – was the quiet strength seen in so many Chisholm's. No matter what hardships are thrown at her and her family, they not only survive, but thrive. Her attention to detail impressed me when she created a family tree – a physical mapping out of the family – so large it towered above us when placed for display. But, it wasn't that she created the large visual (that helps folks like me who are visual learners and still struggle to get it all straight) but that Allie cited each item, each picture, each story, making it easier for all of us to document and track our heritage. And Allie never gave up from our trip to Clinton, TX. She stayed in touch via email, shared her findings with others and kept the fires fueled.

Christen Morris is a Chisholm rancher in Northern California who, although much younger than me, I look up to. She is out roping cattle, raising her girls, volunteering in her community on more charities than I can keep up with, and is always sure to share the stories and heritage with her girls – passing it forward.

Wayne Taylor, my fourth cousin once removed, is from our Taylor side of the family, Hardina Taylor Chisholm. I only ever met Wayne through email and we spoke on the phone a few times, but he was an encourager. He documented and worked on the Taylor Family Heritage book and gave me many tips on the very practical of converting Zenna's research into book form. We recently lost Milburn Wayne who passed away. Wayne got me…he would often "spell it out" for me – putting the answers to my questions in charts I could see. "How are we related?" was answered with a chart.

Josiah Taylor – Hepzibeth Luker	Josiah Taylor – Hepzibeth Luker
Hardina Taylor - Richard Henry Chisholm	William Riley Taylor - Elizabeth Tumlinson
Glenn Thornton Chisholm – Jane P Fore	Joseph Taylor – Elizabeth Ann Silcriggs
George Langford Chisholm – Mary Magdalene Willliams	Charles Leslie Taylor – Minnie Alice Yeater
Stanford Dalton Chisholm – Elizabeth Nadine Simmons	Milburn Lee Taylor – Ann Theresa Jordan
Boyd Langford Chisholm – Anita Jean Ewing	Milburn Wayne Taylor
Dana Suzanne Chisholm (You)	

Raquel Lindaas is an actual professional in heritage research. Our family is lucky to have her. She coordinates DNA testing for our family and finds the most interesting little facts that lead to another that lead to another. "Rocky" is always available to answer a question or set me straight on some facts and fill in with rich details – she is so generous and reminds me so much of Zenna.

Clarence Chambers is the big bear of our family and the keeper of all our knowledge, stories, and the rifle of Daniel Fore Chisholm. Clarence shares documents and stories in the family social media group and when we can get him in person, he shares stories I could listen to all day and night. What a treasure to find this relative and add him to our family collective.

One other very important person to our family history may not be a relative by blood, but part of the family by passion for the history of the RH Chisholm land. Pastor Terry Brown (and wife Barbara) have been a huge support and wealth of knowledge of the history of the town of Clinton and the history of the entire area during the 1800's. Pastor Terry regularly shares RH Chisholm's town with history buffs and treasure hunters so people are still enjoying the finds of Civil War Era relics even in 2018 and 2019 and beyond. His love for the people in the area where Clinton once stood extends our Chisholm family into the entire community that surrounds Clinton, and I think that is the very thing that RH Chisholm intended as I read Zenna's research.

From all these amazing people there may be many, many books in the future. I would love to read them all. But, for now, this is Zenna's book. This is the book we always talked about. This is the book of her painstaking research of nine generations of Chisholm history. This is our start forward by looking back. From here we can take it and keep researching and sharing our findings and stories.

I have not changed Zenna's research if we have since learned something new but added an asterisk if there is especially pertinent information. I have also added some information on folks who have passed, and hope to do more of that in future versions. I also used Zenna "Chisholm" Snowden as her name because she signed per personal stories and notes in her research this way...although once when we were talking I referred to her as "Zenna Chisholm Snowden" and she said, "well, you know my legal middle name is not Chisholm" and we laughed and said that might not be her middle name, but it is at her heart and center of her life. Other than these few notes this is Zenna's book and research, a gift to us all.

Please join our family discussion on social media and add to our story.

Zenna's work isn't exhaustive. It is a start. This first printing will be as much as Zenna was able to accumulate in her lifetime, and as family members add information and see lines that can be expanded we can work to publish an updated version in the coming years. So, please join us!

Note: The "HC" brand at the top of each chapter is the Richard Henry Chisholm brand
        The "TC" brand at the top of each chapter is the Glenn Thornton Chisholm brand

Note: The DVD Zenna produced has a great number of pictures. In future editions of this book we will add additional documents and as many photos as possible.

RESEARCH AND LEGEND

Zenna used a program, PAF5 https://www.familysearch.org/paf/?icid=home-PAF-Retire
Personal Ancestral File (PAF)
Website notice: Downloads and support for PAF end **JULY 15, 2013**

"Advances in technology, strong alternatives from third parties, and the need to focus on the latest FamilySearch initiatives have diminished the need for PAF as part of the FamilySearch offering."

REGISTER NUMBERING EXAMPLE

The following example shows the most common (excluding Henry numbers) numbering conventions which can appear in the register report. Your register may print some or all of these numbers and symbols depending upon which report options you select.

--------------- Example Only ----------------

1. **John**^{3} **Smith**^{6} [17] (Robert^2, Scott^1) born 17 Feb 1849 in New York, NY, died 3 Jan 1930^7. He married 30 Jun 1870 **Mary Jones**, daughter of Albert and Samantha Wiggins.

Their children were:
+ 2 i **Bobby**^{4} [43]
   3 ii **Susan**^{4} [44], born 25 Dec 1871.

_____

^{6}Smith Family Bible, p. 2
^{7}U.S. Social Security Death Index

Explanation:
John^3 John Smith is a third generation ancestor (^{3}).
Smith^6 Citation^6 referring to source of information.
[17]   Record Identification Number (RIN)
died 3 Jan 1930^7 Citation^7 referring to source of information for this event.
(Robert^2, Scott^1)   Lineage: John is son of Robert. Robert is son of Scott.

+ 2 i **Bobby**^{4} [43]
     Bobby had issue (+). His paragraph number is two (2), he is the first (i) child in the family, and of the fourth (^{4}) generation. Bobby's RIN number is [43].
--------------- Example Only ----------------

For questions additions or corrections please find the family group and/or email
https://www.facebook.com/groups/ChisholmFamily
Facebook.com/DanaS.ChisholmAuthor
Admin@ChisholmFamilyFoundation.org

HC

CHAPTER ONE

FIRST Generation

In what we call the early days, the Chisholm's never found their existence dull.
As a youngster and even older, you think about your big robust pioneer ancestors, tall and handsome
who helped conquer the west. Now I long to see a picture of Richard in his younger days. At least Hardina Taylor thought he
was a prize, they married and raised four children one of whom helped to bring many of us into this world.
Zenna Chisholm Snowden

1. **Richard Henry Chisholm** "Uncle Dick" was born in 1799 in Georgia, USA. He died on 8 Apr 1855 in Old Clinton Ranch, Clinton, DeWitt, Texas, USA. He was buried in Old Clinton Cemetery, Clinton, DeWitt, Texas, USA. He married on 7 Oct 1827 in Texas **Hardina Taylor**, born 1812 in Clark County, Georgia; died 1853/55 in DeWitt County, Texas, USA, daughter of Josiah Taylor and Hephzibeth Luker.

Richard Henry Chisholm

The earliest record that I have found of Richard H. Chisholm is in the 1826 Atascosita Census of Texas. He was an unmarried 27-year-old blacksmith from Georgia. The following information is from the "DeWitt Colony Biographies of Texas." The people who knew Richard or heard the stories about him said that he came to Texas with a sister, Lourena, and a brother, Richard A. Chisholm, and that they came from Scotland. Since we have been unable to find any records before the 1826 census, we do not know how many generations back it may have been that our ancestors came from Scotland.

After the War of 1812, the East had become over populated and expansion West was inherent. Treaties with the Indians had opened new lands for settlement and the serious economic depression after the war caused westward migration to increase rapidly. Although Texas was still a part of Mexico, many American settlers moved there because land could be bought for 12 ½ cents an acre and in the United States it was selling for $1.25 an acre and more. Mexico encouraged the settling of Texas by giving land grants to certain individuals to form colonies. The leaders of these colonies were called Empressrio.

In the DeWitt County Land Records, Richard (Dick) H. Chisholm received a sito of land on the west bank of the Guadalupe River in February 1829. He was registered as having a family of four. Since he was married October 7, 1827, it seems logical that his sister and brother were living with him as a part of his household. His first son, Thornton, was not born until 1831.

His sister, Lourena, married James Hallmullen on March 15, 1849. On a trip to Goliad for supplies, she mysteriously disappeared and was never found. Brother, Richard A. Chisholm, was mentioned in some of the records but I have not found the date of his death. When Thornton was settling the estate of his father, they were also dividing the property that Richard A. had owned. His holdings were given to the six children of Thornton.

In the year of 1828, Richard H. was admitted by Empressrio DeWitt Green to settle the land of his colony in accordance with the State Colonization Law. On September 6, 1831, Richard received title and full ownership of a league of land on the southwest margin of the Guadalupe River.

In the 1970's when I was researching our family history, I became well acquainted by mail with Louise Robertson, who lived in San Antonio. She made many trips to Cuero to search records for me. On August 7, 1970, she wrote to say she had found where Richard H. Chisholm had received a Bounty Land Grant for 1280 acres on December 7, 1838 and that he had sold the certificate. She did not say when he sold it, but it is another interesting item on how he bought and sold land.

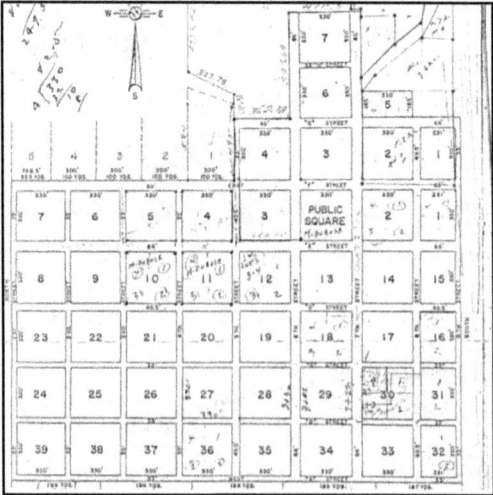

Survey of the town of Clinton

Most of the following information is from the "Handbook of Texas." As a cattle rancher, Richard registered his brand HC in Gonzales County in 1832, one of the first to register a brand in Texas. On October

2

7,1846, he and his son, Thornton, both registered their brands in Clinton, DeWitt County. Richard decided to live on the banks of the Guadalupe River where he started the Town of Clinton, named for Empressrio DeWitt's son. He and DeWitt must have become very good friends. He soon opened a store and a horse driven gristmill that was used by settlers from as far away a Myersville.

On January 1, 1847, Richard rented land from Joseph Tomlinson and Mr. Neill for a ferry landing on the east side of the Guadalupe River for three years. Rent for the land was $75 payable in equal portions of years rent. The document was recorded before the clerk, James Smith.

The founders of the Town of Clinton wanted to be an important part of the new area. Richard gave land for the town center and five acres for the courthouse and jail. He and his wife, Hardina, made a sworn statement donating the timberland for the town of Clinton. After several locations, the Courthouse finally moved to Clinton on November 28, 1850 and remained there until the 1870s. On the 27th of July, R. H. Chisholm did subscribe to and take the oath of the office as Magistrate for the Precinct No.1 for DeWitt Co. State of Texas done at the office of V.V. Poinsett.

Along with all the politics and other enterprises, Richard was also a blacksmith. He cast the first cannonball in the Texas Revolution. This is from the

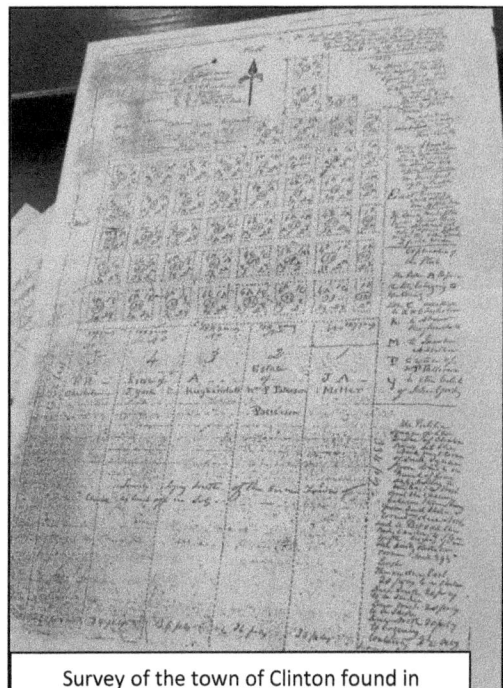

Survey of the town of Clinton found in Cuero, TX Historical Records 2015

book: "Indian Wars and Pioneers of Texas." He served in the Texas Revolution as Capt. Richard (Dick) Chisholm. According to the 1850 Federal Census of DeWitt County, Richard was worth $15,000. That was no doubt a nice sum in those days.

The Town of Clinton prospered and became a good sized community until the war was over. Traditional interpretation says, bad times contributed to the notorious Sutton-Taylor feud which started on Christmas Eve 1868 and ended in Clinton in 1875. The feud developed into the longest and most bloody in Texas History. Many residents moved away. The most significant cause of the town's decline was the extension in 1875 of the Gulf Western Texas and Pacific Railway to Cuero.

When I visited Clinton in the 1960s, you would have never known there had ever been a town there. There was a house that had been built by our cousin, Fannie G. Chisholm[1], and, of course, the Old Chisholm Cemetery was close by. Fannie and some of her family are buried there. Fannie was very dedicated in researching the history of our Chisholm ancestors.

One very important thing I learned from Brice Willis of Safford, Arizona, was that he had found, in some of the court house records, that Richard's middle name was Henry.

The author, Uncle Nathan Boone Burkett, in his memoirs, "Early Days in Texas" was a good friend of Capt. Dick Chisholm. He relates a story of an encounter of Richard's with Indians from which he escaped unharmed.

Robert Hall in his memoirs, "Life of Robert Hall" in the "DeWitt Colony Biographies" related this somewhat exaggerated version of Burkett's story.

> About the time the Comanches were trying to make a treaty with the Texans they spared another man's life. Old man Chisholm was a blacksmith at Old Washington. He was a funny little old man, and regarded by everyone as the ugliest and most harmless man in the world. He was at Old Washington first, and was a great favorite with Gen. Houston and all other prominent men. He was a little dried-up old man and would not have weighed much over a hundred pounds; but his muscles were of iron and his sinews of steel, while he had the heart of a lion. After the capital had been moved from Old Washington, old man Chisholm concluded he would go out west, where there was some chance of having a little fun occasionally. He had some fun. He was riding his old pony along the trail headed for Col. King's ranch, when suddenly looking around, he saw an army of warriors almost at his heels. He knew his old pony could not run, but he spurred him into a gallop and managed to keep ahead of his pursuers for two or three hundred yards. The warriors rode up on him and dragged him off of his horse and then cut his saddle off and threw it on the ground.
>
> They began to jabber among themselves, little dreaming that he understood their language. All at once they began to clap their hands and laugh. One had said, "D--n him, he is too ugly to kill.' Another said 'He is too ugly to eat; he would give an Indian the belly-ache.' They danced around him and laughed a great deal. Finally they put him back on his pony, bareback, with his face towards the animal's tail, and then two led the pony and the balance set up a shout and whipped him with quirts all the way to camp. When they got into camp they all surrounded him and laughed as if they would kill themselves. They got an old silk plug hat and put it on him, and then they would pry open his eyes and blow in them and ask him how he came to be so awful ugly. Some said, 'Maybe he is the devil'. The squaws and the little Indians stuck arrows in him and said to him, 'They won't hurt you; you are too ugly.' After they had exhausted themselves with laughter, the chief told the warrior that they

---

[1] Chisholm Hurst, Fannie G. (1966). *The Four State Chisholm Trail.* Munguia Printers.

might decide what should be done with the old man. There were twenty-five Comanches and fifteen Wacos in camp. The Wacos wanted to burn him, but the Comanches voted to spare his life. They still jokingly said he was too ugly to kill, but the real fact was the Comanches were becoming alarmed at the growing power of Texas, and they were afraid of being driven entirely out of the country and they wanted to make a treaty of peace. They had another frolic around old man Chisholm; the squaws pulled his nose, and the boys blew in his eyes. Then they told him to 'get on his pony and vamoose to h--l, where he belonged.

As youngsters some of us were told the following story, I do not know if it is a part of the above story. We were told that, "Richard H. was once captured by the Indians and since he had bright red hair they tried to wash the red color out. When they could not remove the color, they let him go saying he was too brave to die and too poor to eat. He was raw boned and homely."

We can't leave this tale as an ending to our story. In what we call the early days, the Chisholm's never found their existence dull. As a youngster and even older, you think about your big robust pioneer ancestors, tall and handsome who helped conquer the west. Now I long to see a picture of Richard in his younger days. At least Hardina Taylor thought he was a prize, they married and raised four children one of whom helped to bring many of us into this world.

One of the many good deeds of Richard H. Chisholm was: in 1848 he was appointed guardian to Pleasant L. and Bartley S. Gilbert, the young children of Sarah E. and Jasper L. Gilbert. Jasper L. Gilbert filed a petition to be appointed Guardian to the minor heirs of him and his wife, who were under the age of fourteen. Documents found in the DeWitt County filed September 13, 1847 in the Sarah E. Gilbert file gave the Guardianship to Richard H. Chisholm. It takes a good and honest person to be entrusted with someone's children and to manage their money.

I am thankful for my courageous men and women ancestors whom I have learned to love and respect through my research of them.

2007 Sept 3 – Sitio is a Spanish term meaning space or parcel. In early Texas, the term referred to the amount of land required for ranching horses, mules and cattle. A sitio or league is 6.8 square miles. http://www.oldcardboard.com/lsj/texians/measures.htm

Zenna Chisholm Snowden
November 2006

Richard Henry "R.H." married Hardina Taylor daughter of Josiah Taylor and Hephzibeth Luker on 7 Oct 1827 in Texas. Hardina was born in 1812 in Clark County, Georgia, USA. She died in 1853/1855 in DeWitt County, Texas, USA.

Richard and Hardina had the following children:

+ 2 M i. **Glenn Thornton Chisholm** was born in 1831. He died in Mar 1868.

+ 3 M ii. **Bradford A Chisholm** was born in Apr 1835. He died in 1913.

+ 4 F iii. **Maryann Chisholm** was born in 1842. She died about 1876.

  5 M iv. **Richard A Chisholm** was born in 1850. He died on 24 Dec 1868.

   *Richard was killed along with cousin Buck Taylor in Clinton by Bill Sutton and Dock White. (From Fannie G. Chisholm book)

Sources for Richard Henry Chisholm

Chisholm Family History of Richard Henry. Richard Henry was listed in the Atascosita Census of 1826. The family was listed in the Texas Census of 7 Oct 1850

Many articles were written of his activities in The Hand Book of Texas. Published by the State Historical Association, in Austin Texas in 1952.

1847 Oct 25 - Richard H Chisholm's hand written paper for rental of land for ferry.

Life: Ibid., 1847 Oct 25 - Richard H Chisholm ferry rental paper typed for easier reading.

Life: Ibid., 1848 Oct 29 - Richard H. Chisholm Bond for ferry.

Notes for Hardina Taylor

The 1826 Anacosita Texas census has Hardina born in 1812.

The 1850 census has her born in 1804.

I received an e-mail from a friend, Judith Alef, posing this question. Have you ever heard that Hardina was named after the surname Hardin/Harden. It is a big mystery because her mother's sisters also named their girls that which leads me to think that Luranah, Hepzebeth's mother was a Cherokee Harden with a little Smith thrown in also..(Interesting)

Sources for Hardina Taylor

Life: Taylor Family History received from Luther Hill Jr.in 1970. (Newsletter of Kimble County Historical Survey Committee Junction City Texas May/June 1967). 1 also received information from Louise B Robertson of San Antonio, Texas on the Taylors in the1970s.

See Epilogue for more on Clinton, TX

TC

CHAPTER TWO

SECOND Generation

I am sure all members of the family had their duties but she was their stability.
My Dad said his grandmother, Jane, was a very religious woman. Their home was always open to all who came there.
Zenna Chisholm Snowden
August 2007

2. **Glenn Thornton Chisholm**   (Richard Henry) was born in 1831 (*or 1828) in Old Chisholm Ranch, Clinton, DeWitt, Texas, USA. He died in Mar 1868 in Burnet, Texas, USA. The cause of death was Breast Chain on wagon broke and wagon rolled over him.. He was buried in Burnet, Texas, USA.

Glenn Thornton Chisholm

Glenn Thornton Chisholm, son of Richard Henry and Hardina Taylor Chisholm, was born in 1831 on the Old Chisholm Ranch in the Town of Clinton founded by his father. Fannie G. Chisholm tells in her book, "Four State Chisholm Trail," that Thornton was only eight years old when he started working with cattle on the Ranch. They worked long, hard hours. As a youngster, Thornton learned to ride and rope as well as the next man. Even though he carried a heavy work load, his mother saw that he attended a little country school several miles from home.

While growing into manhood, he also helped his father operate the first ferry across the Guadalupe River which ran along the town site of Clinton, Texas. Since his father was very involved in politics and getting Clinton as the County Seat, Thornton had to take on

4   THE FOUR STATE CHISHOLM TRAIL

Thornton Chisholm, the son of R. H. Chisholm and wife Hardeney Taylor, of DeWitt County, Texas. The founder of the famous Chisholm Trail.

many of the ranching chores.

His brother, Richard A.. had bought several pieces of land shortly before he died in 1850. Thornton and brother, Bradford, had to settle his estate. The estate was divided among the six children of Thornton and Jane. In those days, it was not as big a hassle as it is today to settle estates. They were personal friends with all the judges and knew everyone and trust was a thing of the day.

> *Note: this is confusing – it is unknown if Richard A. was RH's brother who died, or Thornton's brother who died, as the Richard A. who is Thornton's brother was *born* in 1850 and died 1868. This needs further research to clarify – Dana S. Chisholm

Thornton's mother and father had died in 1855. Land had been bought on Coletto Creek by Thornton's father, Richard (RH), on February 7, 1855. He delivered a down payment on a certain tract of land situated in DeWitt in DeWitt County, Texas. The property was located on the stage road leading from Victoria to San Antonio about 12 miles southeast of Clinton. Richard (RH) died on April 8, 1855 only two months after he had purchased the property. Thornton, as administrator of his father estate, sold the property of two hundred and sixty acres for the sum of two thousand and fifteen dollars on May 5, 1855.

In 1852 Thornton married Jane P. Fore, he was 21 and she was 14. They married on the Ranch in Clinton.

The Thornton Chisholm home was the center of hospitality where all friends and strangers were welcome. One night a stranger came and ask to stay all night. Thornton said, "He was afraid he could not let him stay all night." The fellow was very surprised and said, "He had heard that the Chisholm house was always open to strangers." " Well," Thornton said, "I can't let you stay all night but you are welcome to stay the rest of the night."

Another time, a man came and spent a long time with Thornton. He overstayed his welcome and Thornton was very tired of him and tried in several ways to get him to leave. One day in a joking way Thornton said to him, "You take the corner of a red handkerchief and I will take the other." The fellow thinking he was serious said, "Give me one of your good horses and ten dollars and I will go." Thornton gave him what he wanted and was not bothered with him anymore.

The King and Queen of Spain introduced longhorn cattle to Texas through the first Spanish settlers. Over the vast Texas plains, roamed great herds of lanky longhorns.

Wayne Gard in his book, "The Chisholm Trail," said;

> After the Civil War, 5 million longhorns roamed the Texas grasslands. Under a loose form of ownership, they ran wild as 'Texas Steers.' Before 1865 the longhorns were raised mostly for their hides and tallow. When northern and city dwellers began demanding more beef, the cattlemen started to look for some way to get their cattle to market. The steer that could be bought for three or four dollars in Texas was worth ten times as much in New York.

> The long drive was organized from Texas to the Canadian border, where stretched endless miles of unfenced plains; therefore, the cattlemen moved their herds through these great open spaces. Each spring, cattle ready for market were separated from the rest of the herd at a roundup. Those tame enough to be rounded up were called mestenas and those too wild for human control were called cimarrones. They started north under a boss with a gang of cowboys and a cook. The cattle were driven slowly across unoccupied lands toward a railroad shipping point. Routes were determined by the supply of water and grass. Probably the most famous of these was The Chisholm Trial.[2]

The Chisholm family had thousands of longhorn cattle. The ranch was flat and dotted with Live Oak Motes. It was said that on one roundup of Thornton's the cattle they were lined from Clear Creek to the Chisholm Ranch which was about five miles. Many cowboys were required to move such a large herd.

Thornton's brand was Quarter Circle TC and was recorded in Clinton, Texas on October 7, 1846. At this same time, his father registered his brand HC in DeWitt County.

Michael Power Hill told this story to Fannie G. Chisholm and she put it in her book: "The Four State Chisholm Trail".

> My father was on the first Trail Drive. His trail boss was Thornton Chisholm, all the cowboys just called him "Chisholm". We use to visit in their home there in Clinton. They had a large family, girls, good looking ones, and I shall never forget the big table and long benches they had, and table covered with the best food, on a Sunday evening we would have some of the best good old singing. It just did your heart good, one of the girls would

---

[2] Gard, W. (1979). *The Chisholm Trail*. University of Oklahoma Press.

play the organ, and the boys would play guitar and fiddle. There was never a stranger that came to their house that didn't leave full of good food.[3]

I had a good time with the two boys, the oldest was George Chisholm, the other one was Daniel Chisholm, we called them by their nick name, Top and Tots. In 1884 the Chisholm boys and me helped drive cattle for George Sanders and Charlie Lifford to Dodge City, Kansas. We worked hard and pounded leather all day long. We were so tired at night, when we would lay our weary bodies on the ground and our head on the old hard saddle it felt good. Sometimes it was a wet pillow as we were in some of the worst storms. The lightning was so bad we would remove our spurs and wrap them in our bed roll. The cattle would run into each other and when their horns would touch you could see sparks fly. It would look like little string of stars going straight up. Sometime it would run right down an old cow's back bone and take the hair off right down to her tail tip. We lost a few men on this trip while fighting the Indians. We sure ate a lot of sow bellie, corn pones and red beans and drank corn whiskey from an old jug.

This drive started in San Antonio, Texas and we went by the way of New Braunfels, Austin, Taylor, Ft Worth, on to Red River. We lost several head there in that river getting the herd across. I made several trips on this old Chisholm Trail. The last one was to Ft. Worth, Chisholm's wasn't with me on this drive, I heard they were on a trail to Arizona, do hope to see them again someday. There was a many a cowboy that drove cattle over this old Chisholm Trail, made by Thornton Chisholm a real cowboy of yesterday. Now to the outstanding men of my time, Thornton Chisholm with his big ten gallon hat and high top boots, was one of them. He was the founder of the Old Chisholm Trail, he just threw out his lariat and roped those Texas longhorns in, and found them a new home with men in the north that needed them. The Chisholm name was on the lips of every man, woman and child throughout this land of ours. He was a Cowboy King.[4]

In 1866 Crockett Cardwell decided to send a herd of cattle to the northern market. In preparation for the trip, cattle were bought from all over the territory. They had to be hardy enough to make the seven hundred and twenty eight mile trip from the Starting point of DeWitt County to the nearest railhead at St. Joseph, Missouri. They traveled through sometimes waterless and weather torn country. Crockett chose Thornton Chisholm to be the bossman of this expedition. He was a well-seasoned cowboy with compassion for his men and the skill of getting the herd there in the best condition possible. The beginning of the trip was delayed because Thornton's wife was due to have

---

[3] Chisholm Hurst, Fannie G. (1966). *The Four State Chisholm Trail.* Munguia Printers.
[4] Chisholm Hurst, Fannie G. (1966). *The Four State Chisholm Trail.* Munguia Printers.

a baby and he would not leave until the child was born. On the first day of April 1866, Daniel Fore was born and shortly afterwards the drive began.

Following are some writings from Fannie G. Chisholm's book, "The Four State Chisholm Trail" on the beginning of the trip and the route taken.

At the first light of day at Cardwell Flats, two miles east of the present day town site of Cuero, Texas, 1800 head of the toughest Texas longhorns were started moving. Amidst the smell of smoldering campfires and coffee, the cowboys gave their first yell of the famous movement. The herd was moved in two parts and the two men selected by Chisholm to lead each herd of nine hundred head were Dave Augustine and Frank White.

Who can say what was in the mind of each of the thirty men in that group as they looked in awe over the vast sea of moving cattle! No one can be sure what was in the thoughts of each individual, but one can safely say that in each man there was something more than mere determination. There was a courage unmatched, for without this their goal could not have been achieved. We can only imagine the expression on Thornton Chisholm's face as he looked over that mass of animals and the men with him. How many times did he glance back and wonder if any of them would see this land again? What were the thoughts of Please Smith, a negro who was the cook for that trip? He could not have known that he was destined to make seven trips in all up the trail. We can only guess how many men have accepted the food that he prepared on those many trips over the miles of hardship. How many of these men knew they were on their way to make history? Men like Jack Lowe, Gus Guilminot, Gene Guilminot, Eli Newman, Joe Newman, Pack Augustine, G.M. (Tip) Alexander, Jim Hickey, Bingham White, Doly Davis, Cruse and others. The people along the way must have seen quite a sight as that herd made its way north as they stood and watched cattle pass for hours on end, the drone of hooves which could be heard for miles must have sent many a mother to quiet her frightened children.

The drive as near as can be traced today went by way of Gonzales, San Marcos, Austin, Round Rock, Georgetown, Gatesville, Glen Rose, Mineral Wells, Graham, Olney, Seymour, Vernon, across the Pecos River and on the Red River crossing (Doan's Store).

By crossing the river they entered Oklahoma and moved on by the way of Frederick, Lawton, Chichasha, Blanchard, Norman, Oklahoma City, Chandler, Bristow, Sapulpa, Tulsa and Collinsville, then into Kansas through Tatala, Parsons and Topeka and on to St. Joseph, Missouri. This was called the Western Trail (the towns listed being as they are on the map today). Most of these places mentioned above were not even towns at the time this took place but were mere water holes or the sites of stores where supplies could be obtained. It took these men seven months and ten days in the first drive. Many stories have been written about all the hardships and swollen river to cross. Thornton looked after and took care of all his men through trying times. If food was scarce he would see that the men got their portion first. If a swollen river was to cross he was the first to try it. You

11

read about the parties that were thrown when the cattle were all sold but you don't read about the trip home. No cattle to worry about, a faster trip but many miles to cover with home and family on your mind.[5]

After Thornton returned home from the drive, he did some freighting. He had gone to Mexico for gingham and other goods. Coming from one of his trips, he met a group of Mexicans and encountered a fight. He sent his buddy on for help eighty miles away. If you ride your horse steady, you can be there by morning he promised his buddy. Thornton had bought a bay horse and tied two bolts of cloth on the saddle for protection. He left the wagons and tried to outrun the Mexicans. The horse was weighted down and he was having trouble keeping ahead of them; he threw six hundred dollars in a Meleta (murrol) into the cactus. The less weight let him get ahead until he found a place of protection.

He fought until dark, three or four hours. The Mexicans burned the wagons. His buddy made it home and came back with help. They found the Mexicans in a mote of timber and killed some of them. They looked for the money but were unable to find it.

In March of 1868 on one of his freighting trips, Thornton was killed at the age of 37. While his team was pulling the wagon up a steep hill, he was riding the wheel horse named Ned. The trace broke and Thornton was thrown in front of the wagon wheel and it ran over him. He was injured at four o'clock in the afternoon and they sat him up in the middle of the road. He was never able to say a word and he died at two o'clock in the morning. The friends with him made a casket of the side boards of his wagon. They buried him between four Oak trees in Burnet County, Texas.

Zenna Chisholm Snowden
October 2006

Zenna notes:
Some of my older records show he was born in 1828.

Glenn Thornton married Jane P Fore daughter of Daniel Fore and Mary Pollard Wofford on 21 May 1852 in Clinton, Dewitt, Texas, USA. Jane was born in Mar 1838 in Mississippi, USA. She died

---

[5] Chisholm Hurst, Fannie G. (1966). *The Four State Chisholm Trail.* Munguia Printers.

on 27 Sep 1903 in Uvalde, Uvalde, Texas, USA. She was buried on 28 Sep 1903 in Uvalde, Uvalde, Texas, USA.

Jane P. Fore

Jane P. Fore was born in March of 1838 in Mississippi where both of her parents died when she was very young. I do not know when or how she came to Texas. According to their marriage license, Jane married Thornton Chisholm on May 27, 1852 in DeWitt County. She was 14 years of age. Since both of Thornton's parents had passed away, they moved into the beautiful home on the ranch where their first child, George, was born. Jane was eighteen years old. They had five more children before the death of Thornton. They were Effie L., Cora, Jessie, Annie Elizabeth and Daniel Fore.

After the death of their parents, Thornton and his brother, Bradford, were the executors of the estate. Besides taking care of the ranch, Thornton did some freighting and, of course, the trip up the 'Trail,' all of which often took him away from home. Jane became a large woman after her marriage and was not able to do all the chores around the home; therefore, she had a Negro servant to help her with the chores as well as drive her surrey.

In Fannie G. Chisholm's book, "The Four State Chisholm Trail," Michael Power Hill told Fannie G. this story:

> My father was on the first Trail Drive. His trail boss was Thornton Chisholm, all the cowboys just called him "Chisholm." We use to visit in their home there in Clinton. They had a large family. Girls, good looking ones, I shall never forget the big table and long benches they had, and the table covered with the best food. On a Sunday evening, we would have some of the best good old singing. It just did your heart good, one of the girls would play the organ, and the boys would play guitar and fiddle. There was never a stranger that came to their house that didn't leave full of good food. I had a good time with the two boys, the oldest was George Chisholm, the other one was Daniel Chisholm, we called them by their nick names, "Top and Tots."[6]

Jane and Thornton were married for sixteen years when Thornton was killed. She was left with the six children, the oldest twelve years and youngest two. During this time, her sister-in-law, Maryann, had married John Kelso and began to raise her family. They had seven children. Maryann

---

[6] Chisholm Hurst, Fannie G. (1966). *The Four State Chisholm Trail.* Munguia Printers.

died in 1876 while giving birth to Jesse and leaving John with this large family to care for.

Jane had been raising her family alone for eleven years. Her sister-in-law, Maryann, had been deceased for one year when Jane married John Kelso, and took on the responsibility of his seven children along with the five that she still had at home.

I have no information on how financially well off John was. Since Jane left the comforts of her home in Clinton to move to Uvalde with the extended family, John must have had a large home there. *Effie Pridgen 1880's*

Jane had a dear friend who died and she took her baby girl, Effie Pridgen, to raise. Effie was born in 1873. I do not know the exact date she came to live with Jane. She was listed in the 1880 Denton County, Texas Census as seven years old and living with the family. Jane must have been a wonderful and loving woman to take on another child.

Jane and John had a son of their own, John Clyde, born in May 1880. Jane died May 27,1903 at the age of 65. She had raised a large family. I am sure all members of the family had their duties but she was their stability. My Dad said his grandmother, Jane, was a very religious woman. Their home was always open to all who came there.

Zenna Chisholm Snowden
August 2007

Zenna Notes:

In Tenn (1860 Denton Co Census)

Feb 1837 in Rankin Co Miss as found by Clarence Chambers

Funeral Notice as to where she died.

1880 Census says she was born in Mississippi.

The Fore's were of French descent.

Marriage Source: CERTIFICATE OF MARRIAGE 1852 May 21 - Marriage License for Glenn Thornton Chisholm to Jane P Fore in Clinton, Texas.

Pictured: Effie Pridgen married Ben Fox, and daughter Lucy

Glenn Thornton and Jane had the following children:

+ 6 M i.   **George Langford Chisholm**   was born on 23 Jun 1856. He died on 15 Sep 1938.

+ 7 F ii.   **Effie L Chisholm**   was born about 1868. She died on 11 Jul 1891.

+ 8 F iii.   **Cora Chisholm**   was born in 1859. She died about 1900.

+ 9 F iv.   **Jessie Chisholm**   was born in 1862.

+ 10 F v.   **Annie Elizabeth Chisholm**   was born on 8 May 1864. She died on 10 Oct 1931.

+ 11 M vi. **Daniel Fore (Jim) Chisholm**   was born on 26 Mar 1866. He died on 1 Oct 1954.

Jane P. Fore Chisholm married John Kelso about 1877. Jane and John had a son of their own, **John Clyde**, born in May 1880.

Glenn Thornton Chisholm (1831-March 1868) Married May 21, 1852 Jane "Jennie" Fore (March1838 - 5/27/1903)	Maryanne Chisholm(1842-1876 birth of Jessie) Married August 14, 1857 John Roebuck Kelso (1835-4/20/1891)
George Langford Chisholm was born on 23 Jun 1856. He died on 15 Sep 1938.	Winchester[3] Kelso, born abt 1858.
Cora Chisholm was born in 1859. She died about 1900.	Frank Hubert[3] Kelso.
Jessie Chisholm was born in 1862.	Dennie[3] Kelso.
Annie Elizabeth Chisholm was born on 8 May 1864. She died on 10 Oct 1931.	Hardina[3] Kelso.

Rhoda[3] Kelso, born 1867 in Texas, USA. |
Daniel Fore (Jim) Chisholm was born on 26 Mar 1866. He died on 1 Oct 1954.	Fannie[3] Kelso, born 1874 in Texas.
Effie L Chisholm was born about 1868. She died on 11 Jul 1891.	Jessie[3] Kelso, born 1876 in Texas, USA.
Effie Pridgen abt 1873 in the 1880 Census living with Jane	
Jane "Jennie" Fore Chisholm Married 1877 (or 79…11 years as a single mom would be 1879) **John Roebuck Kelso**	
John Clyde Kelso b. 1880	

Dana S. Chisholm 2018 notes

Sources for Jane P Fore

Marriage: Ibid., 1852 May 21 - Marriage License for Glenn Thornton Chisholm to Jane P Fore in Clinton, Texas.

Death: CERTIFICATE OF DEATH. 1903 Sept 27- Death Certificate for Jane P (Jennie) Fore Chisholm Kelso.

Burial: FUNERAL NOTICE . 1904 Sept 28 - Funeral Notice for Jane P Fore Kelso. This paper gives a different date than Death Certificate. By the age they have on this it may be the right date.

Photo Right: 1883 John Roebuck & Jane P. Fore Chisholm Kelso

Photo Left: Effie Chisholm, Jessie Kelso, Fannie Kelso, John Clyde Kelso

3. **Bradford A Chisholm** (Richard Henry) was born in Apr 1835 in Clinton, DeWitt, Texas, USA. He died in 1913 in Carrizo, Springs Dimmitt, Texas, USA.

Fannie G said is name was Bradford C

In 1850 Texas Census he was 14 years old

He had a Grandson (Bradford Carr) in San Diego, California in 1966 (Clarence Chambers' notes)

I have a copy of Marriage License (Zenna notes). Photo 1900 Bradford and Harriett.

Bradford and Harriet 's marriage license was issued 3 Oct 1866 at Clinton, before Tom C Smith DeWitt County Clerk. They we married on the 4th before O H Stopp and acting Justice of the Peace for Precinct No 1 in presence of John M Rustin.

On 5 Jan 1858, Bradford and his brother Thornton paid off a promissory note to James C Tyson No 77 – 2117.

The 1910 Federal Census gave me the names of the two daughters, Ethel and Jodie and confirmed the ages of all remaining in the household at that time.

Bradford Chisholm, brother to Thornton Chisholm. Married Harriett Courtney, had four children, Ida, Ollie, Emma, and Richard Thornton. This picture was given to me by Bradford Carr grandson of Bradford Chisholm, San Diego, California.

Bradford married Harriett Aneda Courtney daughter of John Courtney and Aneda Gary on 3 Oct 1866 in Clinton, DeWitt, Texas, USA. Harriett was born on 21 Nov 1839 in New York, New York, USA. She died on 18 Jan 1914 in Victoria, Victoria, Texas. USA. She was buried Evergreen Cemetery, Victoria, Victoria , Texas, USA.

They had the following children:

+ 12 F i. **Olive Ann Chisholm** was born in Jun 1869. She died in 1930.

　13 M ii. **George B Chisholm** was born in 1876 in Texas, USA.

　14 F iii. **Alice M Chisholm** was born in 1978 in Carrizo Springs, Dimmit, Texas, USA. She died in 1929 in Pod, , California, USA.

　　Alice married (1) **Bill Armstrong**

　　Alice married (2) **W Handel**

+ 15 F iv. **Emma Chisholm** was born in Jun 1875. She died in 1932.

16 M v. **Seymour Chisholm** was born in 1874. He died about 1900.

17 F vi. **Ida Mae Chisholm** was born in 1878 in , Kerr, Texas, USA. She was christened in 26 Apr 1959.

Ida married **Joel Allen English** in Carrizo Springs, Dimmit, Texas, USA.

+ 18 F vii. **Nina Maud Chisholm** was born on 30 Aug 1881. She died on 27 Sep 1923.

19 M viii. **Richard T Chisholm** was born in Sep 1889 in , , Texas, USA.

Richard married **Ethel Day** on 6 Nov 1908 in LaSalle, Texas, USA

Richard T "Dick" Chisholm and his second cousin, William P "Buck" Taylor were shot and killed by Bill Sutton and his friends on Christmas Eve, 1868 in Clinton, Texas. There was a disagreement between the Taylors and Suttons factions about the reason for the killings , but there was no question on who did the Killings.

"Dick" Chisholm was 20 years old when the shooting took place.

(*Note: This is actually not the right Richard Chisholm. It was Richard A. Chisholm born in 1850 and shot in 1868 on Christmas Eve. Richard T. Chisholm wasn't born until 1889. Dana S. Chisholm)

Zenna notes for Bradford A Chisholm

Fannie G said is name was Bradford C
In 1850 Texas Census he was 14 years old
He had a Grandson (Bradford Carr) in San Diego, California in 1966 (Clarence Chambers' notes)
I have a copy of Marriage License

Bradford and Harriet 's marriage license was issued 3 Oct 1866 at Clinton, before Tom C Smith DeWitt County Clerk. They we married on the 4th before OH Stopp and acting Justice Of the Peace for Precinct No 1 in presence of John M Rustin.

On 5 Jan 1858, Bradford and his brother Thornton paid off a promissory note to James C Tyson. No 77 - 2117

The 1910 Federal Census gave me the names of the two daughters, Ethel and Jodie and confirmed the ages of all remaining in the household at that time.

Sources for Bradford A Chisholm

Chisholm Family History of Bradford A. Updated by Bobby Christall Jr. 26 Mar 2007. on extended families. (1900 CENSUS TEXAS twelfth). 1880 CENSUS TEXAS Census used also..
1910 CENSUS TEXAS Dimmitt, County, Salt Creek.

Marriage: CERTIFICATE OF MARRIAGE . 1866 Oct 3 - Marriage License of Bradford A. Chisholm to Harriett Courtney in Clinton, Texas.

Notes for Harriett Aneda Courtney

MARRIAGE: Their license was issued 3 Oct i866 at Clinton, Texas before Tom C Snith, DeWitt County Clerk. They were married before O H Stapp an acting Justice of the Peace for Precinct No 1 DeWitt County Texas in the presence of John M Rustin.

Sources for Harriett Aneda Courtney

Chisholm Family History of Bradford A. Updated by Bobby Christall Jr. 26 Mar 2007 on extended families. (1900 CENSUS TEXAS twelfth). 1880 CENSUS TEXAS Census used also. 1910 CENSUS TEXAS Dimmitt County, Salt Creek.

Marriage: CERTIFICATE OF MARRIAGE 1866 Oct 3 - Marriage License of Bradford A. Chisholm to Harriett Courtney in Clinton, Texas.

Death: CERTIFICATE OF DEATH 1914 Jan 18   Death Certificate for Harrett Aneda Chisholm.

4. **Maryann Chisholm** (Richard Henry) was born in 1842 in DeWitt, Texas, USA. She died about 1876 in DeWitt, Texas, USA.

Born in 1842 according to the 1850 DeWitt County Census. Died at the birth of her daughter Jessie.

Maryann married John Roebuck Kelso son of James Kelso and Rhoda Roebuck on 14 Aug 1857 in Dewitt, Texas, USA. John was born in 1835 in Rankin, Mississippi, USA. He died on 20 Apr 1891. Obituary notice   (Age 56)   From Fannie G Chisholm.

John and Maryann had the following children:

    20 M i. **Winchester Kelso** was born about 1858.

    21 M ii. **Frank Hubert Kelso**

    22 F iii. **Dennie Kelso**

    23 F iv. **Hardina Kelso**

    24 F v. **Rhoda Kelso** was born in 1867 in Texas, USA.

    25 F vi. **Fannie Kelso** was born in 1874 in Texas. USA.

Fannie married **Parker**.

26 F vii. **Jessie Kelso** was born in 1876 in Texas, USA.

Notes for Maryann Chisholm

Born in 1842 according to the 1850 DeWitt County Census. Died at the birth of her daughter Jessie.

Sources for Maryann Chisholm

Chisholm Family History of Maryann daughter of Richard Henry Chisholm. Maryann married John Roebuck Kelso and they had a family of seven children. She died at the birth of Jessie Kelso in1876.

Notes for John Roebuck Kelso

Obituary notice (Age 56) From Fannie G Chisholm.

5   **Richard A Chisholm**, born 1850 in Texas, USA; died 24 Dec 1868 in Texas, USA; buried in Texas. Richard was killed along with Buck Taylor at Clinton by Bill Sutton and Dock White. (From Fannie G. Chisholm book)

HC

CHAPTER THREE

THIRD Generation

In 2002, my sister, Bonnie, made the trip into Havasupai Canyon on her horse, Warrior, riding the same trail that Uncle Jim had taken the first tourists over in 1891. The pictures she took of Havasu Falls and Moony Falls were beautiful and the blue-green water in the ponds below was a sight to behold.
Zenna Chisholm Snowden

6. **George Langford Chisholm** "Top" (Glenn Thornton, Richard Henry) was born on 23 Jun 1856 in Clinton, DeWitt, Texas, USA. He died on 15 Sep 1938 in Dos Palos, California. The cause of death was Arterial Sclerosis, Myocardial failure. He was buried on 17 Sep 1938 in Evergreen Memorial Park, Dos Palos, California.

In 1920 Census his residence was Peoria, Maricopa, Arizona, USA. In 1930 Census his residence was Casa Grande, Pinal, Arizona.

He married (1) abt 1881 in **Fannie Maude King**, born 15 Oct 1863 in Texas, USA; died 15 Sep 1917 in Peoria, Maricopa, Arizona; buried 16 Sep 1917 in Rest Haven Park, Glendale, Maricopa, Arizona; (2) married **Mary Magdelene Williams** on 21 Nov 1918 in Peoria, Maricopa, Arizona, born 22 Oct 1879 in Grosbeck, Limestone, Texas; died 20 Feb 1954 in Glendale, Maricopa, Arizona; buried 24 Feb 1954 in Resthaven Cemetery, Glendale, Maricopa, Arizona, USA, daughter of Benj R Williams and Margaret Vienna Foster.

In the family picture taken in Granite, Oklahoma in 1910 here is the lineup of the individuals.

Back Row (corner L- R)

Top Chisholm, (2 friends on horseback (Shumaker with white shirt), Calvin Chisholm, Richard (Dick) Chisholm (standing), W.R. (Doc) Jordan - husband of Maude Chisholm, Bill Evans - son of Jennie Chisholm, Martin Chisholm, Thomas Chisholm

Front Row (L-R)

Jess Chisholm, Albert Chisholm, Quillar Evans - husband of Jennie Chisholm, Ted Evans - son of Jennie, Totsie Chisholm, Jennie (Chisholm) Evans, Georgia Evans - daughter of Jennie, Virgie Chisholm, Narnie (Simmons) wife of Dick, Bradford Jordan - son of Doc and Maude, Fannie (King) Chisholm - mother and grandmother - (holding picture of Maude), George Langford Chisholm -father - grandfather

George Langford Chisholm

On the 23 of June 1856, George was born in Clinton, Texas on the "Old Chisholm Ranch." His father, Thornton, was involved in several businesses as well as cattle ranching. George's paternal grandparents, Richard and Hardina, had both passed away a year before his birth; so, he never knew

them, although, he remembered all the tales told about them.

George Langford Chisholm married Fannie Mande King, her father was Martin J. King, They had eleven children, Mart, Maude, R. A. (Dick) Top, Tom, Jess, Jennie, Virgie, Albert and Totsie.

George grew up on the ranch building fence, gathering and branding cattle. When he was twelve years old, his father, Thornton, was killed. He had plenty of family and friends to help him through the hard times. In 1872, at the age of 16, he went to work for his Uncle Creed Taylor, a frontiersman, who was well known throughout Texas. He was one of George's favorite people. He spent three months there and then went home to Old Clinton and spent the winter with his mother.

In 1874, he worked on the O N Ranch. With plans to go up The Chisholm Trail, he and his buddies, Hun and Bunk Tuggle, joined a herd owned by Bob Murphy, but the trip did not work out. It was at this time that he met Jessie James.

After the last job, he and his friend, Hun Tuggle, went from Corpus Christi back to Uncle Creed Taylor's which was many miles away. The Taylor's were from his maternal grandmother's side and the family was a large one; therefore, he had a lot of cousins to work and play with. Roping and target practice were probably the competitions of the day.

In the 1960's, while I was working on our ancestry, I received a call from someone in the town of Peoria, Arizona. They had found my Grandfather's writings and wanted to know if I would like to have them. I was more than pleased to receive them. I did not know he had written them and had left them with a lawyer friend. How fortunate, that the one who found them knew us and knew we still lived in the area.

In 1879, he again started up The Chisholm Trail with Wofford and Johnny Bell's cattle, but they only got to Fort Forth, Texas on this try. In 1880 at the age of twenty four, with the Kimble Cattle Company, he finally made the trip up The Chisholm Trail all the way to Caldwell, Kansas.

In 1879 his mother, Jane P. Fore Chisholm, and John Kelso were married and moved to Uvalde, Texas.

Please read Jane P. Fore's story to see what may have been another sacrifice of love for family.

Sometime in 1881, **George married Fannie Maude King**. He settled down to farming in DeWitt County, on land rented from John Taylor. As a young boy growing up without a father, he had never stayed long in one place, and he did not change that kind of living during his married life.

Please read his wife, Fannie Maude King's, biography to understand the sheer wonder of the endurance of our women pioneer ancestors.

While in Texas two of their sons were born a good distance from The Old Chisholm Ranch, and I often wondered why. In 1886 Richard (Dick) was born in Pearsall, not too far from Uvalde and in 1890 Top was born in Uvalde. My thoughts were answered when I realized, that was where his mother lived after her marriage to John Kelso. After that, he move to Bastrop County, the area where the other children were born. His son, Jesse, said the family was in Del Rio, Texas when he was two years old. That would have been in early 1899. Shortly thereafter, George took his family to Geronimo, Arizona by covered wagon where his sister Annie lived. George kept in touch with Annie, his favorite sibling. While George and family were there, his daughter, Virgie, was born in Sept of 1899. They spent a year in Arizona and returned to Texas where they farmed for a while. He took his family to Oklahoma in 1907.

They were there about five years, went to Arizona again and then back to Texas. Finally in 1917, they settled in Peoria, Arizona.

After four months in Arizona, Fannie went to Paducah, Texas to be with her oldest daughter, Jennie. I do not know why she went to Texas, but after four months George went and brought her home. They returned to Arizona on the July 14, 1917. These trips had to have been by train. Two months later on September 15, 1917, Fannie passed away of Pelegra. One year later **George married Maggie Damron Moon**, my mother's mother. It was another one of those times when we became double related and had a hard time explaining it; however, it was fun for us because we had an aunt and uncle our age when Mae and Stanford were born.

I can remember them living in a home on an acre of land they had bought. It was located near what is now 91st Avenue and Peoria Avenue in an area called Altaloma. When Grandpa was in Arizona in 1913, he purchased this property with the help of a friend, B L Whitney. The property was put in Whitney's name and Grandpa sent payments to him. When Grandpa came to Arizona in 1917, Mr. Whitney for the payment of one dollar signed the contract over to him. The payments were $5 a month and the interest was 8%.

On March 14, 1918, George had a disagreement with a Mexican whom he shot and killed. His trial was March 22, 1918 in Phoenix. Grandpa was so pleased with the fact that Judge Stanford got him out of the ordeal without any consequences, he named his youngest son for him.

They were living in Altaloma in 1924 when George's brother, Jim (Daniel Fore), and his wife, Fannie M., came to live or visit. While they were there, she committed suicide in a little building. She was buried in the Glendale Cemetery. I was only three when it happened, but Grandpa must have lived there awhile because we kids grew older and knew what had happened. We were always curious about that little building. I can remember it was built across an irrigation ditch and I often wondered why. It was probably built as a storage for keeping their perishable foods cool.

I do not know how long they lived at Altaloma. In his little contract payment book, he had written that he was at a road camp job in Flagstaff on July 10, 1929. He noted that he left Phoenix on Friday the 5th and got to Flagstaff Thursday the 9th at noon. In 1932, they were living at the 'Old Olive Orchard', north of Marinette, and lived there for six years.

Grandpa went to California a few times but spent most of the rest of his life in Arizona. In 1938, while on a trip to California to visit his family, he died from a heart attack and was buried in Dos Palos, California. Grandma came back to Arizona and lived with different ones of the family, but spent most of the time with her daughter, Marie.

Zenna Chisholm Snowden
January 2007
(Dana's note: I am unsure who committed suicide. Fannie Maude was married to George, not Jim, and died in 1917. Need to see who committed suicide in 1924.)

George married (1) Fannie Maude King daughter of Martin V King and Margaret Lowrence about 1881. Fannie was born on 15 Oct 1863 in Texas, USA. She died on 15 Sep 1917 in Peoria, Maricopa, Arizona, USA. She was buried on 16 Sep 1917 in Rest Haven Park, Glendale, Maricopa, Arizona, USA.

Picture circa 1881 Uvalde

Fannie Maude King

Come with me now on a journey of love, travel and children. Fannie knew the Chisholm's well. There were four pretty young sisters and two brothers, one a frisky youngster of about fifteen, but it was the oldest who caught her attention. He was short and rather handsome, but the swagger and the gun he wore on his hip would make any girl's head turn. He was a little old for her but that was alright. He could take care of her and give her a good home; so, at about the age of eighteen she married this older man, George Langford Chisholm, nicknamed Top.

They settled down on a ranch in DeWitt County, Texas. They were farming on land they rented from a cousin, John Taylor. Now this was not exactly the life of a Chisholm. They lived there long enough to have their first child, Jennie. She was the first of eleven children. A covered wagon was bought and prepared for a trip. I find that the second child, Mart, was born in Oklahoma in 1884. Oklahoma did not offer what George wanted. I would think that Fannie was not really pleased traveling across country in a covered wagon and having her children.

25

Their next home was in Pearsall, Texas where Richard (Dick) was born in 1886. Maud was born in 1887 and they were living around Uvalde at that time. She may have been born there. Top was born in Uvalde. Tom was born in Middleton. Even though they moved to different towns, they were spending some time in the vicinity of George's mother since she had moved to Uvalde when she married John Kelso. In 1895, they were at Bastrop a town near Austin. They stayed there for the birth of Calvin and Jesse.

Some of the boys were now old enough to help, and the west was calling. After George's brother, Jim, had been in Arizona Territory, he had some great tales to tell; so, in 1899 they saddled up some horses, hitched the team to the covered wagon and were on another adventure this time to Arizona. After fifty-one days, they were in Geronimo, Arizona. While in Geronimo, a beautiful little girl was born. She was named Virgie.

My father, Tom, was on all the trips; so, I wrote down what he told me about them. They stayed in the Geronimo and Solomonville area. After about a year, the family went back to Taylor, Texas by wagon where they farmed for a few years. The last two children of the family, Totsie and Albert, were born in Texas.

My Dad did not say it was the same covered wagon, but if it was the same, it was to be in use again. In 190X, George's entire family was on their way to Oklahoma again. Mart was married there and all three of his children were born in Oklahoma. The family spent four years there then returned to Thrall, Texas.

In 1907 in Granite, Oklahoma daughter, Maud, and husband, Dock Jordan, had a son, Bradford, and Maud died in childbirth.

Uncle Albert told me these stories about his mother. He said she weighed about 250 pounds. When she would get angry with them, she would throw shoes at them. One of the pranks that he remembered was a time she was milking the cow and Tom was holding the calf. Top had a "nigger shooter" and shot the cow. Things got a little serious but he didn't give me the consequences, but they thought it was really funny. One time while they were playing cards, their mother decided to go to bed, and when she laid down she fell through the slats. You can just imagine how mad she got with a group of young upstarts laughing their hearts out. Dad said his Mother was very religious so her remarks were no doubt held in check.

In October 1916 from Thrall, Texas, Fannie was to make her last long trip, but this time it would be in a surrey instead of a covered wagon. Along with family and friends, another caravan of pioneers was on the way west again. They arrived in Glendale, Arizona on January 7, 1917. With the help of his family, George settled in a little home in Peoria, Arizona.

After eight months of living in Arizona, at the age of fifty-four, Fannie was laid to rest in the Glendale Rest Haven Cemetery.

In researching and writing this story about my Grandmother, I am feeling very sad. Did she have a good life or was raising a large family, much of the time in a covered wagon, a very stressful and hard life?

Zenna Chisholm Snowden
May 2007

George and Fannie Maude had the following children:

+ 27 F i. **Jennie Chisholm** was born on 28 Jul 1882. She died on 15 Jul 1951.

+ 28 M ii. **Martin Gaines Chisholm** was born on 24 Feb 1884. He died on 4 Feb 1942.

+ 29 M iii. **Richard Akley Chisholm** was born on 15 Dec 1886. He died on 5 May 1968.

+ 30 F iv. **Maud Chisholm** was born in 1887. She died about 1907.

+ 31 M v. **Top Chisholm** was born on 11 Feb 1890. He died on 4 Jul 1965.

+ 32 M vi. **Thomas John Chisholm** was born on 1 Apr 1892. He died on 21 Sep 1966.

+ 33 M vii. **Calvin Alonzo Chisholm** was born on 17 Feb 1895. He died on 6 Aug 1956.

+ 34 M viii. **Jesse Chisholm** was born on 9 Apr 1897. He died on 13 Aug 1985.

+ 35 F ix. **Virgie Eliza Chisholm** was born on 23 Sep 1899. She died on 6 Nov 1968.

+ 36 M x. **Albert Vivian Chisholm** was born on 12 Mar 1902. He died on 13 Dec 1971.

+ 37 F xi. **Totsie Lee Chisholm** was born on 8 Mar 1905.

Pictured above: Jennie, Martin Gaines, Richard Akley, and Maud.

George married Maggie Damron Moon (Zenna's Notes above)

George married (2) Mary Magdelene Williams "Maggie" daughter of Benj R Williams and Margaret Vienna Foster on 21 Nov 1918 (picture from wedding) in Peoria, Maricopa, Arizona, USA. Mary was born on 22 Oct 1879 in Grosbeck, Limestone, Texas, USA. She died on 20 Feb 1954 in Glendale, Maricopa, Arizona, USA. She was buried on 24 Feb 1954 in Resthaven Cemetery, Glendale, Maricopa, Arizona, USA.

Mary was in Limestone County for 7 months, on 1 June 1880 they moved to Grosbeck county. In 1910 Census Maggie was in Milam county Texas.

George and Mary had the following children:

+ 38 F xii. **Mae Chisholm** was born on 8 Sep 1919. She died on 6 Dec 1977.

+ 39 M xiii. **Stanford Dalton Chisholm** was born on 21 Feb 1921. He died on 10 Jul 1958.

Zenna's notes: Chisholm Family History of George Langford and his extended family by Zenna Chisholm Snowden. George was my Grandfather and the family lived close to us until he passed away. The older generations names and dates came from searches at the Morman Church Genealogy Library.

1877 Nov 15 - George Langford Chisholm registered his stock mark and brand in Cuero, Texas. Letters, notes and contracts of George Langford Chisholm.

1917 - Altaloma Real Estate Contract he made on a trip to Arizona and where he lived when he settled in Arizona.

Ibid., 1917 Jun 6 - Altaloma property was transferred to George. He also transferred some of his thoughts to the pages later.

Ibid., 1917 Nov 16 - George belonged to Hare I.O.O.F Lodge and when they heard of the death of his wife, Fannie, they sent him money for funeral expenses.

Ibid., 1905 Mar 8 - Religious thoughts penned by George and a notation of the birth of his youngest daughter, Totsie.

Ibid., 1907 Mar 17 - Names and some ages of family members written in his little contract book - George L Chisholm.

Ibid., 1904 Mar 17 - Some jottings of memories of friends and dates by George.

Ibid., 1929 July 10 - George uses his little contract book again to record his working at a road camp in Flagstaff. George Langford Chisholm, 1932 Hand written Memoirs of George Langford Chisholm. This tablet was kept by a lawyer friend of George's until given to me, Zenna Chisholm Snowden, in the 1970s.

1932 - This is the cover of the Tablet George used to write his memoirs in. It belonged to his daughter Mae.

Ibid., 1932 - Page 1 of 24 - of George Langford Chisholm Hand Written 1932 Memoirs. It starts out about his Uncle Creed Taylor, one of his favorite people. Letters, notes and contracts of

George Langford Chisholm. This tablet was kept by a lawyer friend of George's until given to me, Zenna Chisholm Snowden, in the 1970s.

1932 - Page 3 - George's Memoirs.

Death Source: Funeral Service Notice.

Funeral Service notice from newspaper. 1938 Sept 15. Death Certificate of George L Chisholm in Dos Palos, California.

7. **Effie L Chisholm** (Glenn Thornton, Richard Henry) was born about 1868 in Clinton, DeWitt, Texas, USA. She died on 11 Jul 1891 in Stratton, Texas, USA. She was buried in Clinton, DeWitt, Texas, USA.

Effie married William W McKissack on 29 Dec 1888 in Uvalde, Uvalde, Texas. USA. William was born in Mar 1862 in Tennessee, USA. Burial Source: FUNERAL NOTICE. 1891 July 13 - Funeral Notice to tell that Funeral for Effie Chisholm McKissack was to be in Clinton, Texas.

They had the following children:

    40 M i. **William Wood McKissack** was born in Feb 1890 in Texas.

8. **Cora Chisholm** (Glenn Thornton, Richard Henry) was born in 1859 in Clinton,

DeWitt, Texas, USA. She died about 1900 in Seymore, Baylor, Texas. USA. She was buried in Seymore, Baylor, Texas. USA.

Cora married Charles Middleton. Chisholm Family History of Cora Chisholm from Ancestry.com and Marie Damron Chisholm.

They had the following children:

    41 M i. **Tom Middleton.** Tom married **Unknown**.

  +42 F ii. **Frankie Middleton.**

    43 F iii. **Jennie Middleton.** Jennie had one boy - Told to me by Marie Chisholm

    44 F iv. **Fannie Middleton.**

  +45 F v. **Georgia Middleton.**

    46 M vi. **Less Middleton.**

        Less had three children (Information From Marie Chisholm)

9. **Jessie Chisholm** (Glenn Thornton, Richard Henry) was born in 1862 in Clinton, Dewitt, Texas, USA.

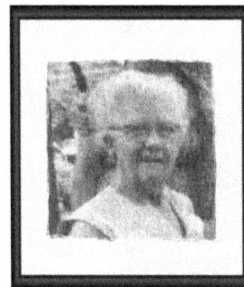

Jessie married John Parker Denham son of James DeJarnette Denham and Ann Elizabeth Benham about 1884 in Dewitt, Texas, USA. John was born on 7 Nov 1861 in Goliad, Goliad, Texas, USA.

Picture Left: James Denham and Ann Elizabeth 1880's

John Parker was listed as a salesman in the June 30, 1900 Texas Census and as a Carpenter of house building in the April 28, 1910 Texas Census. He spent two years in the

Confederate Army as a member of the Chisholm regiment, in Majors' Brigade of Texas Cavalry, and was attached to Green's Division in the Trans-Mississippi Department.

In the 1910 Harris County, Texas Census the three oldest Girls were not on the census and the two younger sons were there. They no doubt had gotten married.

John and Jessie had the following children:

    47 F i.   **Pearl Denham** was born in Oct 1885 in , , Texas, USA.

    48 F ii.   **Elizabeth Denham** was born in Jan 1890 in , , Texas, USA.

    49 F iii.   **Allie Denham** was born in Jun 1892 in , , Texas, USA.

    50 F iv.   **Anne Denham** "Annie" was born in Apr 1896 in , , Texas, USA.

           Anne married **Unknown** .

    51 F v.   **Gertrude Denham** was born in Apr 1898 in , , Texas, USA.

    52 M vi.   **Parker Denham Jr** was born in 1901 in , , Texas, USA.

    53 M vii. **John Denham** was born in 1904 in , , Texas, USA.

---

10. **Annie Elizabeth Chisholm** (Glenn Thornton, Richard Henry) was born on 8 May 1864 in Clinton, DeWitt, Texas, USA. She died on 10 Oct 1931 in Morenci, Greenlee, Arizona, USA.

Annie Elizabeth Chisholm

Annie Elizabeth, the 5th child of Glenn Thornton and Jane P. Fore, was born in Clinton, Texas May 8, 1864. On May 2,1889, she married John Joseph Filleman in Uvalde, Texas. The family had moved to Uvalde after her mother married John Kelso. In the following letter, Brice Willis, Annie's great-grandson, tells us that he believes Annie and John were introduced by Annie's brother. The two men were on a cattle drive together to Arizona. They may have

known each other before since they only lived about thirty miles apart. This brother would have been Daniel (Jim) Chisholm. He tells of his trip on the cattle drive to Arizona in 1885 in his book, "Memoirs of Daniel Fore (Jim) Chisholm."

Pic May 2, 1889

1880's Annie Elizabeth

When Annie's sister, Effie L. McKissack, was ill in Texas, Annie went to Stratton, Texas to be with her. Effie died July 11, 1891. Annie was pregnant while on this trip and six days after Effie died Annie's daughter, Effie Lucille, was born July 17, 1891 in Uvalde, Texas. This was still the home of Annie's mother, Jane.

From this trip to Texas, Annie brought a cutting of a rose bush back to her home in Arizona. The rose bush is still in the Filleman family and blooms once a year in June or July. In 2006, the rose bush was 105 years old.

What a treasure to behold!

The following was sent to me by Brice Willis of Safford, Arizona, the great-grandson of Annie Elizabeth Chisholm Filleman.

You might like a little more on Annie - I do believe they were introduced in Uvalde by one of her brothers. This would have been after a cattle drive to Arizona. Like you said they probably attended some dances and other social events together because Annie really enjoyed dancing and being with people.

When Annie lived in Solomonville, she helped at the Solomonville Hotel owned by Mrs. I. E. Solomon. She cooked, cleaned and did general hotel work. When they moved to Ft. Thomas, she continued doing the same work for J. N. Porter, a large rancher and owner of a boarding house in Ft. Thomas. She had full rein of the boarding house. One day some cowboys were in town and were chasing and lassoing any Indian they could find. Annie was not tolerant of that type of behavior and went right out in the middle of it all. She gave the drunk cowboys a piece of her mind and suggested they hightail it out of town. A young squaw cowered behind Annie during this episode. Afterward, Annie couldn't get the young girl to leave. She had been frightened badly; so, Annie took her in and cared for her until she was in better condition. After that incident, the young girl came to the boarding house every day and did chores for Annie. She called Annie Shahliman (which was supposed to be "Friend", but no Apache I have met could ever recognize the word). Anyway, she was devoted to Annie. I still have a nice Apache basket given to Annie by the young girl.

Another boarding house incident involved the four oldest children, Clara, Effie, Howard and Joe. The children had been out in the desert near the fort picking poppies and looking for pretty rocks. They happened to find two pretty rocks! One was an amethyst ring in a gold mounting and the other a large diamond in gold wires. How these things got into the desert is a mystery, but they were probably loot taken by Indians and discarded there. Well, the kids took them back to their mom. She showed them to some salesmen who happened to be numerous in the area at that time. One she trusted told her about the diamond and offered to take it to Mexico City. It was cut into four smaller diamonds for each of the children. Annie was proud of the stones and showed them to anyone who stayed in the boarding house. As you can guess, one morning the safe was open and the stones were gone - but the amethyst ring was still there and has been passed down to my daughter, Emily.

Annie enjoyed the social life of Ft. Thomas, but she realized she and John needed to do more for their family. This was when they purchased the ranch in Geronimo. It was located on the border of the Apache Reservation. John had made good friends with many Apache men over the years and had gained a little knowledge of the language. Howard and Joe learned a lot of the language and had many friends on the reservation. Apaches were always helpful and friendly with the Filleman Family.

Unfortunately, the ranch at Geronimo never was enough to support the family. John bought a ranch on Eagle Creek - he was familiar with the area. The family moved from Geronimo by horse and mule with all the family possessions they could take. The trail was over fifty miles, and wagons could not be used. Annie had to give up all her furniture and most of her possessions that weren't necessities. The whole family including my grandmother and her husband and my mother, Geneva, who was under two at the time all made the trip to Eagle Creek. It took several days for the journey. When they got there, Annie found her new home. It was a two room log cabin with hardly a roof. It didn't take long for them to get things in shape. Annie cooked around a fire in front of the cabin. They all came together to do what was needed as that was the way people did things then. Neighbors came with fresh meat and vegetables.

John learned of a sawmill opening nearby and immediately ordered enough lumber to build a better house up on the hill. The decision was good, because soon after they were situated in the cabin, a cloudburst came and the cabin was under water. My Aunt Nina described it as devastating. The few things they had were washing out the front door of the cabin. Nina was most concerned because she saw her enamel potty wash away.

The new cabin was started as soon as possible. My grandfather, George Wyatt, was a carpenter and organized the men into a building crew. They put together a larger three room clapboard house. It was a mansion to the Filleman family after where they had been living. The home had a large open dogtrot through the center. This was an area where people could wash up or just sit out of the sun in the breeze. Soon after the house was built, neighbors said the Filleman's had to have a dance to get to know the neighbors. Well, the closest neighbor was miles away and they didn't think there were too many people in the area. Annie was excited about the prospect of having some fun for a change as I'm sure the others in the family would have liked the same. Neighbors started showing up - close one's first - then it just grew and grew. Whole families on horseback, a foot, and in buggies! People came from as far as Blue River about thirty miles away. The dance floor was the dogtrot. This proved to be too small, so the boys dismantled the new wall into the bedrooms and increased the dance floor. Every rancher and cowboy on Eagle Creek was there along with every young lady interested in finding a young man! The celebration lasted for three days and two nights. This was the way people socialized and visited in those days. When you went to visit, you had to stay a spell and Annie welcomed everyone!

Every fall up until the late 1920's, John and Annie's Apache friend, Chino, would make a special visit to the Filleman Ranch. Chino was like a chief, and had thirty or forty followers. The Indians came to the area to gather pinyons and acorns. They would camp at the Filleman orchard. John told them which trees they could pick from and they never touched anything but those. Also, during the fall they had plenty of squash and pumpkins and they let the Indians have all they wanted. Annie would have the boys bring in some turkeys. The boys always knew where the wild turkeys roosted. Annie would pit roast turkeys and feed all the Indians. In a way, it was like a Thanksgiving every fall. Chino and John would sit on the porch of the house and visit. The rest of the tribe would sit outside the fence of the yard. The boys liked visiting with their old friends - they traded and had a lot of fun together. One time when Nina and Geneva were about ten years old, the boys told them they were going to give the girls to the Indians. The boys tied the girls up in gunny sacks and handed them over to the Indian boys. Nina and Geneva were screaming and yelling. Old Chino came to their rescue and opened the bags. Unfortunately, the girls thought he was after them! They ran away and wouldn't go near the Indians again. Days later the girls got even with the boys when they baked some cookies spiked with a laxative!

John and Annie had finally found a way to support their family and they lived frugally and happily the remainder of their lives on Eagle Creek. Their son, Carl, was killed in a horse accident, and their daughter, Mary, died from the results of a cancer from a rattlesnake bite. Howard and Joe remained on their ranches on Eagle Creek. Their daughter, Coralea, with her husband, Bill Edwards, also ranched the Eagle Creek area. Effie divorced George and married Harris Martin, they lived and worked in Clifton, Arizona. Clara moved to California. Mike enjoyed the rodeo circuit and died of pneumonia in Prescott white attending a rodeo. My mother, Geneva Wyatt Willis, lived with John and Annie most of her young life. She and Nina were almost the same age and grew up like sisters. All these people are gone now and the thing I remember most is that their lives were never about money or fancy clothes. It was about love of family and providing for one another and their friends.

Annie lived a long and rich life with family and friends. She had nine children and died October 10, 1931 at the age of 67 in Morenci, Arizona.

"On My Way"

Brice Willis   *Pic about 1914*

Chisholm Family History of Annie Chisholm from Brice Willis of Safford, Arizona. Genealogy work sheets received Aug 2006. Information on Chisholms, Fillemans, Woffords, and extended families.
Zenna Chisholm Snowden
October 2006

Annie married John Joseph Filleman son of John Anselmo Filleman and Marie Zerr on 2 May 1889 in Uvalde, Uvalde, Texas, USA. John was born on 2 May 1861 in D'Hanis, Medina, Texas, USA. He died on 10 Jul 1942 in Phoenix, Maricopa, Arizona, USA.

They had the following children:

+ 54 F i. **Clara May Filleman** was born on 20 Feb 1890. She died on 10 Oct 1968.

+ 55 F ii. **Effie Lucille Filleman** was born on 17 Jul 1891. She died on 4 Jan 1961.

+ 56 F iii. **George Joseph Filleman** was born on 14 Oct 1893. She died on 29 Aug 1960.

+ 57 M iv. **William Howard Filleman** was born on 30 Jun 1895. He died on 9 Feb 1973.

+ 58 F v. **Coralea Filleman** was born on 1 Aug 1897. She died on 18 Mar 1981.

+ 59 F vi. **Mary Annie Filleman** was born on 15 Aug 1899. She died on 13 Feb 1920.

  60 M vii. **Carl Otis Filleman** was born on 23 Feb 1902 in Geronimo, Graham, Arizona, USA.
  He died on 16 Jan 1924 in Eagle Creek, Greenlee, Arizona, USA.

+ 61 M viii. **Walter Jake Filleman** was born on 2 May 1904. He died on 25 Apr 1947.

+ 62 F ix. **Nina Elsie Filleman** was born on 13 Jan 1909. She died on 23 Sep 1978.

11. **Daniel Fore Chisholm** (Glenn Thornton, Richard Henry) was born on 26 Mar 1866 in Old Chisholm Ranch, Clinton, Texas, USA. He died on 1 Oct 1954 in Needles, San Bernardino, California, USA. He was buried on 8 Oct 1954 in Needles, San Bernadino, California, USA.

Daniel Fore Chisholm son of Thornton Chisholm, was a trail driver over the Chisholm trail that was made by his father.

Daniel Fore (Jim) Chisholm

In the early days of our family history, it was necessary to move to

35

different parts of the country to have a better and more prosperous life for families and to open up new frontiers for that purpose. There were some that adventure was their forte, and the one that comes to mind was our great uncle, Jim.

Jim was born March 26, 1866. His father, Thornton, held up his famous trip to blaze 'The Chisholm Trail' until after Jim's birth.

Jim was only a couple of years old when the Taylor-Sutton feud started but it lasted seven years; so, at the age of nine he had vivid memories of the fighting. As youngsters, we listened to many stories about the feud from him and our Grandfather George. History books have many of these; so, we will not focus on that part of Jim's life.

As a young man of fifteen, he was a true cowboy with all the skills that went with it, including carrying a gun. As was often said about him, he could rope a steer and shoot a gun with the best of them. When his father was killed, Jim was only two and his brother, George, was 12; so, relatives, including the Taylor boys, helped show them the ways of work and play.

In 1884, Jim hired on with the King and Kennedy Cattle Company. The Cattle Company had gathered a large herd of cattle near Corpus Christi, Texas and had started up the Chisholm Trail; at the age of 18, Jim joined them at the mouth of the Nueces Canyon in Uvalde County near his mother's home. He went to Dodge City, Kansas with the herd. One of the men on the trip, Si Eli

Newman, had been with Jim's father, Thornton, on the famous first trip up 'The Trail.' Jim tells of their trials and hardships in his book, "Memoirs of Daniel Fore (Jim) Chisholm." After the cattle were sold, Jim came back to Texas.

In 1885, Jim helped drive 5,000 head of longhorns for the Black Cattle Company from Murphyville (Alpine), Texas westward toward Arizona Territory. This was a disastrous drive, streams and waterholes had dried up due to lack of rain. Many of the cattle and some of the men died of thirst. By the third waterless day, the men were staggering with swollen tongues, eyes fixed in a glassy stare, and instead of guiding the herd were merely following in order to find water; however, these perilous adventures did not diminish their adventurous spirit.

Jim was married February 11, 1886 to **Lulu Rebecah Denham of Goliad**, a town about 25 miles south of his home town, Clinton. Lulu's bother, Parker, married Jim's sister, Jessie. The family had a close relationship. Jim had three children. Anna was born in 1887, Addie in 1890 and Bob in 1892. Our family knew that Jim had two girls although he never talked about them. We did not know about the son until later when Jim's grandson, Adrian Smith, and wife, Bonnie, came to Arizona looking for Jim's family.

Picture Left: Jim and Lulu Rebecah

What a treat it was for us to get to know that side of Uncle Jim's Family.

From Jim's memoirs, we find 'the pioneer blood' came out again. While in Arizona, he helped to pioneer a trail that was to be as equally famous as the one his father blazed in Texas. In 1890, he formed a partnership with W. W. (Bill) Bass to build a trail into Grand Canyon country. The trail was to connect with the Havasupai Trail made by the Havasupai Indians, who lived in a village at the bottom of the Canyon. The purpose of the trail was to take tourists down into the Grand Canyon. After working on the trail for about a year, they took their first tourists over it. Bill, Mrs. Bass and Jim met the two ladies at Williams, Arizona. The tourists were both writers. It was a 60 mile trip into the Grand Canyon; so, they had built and equipped a relay station along the way. When they reached the relay station, they changed from wagons to horseback and used pack mules to carry their supplies. The last twelve miles of the trail, from where it intersected with the Havasupai Indian Trail into the rim of the Grand Canyon proper was not entirely finished; so, they decided when they reached that point to follow the Indian Trail down to Havasu Village at the bottom of Catarrac (or Havasu or Havasupai) Canyon.

They started the 12 mile trip down a steep, narrow and hazardous trail sometimes in single file. What a beautiful and exciting time they must have had. They spent the night, saw all the sights and returned well pleased with their trip.

Bill and Jim finished their trail so that it was wide enough for a Concord Stage to pass over it. Tourists were hard to find. Jim tired of the business and sold his interest to Bill for the sum of $50.

Even today, people going down a much better trail find it very beautiful and exciting. In 2002, my sister, Bonnie, made the trip into Havasupai Canyon on her horse, Warrior, riding the same trail that

Uncle Jim had taken the first tourists over in 1891. The pictures she took of Havasu Falls and Moony Falls were beautiful and the blue-green water in the ponds below was a sight to behold. Attending a Site Steward Conference meeting in Flagstaff, Bonnie met the guest speaker, Jim Babbitt, who owns the Babbitt Ranches that includes a large amount of northwestern Arizona. His topic was about Bill Bass and what he had done for tourism in Arizona. Bonnie was able to get information from him on the approximate area where the relay station was located that Uncle Jim had help to build. By some searching in a four-wheel drive vehicle, she and a friend were able to find where the relay station had been. There were still enough walls left standing and artifacts scattered about that made it possible to recognize the spot. It is still a wilderness of nothing but cedars, cattle and cowboys. As you are looking through Jim's scrapbook, you will see a photo of what is left of the relay station.

Uncle Jim's grandson, Adrian Smith, said his mother, Addie, was one year old when her father, Jim, made his trip into the Canyon.

We have to surmise about his life a little here. Jim went back to Texas in about 1892. He did not stay long. Whether he ask Lulu to come to where he was, or if she decided to follow him on her own, we do not know. In about 1893, Lulu started for Idaho alone in a covered wagon with three small children. On the way, their son, Bob, died at 12 months old. Adrian told us it was in Arizona where he died. He had to have been a little one when she left Texas because it would have taken several months to get that far in a covered wagon. You can read a little of what we know of her trip under Lulu's biography.

During the Gold Rush days in Alaska, Jim helped move a herd of 1,000 head of cattle to Dawson City, Canada. In the spring of 1898, a herd was shipped from Montana to Seattle where they were loaded on boats and sent up the coast to Pearmint Harbor. There they were unloaded and driven inland to the Yukon. Jim stayed in Alaska for two years. He prospected, mined and ran a mule pack-train packing supplies into the mining camps. He tells this in his book and told it to us youngsters who loved to sit and listen.

In about 1900, we find Jim in Junction City, Texas. His brother, George, and family were there. His sister, Jennie, was married there in about 1900 to a deputy sheriff. I have a photograph of Jim in front of the nearly new jail house. After that, Jim spent some time in Idaho working for Governor Gooding until around 1905. At this time, he was able to be with his family. In 1905 when the

Thunder Mountain 'gold strike' hit Idaho, Jim was there. The gold didn't last long and Jim returned to Arizona.

In 1915, Jim was ranching on the Santa Maria River in Yuma County, Arizona. A man by the name of Pete Silk lived on an adjoining ranch. Jim had known him in Idaho and Pete had shot a man there before leaving. Since settling on the Santa Maria, Silk had been in trouble with a number of the ranchers and homesteaders and, finally, he and Jim tangled over an irrigation ditch, that Silk was attempting to dig across Jim's property. They decided to ask in a bunch of neighbors to arbitrate the dispute and both agreed to be guided by that decision; however, when they met Silk started cursing one of the men whom Jim had asked to be present. Jim told him not to abuse the man. Silk went for his gun. Jim said, "Pete, don't do that," but Silk paid no attention to the warning; his gun was already in 'the clear' before Jim went into action. Jim shot from the hip, and his bullet pierced Silk's brain. Silk's gun dropped to the ground without being fired as he fell forward.

Jim saddled up and rode 45 miles to Wenden, Arizona from there he wired Deputy Sheriff Billy De Spain at Bouse. When he was taken to Yuma, the county seat, there were a dozen men already there to go 'his bond.' One man wired from Kingman, Arizona (where Jim was well known, having lived there for many years), and offered to raise $100,000 for his bond if it were needed.

When the trial came up , a verdict of "not guilty" was rendered, and Jim was freed. Shortly thereafter, "he hung his gun on the wall where it hangs today." This story I took from Jim's book because I wanted it to be in his words even though we heard the story over and over many times as we grew up. Just like our boys home from the wars would go over there adventures many times.

Since we knew about Uncle Jim's lady friends, it was a relief to learn he had divorced Lulu on June 1, 1923 in Orange County, California. I can remember when most of our uncles, aunts and all of the kids (and there were lots of kids) were gathered at our home at 'The Old Olive Orchard', located north of Grand Avenue on Lake Pleasant Road, for Thanksgiving 1932; somehow, Uncle Jim knew we were having a 'get together' and decided he would like to join us. He came out alone and left his lady friend, Dora, in the town of Marinette. He ask my Dad, Tom, would it be alright if he brought Dora to the celebration. He was told yes. I was ten years old at the time and I can remember that she brought several heads of cabbage and made a big pan of coleslaw. I can remember how good it tasted and how I would look at the two of them and think something is wrong; they are not married. Stories got around fast among us youngsters.

Some of the fond memories of Uncle Jim that Bonnie recalls are, "I remember as a child, sitting on his knee and being regaled by stories of Billy the Kid and Pat Garrett. This brought the 'old west' right into my life and made me wish I had lived during that era."

Dora and Jim lived together in Wenden, Arizona until she died. She became Aunt Dora to us and we would see them often. Uncle Jim was rather heavy and one of the things that we often laughed about as kids, or even after we were grown was he would sit down and ask us, "Get your Old Uncle a glass of water" or whatever he wanted at the time.

After Dora died, we didn't see him very often; he spent time around Aguila and Bouse and was busy with his mining claims.

In about 1950, we heard on the radio that Jim Chisholm of Aguila, Arizona had befriended a young girl, and that she had stolen his gun and ran away with it. Knowing Uncle Jim, it was no doubt, the same one he had hung on the wall years before. We never heard whether he got his gun back or not.

On June 13, 1951, Jim married Lorna Chambers. They did some traveling in a small trailer and enjoyed life until he died October 1,1954 ten miles south of Kingman enroute to California. He was buried in Kingman, Arizona.

Zenna Chisholm Snowden
July 2007

Daniel married (1) Lulu Rebecah Denham daughter of James DeJarnette Denham and Ann Elizabeth Benham on 11 Feb 1886 in Goliad, Texas, USA. Lulu was born on 16 Apr 1866 in Goliad, Goliad, Texas, USA. She died in Feb 1954 in Picabo, Idaho, USA. She was buried in Hailey, Idaho, USA.

Adrian Smith's wife, Bonnie, Tells of Their Memories of Lulu Denham Chisholm and the Search for Jim Chisholm

I am the widow of Adrian Aaron Smith, and these are some of our memories of his grandmother, Lulu. I will try to write about what Adrian told me of his grandmother and her being married to Jim Chisholm, 'The Chisholm Trail Man.'

When I first met her, she was living in Hailey, Idaho. After Adrian and I married, she lived with Addie, her daughter, and son-in-law in Picabo, Idaho and Twin Falls, Idaho. She passed away at Addie's home in Twin Falls in 1954.

Adrian wondered about Jim Chisholm. He grew up thinking his grandfather had lived and died in Arizona. Grandma Lulu came to Idaho bringing with her two daughters. They came by team and wagon from Texas to Arizona; then over the Humboldt Trail in Nevada; passing through Three Creek, Idaho; then crossing the Snake River Canyon. She told of being alone on the trip in the wagon and having a gun across her lap with Indians peering in at her. After arriving in Idaho, she went to work at the Gooding Ranch. Adrian's mother, Addie Chisholm Smith, did not know the whereabouts of her father until later.

When Adrian was growing up, he always wondered why Lulu never liked Jim or the male gender. The family thought she had gotten the divorce but found out in later years that Jim had filed for it. We thought Jim Chisholm had deserted her while on one of his travels.

On our January vacation, after Grandma Lulu passed away, we decided to find out where Jim was buried and what we could find out about him. Adrian said there are always two sides of a divorce and Grandma was such a man hater and he wondered why. Adrian had a blue book that was the autobiography of Jim that his mother had given him.

We left on vacation in search of Grandpa's history. After visiting the Kingman Cemetery, Then Wickenburg, Arizona; then just shopping around we happened to stop in Bouse, Arizona. What a surprise we found there. We were in the Ocotillo Café and Lounge sitting by an older man, and he told Adrian about Jim Chisholm and about the mines and a lot of tracts. He decided he had given too much information when he ask Adrian what he did and Adrian told him he was an Idaho State Policeman and was on vacation. Things went very quiet after that.

We went to the Chisholm house across the railroad tracks and Dorothy Chisholm, wife of Eugene Chisholm, was there. The blue book that Jim had written identified Adrian as his grandson. We were told about Chet and Gene Chisholm, but they were not at home. They were in Salome on mining business. We did not meet Chet Chisholm and Clarence Chambers until another year. We visited the burial site of Jim in Needles, California; so, with knowing about Grandpa Jim, Adrian concluded that there really was a man in Grandma Lulu's life. The stories certainly added up to a man who lived a very active roaming life, as was told in stories of old, that he rode hard and had a fast horse to cover all the territory he was supposed to have been in.

Time passed and Chet Chisholm, a grand nephew of Jim, invited Adrian and myself to come to Bouse to visit the mines; so, we did and heard more stories about the Chisholm Trail and other relatives. It was at that time that Chet gave Adrian Jim's poker chips and the divorce decree. It was also at that time we found that Jim had been the one to get the divorce. He gave Adrian a letter Attie, Jim's daughter, had written to him and one that Jim's last wife, Lorna Chambers, had written in return. There was contact in later years but they never visited each other. He had visited the family in their younger years. He worked at one time at the Gooding Ranch, and he left from there to go to the Klondike during the gold rush. Adrian was surprised that neither Chet or Clarence knew that Jim had two daughters. Clarence Chambers had spent a lot of time with Jim after Clarence's grandmother became Jim's last wife.

In Lulu's last days, Adrian's brother, Darrel, remembers her saying she was waiting for Jim to come and get her. Adrian and I discovered to our amazement the number of relatives we had on Grandpa's side of the family and they have been very wonderful.

Bonnie Doggett Smith
February 2007

Daniel and Lulu had the following children:

63 F i. **Anna Othoma Chisholm** "Annie" was born on 10 Aug 1887 in Houston, Texas.

She died on 28 Mar 1968 in Venture, California, USA. Anna married **Danks.**

+ 64 F ii. **Addie Bell Chisholm** was born on 27 Jan 1890. She died on 19 Mar 1968.

65 M iii. **Bob Chisholm** was born in Feb 1893 in Texas, USA. He died in Mar.

Bob died when his mother and two sisters were on their way to Idaho, alone, making the trip in a covered wagon. We are not sure it in New Mexico or Arizona. He was twelve months old.

Pictured: Anna & Addie

Daniel married (2) Dora Chisholm unmarried in Bouse, LaPaz, Arizona, USA.

Uncle Jim lived with Dora from the 30's until she died. They lived at Bouse most of the time. He live with her longer than any other woman. We all called her Aunt even though we never new if they married.

Daniel married (3) Lorna Elizabeth Klaholtz on 13 Jun 1951 in Las Cruses, New Mexico, USA.

Lorna was born on 16 Jul 1884 in Wellsby, Ontario, Canada.

Zenna notes: Chisholm Family History of Daniel Fore Chisholm an extended family. Information from Clarence Chambers and personal family contacts.

1923 Jun 1 - Divorce paper of (Jim) and Lulu Chisholm.

Ibid., 1945 Mar 26 - Letter from San Antonio, Texas Express, thanking (Jim) for sending information on the Chisholm Trail.

Marriage Source: CERTIFICATE OF MARRIAGE 1951 Jun 13 - Marriage License for Daniel Fore (Jim) Chisholm to Lorna Elizabeth Chambers in Las Cruces, New Mexico.

Entered into this genealogy on 27 Apr 2007.

Marriage Source: Milam Family History of Walter Burton Milam from wife Snowda Darlene Snowden received Feb 2007. Extended family of Milams and Alfred and Mae Chisholm Snowden.

Copy of the Birth Certificate for Snowda Darlene Snowden issued 21 Sept 1998. Certificate entered into this genealogy 27 Apr 2007.

Death Source: CERTIFICATE OF DEATH 1954 Oct 1 - Certificate of Death of Daniel Fore Chisholm. He died in route to California near Needles, California.

12. **Olive Ann Chisholm** "Ollie" (Bradford A, Richard Henry) was born in Jun 1869 in Carrizo Springs, Dimmit, Texas, USA. She died in 1930 in Pod, California, USA.

Olive married John Rutledge Dickens son of William Dickens and Amanda Burleson on 17 Aug 1886 in Dimmit, Texas, USA. John was born on 8 Dec 1857 in Carrizo Springs, Dimmit, Texas, USA. He died on 18 Mar 1918 in Carrizo Springs, Dimmit, Texas, USA.

They had the following children:

   66 F i.   **Wavie Estelle Dickens** was born in 1887 in Dimmit, Texas.

   67 M ii. **William Bradford Dickens** was born on 22 Dec 1890 in Dimmit, Texas.
             He died on 7 Sep 1957 in Santa Clara, California.

   68 F iii. **Delila Alice Dickens** was born on 27 Jul 1892 in Carrizo Springs, Dimmit, Texas.

   69 F iv. **Ruth Mae Dickens** was born on 28 May 1895 in Carrizo Springs, Dimmit, Texas.

   70 F v.   **Iva Lorraine Dickens** was born on 8 Apr 1899 in Dimmit, Texas.

   71 F vi. **Hattie Dickens** was born on 1 Apr 1904 in Dimmit, Texas.

   72 F vii. **Ophelia Dickens** was born on 17 Apr 1907 in Dimmit, Texas.

Zenna notes: Chisholm Family History of Bradford A. Updated by Bobby Christall Jr. 26 Mar 2007 on extended families (1900 CENSUS TEXAS twelfth). 1880 CENSUS TEXAS Census used also..
   1910 CENSUS TEXAS Dimmitt, County, Salt Creek.

13 **George B. Chisholm**, born 1876 in Texas, USA.

14 **Alice M. Chisholm**, born 1978 in Carrizo Springs, Dimmit, Texas, USA; died 1929 in Pod, California, USA. She married (1) **Bill Armstrong**; (2) **W Handel**.

15. **Emma Chisholm** (Bradford A, Richard Henry) was born in Jun 1875. She died in 1932.

The daughter of Bradford A Chisholm and she lived in Hemet California abt 1966.

Emma married (1) Levi English on 27 Jun 1900 in Carrizo Springs, Dimmit, Texas, USA. Levi died about 1900 in Dimmit, Texas, USA.

Emma married (2) A A Carr in 1903.

They had the following children:

    73 M i.   **Bradford Carr**

Zenna notes: Updated by Bobby Christall Jr. 26 Mar 2007 on extended families. (1900 CENSUS TEXAS twelfth). 1880 CENSUS TEXAS Census used also.

    1910 CENSUS TEXAS Dimmitt, County, Salt Creek.

16. **Seymour[3] Chisholm**, born 1874; died abt 1900.

17. **Ida Mae[3] Chisholm**, born 1878 in Kerr, Texas, USA; christened in 26 Apr 1959. She married in Carrizo Springs, Dimmit, Texas, USA **Joel Allen English**.

18. **Nina Maud Chisholm** (Bradford A, Richard Henry) was born on 30 Aug 1881 in Sierra Blanca, Hudsbeth, Texas, USA. She died on 27 Sep 1923 in Amarillo, Potter, Texas, USA.

Nina married (1) Thomas Frank Watson in 1905 in Del Rio, Val Verde, Texas, USA. Thomas was born in 1879.

They had the following children:

    + 74 F i.   **Winnie Mae Watson** was born in 1905. She died in 1989.

75 F ii.   **Marie Watson** was born in 1908. Marie married **Unknown** .

Nina married (2) Clarence Clinton Duncan.

19. **Richard T. Chisholm**, born Sep 1889 in Texas, USA. He married on 6 Nov 1908 in LaSalle, Texas, USA **Ethel Day.**

TC

CHAPTER FOUR

FOURTH Generation

God blessed our hearty pioneer relatives. They were happy with what they had and where they were.
When they told the stories of their trips, they spoke more of the good times than the hardships.

Zenna Chisholm Snowden

27. Jennie Chisholm (George Langford, Glenn Thornton, Richard Henry) was born on 28 Jul 1882 in , DeWitt, Texas, USA. She died on 15 Jul 1951 in Yuma, Yuma, Arizona, USA. She was buried in Rest Haven Park, Glendale, Maricopa, Arizona.

Jennie married (1) Aquillar Q Evans "Doc" son of George Edwards Evans and Celeste Ann Oden in 1901 in Junction City, Texas, USA. Aquillar was born on 1 Jun 1865 in Gonzales, Texas, USA. He died on 26 Dec 1932 in Riverside, Riverside, California, USA. Twin brother to Laura.

Aquillar and Jennie had the following children:

+ 76 F i.   **Georgia Louise Evans** was born about 1902.

  77 M ii. **Willie Evans** "Bill" was born about 1903 in Junction City, Kimble, Texas. He died about 1952 in California, USA. He was buried in Rest Haven Park, Glendale, Maricopa, Arizona, USA. Willie had two Children. Willie married **Cathryn Brooks** .

+ 78 M iii. **Oscar Tedford Evans** was born on 11 Jul 1905. He died on 15 Jun 1950.

Jennie married (2) Otto Myers about 1943.

━━━◦◦◦━━━

28. **Martin Gaines Chisholm** "Mart" (George Langford, Glenn Thornton, Richard Henry) was born on 24 Feb 1884 in Oklahoma, USA. He died on 4 Feb 1942 in Planet Ranch, La Pas, Arizona, USA. The cause of death was Hemorrhage - Tuberculosis. He was buried on 7 Feb 1942 in Rest Haven Park, Glendale, Maricopa, Arizona, USA.

A Son was stillborn in 1919

The Planet Ranch where Martin died is located northeast of Bouse, Arizona, about 25 miles in the Buckshin Mountains of La Pas County.

Martin married Blanche Currie in 1908 in Oklahoma, USA. Blanche was born in 1892 in Oklahoma, USA. She died on 21 Apr 1920 in Peoria, Maricopa, Arizona, USA. She was buried in Glendale Memorial Cemetery, Glendale, Maricopa, Arizona, USA. Died in a rest home (Living on Sanderson Ranch in Peoria, Arizona before that.)

Martin and Blanche had the following children:
+ 79 F i.   **Vivian Mable Chisholm** was born in 1912.
+ 80 F ii.   **Vestal Chisholm** was born in 1914.
+ 81 F iii.   **Bessie Loraine Chisholm** was born on 18 Jun 1917. She died on 7 Oct 1988.

━━━◦◦◦━━━

29. **Richard Akley Chisholm** "Dick" (George Langford, Glenn Thornton, Richard Henry) was born on 15 Dec 1886 in Pearsall, Frio, Texas, USA. He died on 5 May 1968 in Wickenburg Hospital, Wickenburg, Maricopa, Arizona, USA. He was buried on 11 May 1968 in Glendale Memorial Park, Glendale, Maricopa, Arizona, USA.

Richard was living at Bouse when he became ill.

Information from Funeral Service Brochure.

Richard married Narnie Bell Simmons in 1905 in Thrall, Texas, USA. Narnie was born in 1889. She died in 1974 in Texas, USA.

They had the following children:

+ 82 M i. **Thornton Dudley Chisholm** died on 15 Jun 1944.

  83 F ii. **Vivian Chisholm** died in 1916.

+ 84 F iii. **Fannie G Chisholm** was born on 16 May 1915. She died on 14 Dec 1973.

+ 85 M iv. **Richard A Chisholm** was born in 1918. He died on 2 Jan 1977.

+ 86 M v. **Beldon Hopkins Chisholm** was born on 7 Dec 1918. He died on 23 Apr 1972.

  87 M vi. **Eugene Hayes Chisholm** "Boy" was born on 23 Feb 1922 in Williamson, Texas. He died on 14 May 1986 in Texas, USA. He was buried in Texas, USA. Eugene married **Dorothy Chisholm** on 14 Jun 1947 in Austin, Texas, USA (Baptist Church). Dorothy was born on 16 Jan 1931. She died on 6 Apr 1974 in Glendale, Maricopa, Arizona, USA. She was buried in Cuero, DeWitt, Texas, USA. Information from family and Funeral Service Brochure.

+ 88 F vii. **Frances Charlene Chisholm** was born on 6 Sep 1928.

30. **Maud Chisholm** (George Langford, Glenn Thornton, Richard Henry) was born in 1887. She died about 1907 in Granite, Oklahoma. The cause of death was Died with childbirth.

Maud married Dock Jordan in 1905 in Thrall, Texas. Dock died in California.

They had the following children:

  89 M i. **Bradford Jordan** was born about 1907 in Granite, Oklahoma, USA. He died on 2 Jan 1923 in Glendale, Maricopa, Arizona, USA. The cause of death was burned in starting a fire to keep warm. Grave is Block 107. He was buried in Glendale Resthaven Cemetery, Glendale, Maricopa, Arizona,

USA. Bradford was starting a fire by pouring kerosene on a flame and the fire exploded into the can he was holding, and he was burned and died.

31. Top Chisholm (George Langford, Glenn Thornton, Richard Henry) was born on 11 Feb 1890 in Uvalde, Uvalde, Taxes, USA. He died on 4 Jul 1965 in San Bernadina, San Bernadina, California, USA. He was buried in Merced, Merced, California, USA.

Top married Lillie Amanda Thur daughter of Whilhem Heinrich Thur and Laura Augusta Zielsdorf on 10 Feb 1912 in Granite, Oklahoma, USA. Lillie was born on 3 May 1896 in Fairfield, Jackson, Wisconsin, USA. She died on 15 May 1991 in San Bernadina, San Bernadina, California, USA. She was buried on 20 May 1991 in Evergreen Memorial Park, Merced, Merced, California, USA.

Information from family and Funeral Service Brochure.

Top and Lillie had the following children:

90 M i. **Raymond Stockton Chisholm** "Snooks" was born on 15 Aug 1913 in Ft. Stockton, Texas, USA. He died on 30 Jul 1936 in Dos Palos, California, USA. He was buried in Merced, Merced, California, USA.

91 M ii. **Dobboy Chisholm** was born on 5 Jun 1916 in Thrall, Texas, USA. Died 10 July 2016.

+ 92 M iii. **Vernon Ansel Chisholm** was born on 26 Mar 1918. He died on 2 Dec 1995.

+ 93 F iv. **Oleta Chisholm** was born on 20 May 1920.

+ 94 M v. **William Chisholm** was born on 10 Dec 1922. He died on 4 Apr 2004.

+ 95 F vi. **Josephine May Chisholm** was born on 17 Jan 1925. She died on 23 Feb 2001.

+ 96 M vii. **Douglas Fairbanks Chisholm** was born on 25 Oct 1926. He died on 13 Aug 1955.

+ 97 M viii. **Lloyd Frances Chisholm** was born on 14 Oct 1928. He died on 6 Dec 1959.

+ 98 M ix. **Toppy Monroe Chisholm** was born on 25 Jul 1931.

32. Thomas John Chisholm "Tom" (George Langford, Glenn Thornton, Richard Henry) was born on 1 Apr 1892 in Middleton, De Witt, Texas, USA. He died on 21 Sep 1966 in Glendale, Maricopa, Arizona, USA. The cause of death was emphysema - heart. He was buried Glendale, Maricopa, Arizona, USA in Rest Haven Park, Glendale, Maricopa, Arizona, USA.

Thomas John Chisholm

On April 1, 1882 in Middleton, Texas the sixth child was born to the family of George and Jennie Chisholm. Thomas spent his younger days in Texas working on farms and ranches. The family moved often. As soon as Tom was old enough to ride a horse, he rode many a mile back and forth between Texas , Oklahoma, and Arizona. You can read in his mother's biography about most of the trips he made. With all the traveling, the children were unable to attend school regularly. They learned to work hard and to do whatever was necessary to live. The children stayed close to the family until they were grown and married. I do not know if it was their Mother's influence or their Father's need for them to work.

The family came by covered wagon to Arizona in 1899 when Tom was only seven years old. He remembered the trip vividly. They left from Smithville, Texas, and crossed the Colorado River on a ferry. Dad remembered that the man that ran the ferry was called Hand because he was crippled in one hand. The ferry got loose from the six pairs of mules that were pulling it. A Negro man came with a yoke of steers and pulled for (2 to 3 hours) to get them out. The wagon dropped down into the water to the chuck box on the back. Tom rode all the way on a pack saddle. He would open gates and ride out for water. It is hard to imagine a seven year old riding out alone in unknown territory.

They passed through Leon Springs, Fort Stockton and El Paso, Texas. In El Paso, they saw a street car being pulled by one mule. After one month and twenty-one days, they arrived in Geronimo, Arizona. While they were living in the area, they built a canal at the flour mill in Solomonville. In doing this type of work, they would use their own horses. I know the whole family was on this venture because his sister, Virgie, was born in Geronimo at that time. The family spent about a year in Arizona and then went back to Texas by wagon.

The family went to Taylor, Texas where they farmed for several years. In 1907, once again, the family loaded the wagons and headed for Oklahoma. Since there were nineteen family members who went on this trip, it was a large caravan.

Maud and her husband were with them and while in Granite, Oklahoma they had a son, Bradford, and Maud died in childbirth. This was the first death in the immediate family.

After spending about five years in Oklahoma in the winter of 1913, the family came by train to Congress, Arizona. Tom got a job in Congress and stayed there while the rest of the family went on to the Santa Maria River. Tom stayed in the Congress Hotel and delivered mail by stage from Congress Junction to Stantion and the Octave Mine. After becoming a ghost town, Stanton is once again a booming mining town. The Lost Dutchman Mining Assoc. now owns it. Instead of tents and wagons, the campground now has motor homes and ATVs. The post office building that Tom delivered mail to is still standing and being used by the wannabe prospectors. He also drove a freight wagon from Wickenburg to Sheep Camp near Congress. He remembered that a store in Wickenburg was owned by Deutches.

While Tom was working in the Congress Junction area, his father farmed 40 acres of irrigated land on the Santa Maria River where they built levies, ditches, and flumes. We can check back to Uncle Jim's writings and find that it was during this time that he too was ranching on the Santa Maria River. The brothers had kept in touch and Uncle Jim convinced George to come to Arizona where he could get a ranch.

Farming on the Santa Maria was not meant for George; so, in 1914, he decided to return to Texas by wagon. Tom rejoined the family and they went to Glendale, Arizona and worked in the cantaloupes during the spring before going on to Texas. They went to a place called Hare along the San Gabriel River where they farmed. They grew cotton, corn, and sugar cane. After one year of farming, they moved to Thrall, Texas and lived there about two years.

While in Thrall, Grandpa George planned another trip. Tom and Marie Damron had become good friends. Mom never told me this, but I feel that she did not want the love of her life to leave; so, the two of them helped to persuade Marie's mother, Maggie, and Marie's brothers to go to

Arizona. Maggie was a divorcee at the time.

On a Tuesday afternoon at about 2 o'clock, October 31, 1916, they left Thrall, Texas. In Grandpa

George's family, there were three wagons and a surrey. Grandfather George drove a wagon. His daughter, Virgie, and a cousin, Dena Kelso, both 16 years of age, drove a wagon. Tom drove the third wagon. Grandmother Fannie and daughter, Totsie, who was about ten years old, the youngest child, drove the surrey. This may have been the most comfortable trip Grandma Fannie ever made since there were no little ones to care for and she was riding in the surrey. Son, Albert, and grandson, Bradford, rode horseback. In Grandmother Maggie's two wagons, were daughters, Marie and Fay, and sons, Dude and Cooter.

On the way, Moses Waddle and wife, Leta (Minnie) Taylor, the daughter of Uncle Creed Taylor, joined the caravan with their three sons. The wagon train went through Lampasas, San Saba, where Tom and Marie were married November 6, 1916. At Menard, Texas, Maggie Damron ran out of money; so, she and the boys stayed there to work. After selling their wagons and stock, they later came to Glendale by train.

From Menard the wagon train continued on to Sheffield, there ticks were found on Moses Waddle's stock and the family had to lay over while the stock were dipped. Along the way, all the kids except Virgie had the measles. It did not delay the trip; they kept on traveling. The trip took the wagon train through Van Horn, Sierra Blanca, Fort Stockton, El Paso, Las Cruces, Deming, Lordsburg, Duncan and Ash Springs where they spent Christmas of 1916. The night was cold and it snowed. The next morning the kids made a snowman before they left for Safford, Solomonville, Globe and Roosevelt Dam where they spent another cold night.

While on the trip, when they stopped at night everyone had a job to do. Tom would take care of the stock and the rest would gather wood and cook supper. The girls would take turns making bread. On the back of one of the wagons, there was a chuck box where dishes and cooking utensils were kept. The lid of the chuck box could be let down and used as a table.

The wagon train arrived in Glendale January 7, 1917 after two months and eight days. Tom worked at different jobs in Arizona and sometimes in California.

The last twenty-five years of Dad's working life was spent farming and managing a cattle feed lot for the Glendale Cattle Company, owned by Marion Welborn. The feed lot was located on Bethany

Home Road and Palm Lane. When Tom retired, the family moved to Peoria where he lived until he passed away on September 21, 1966. Tom and Marie raised their family of five girls in Arizona

Zenna Chisholm Snowden
May 2007

Thomas married Marie Damron daughter of John Edward Damron Sr. and Mary Magdelene Williams on 6 Nov 1916 in Lampassas, Texas. Marie was born on 5 Apr 1898 in Dallas, Dallas, Texas, USA. She died on 17 Feb 1987 in Cottonwood, Yavapai, Arizona, USA. She was buried in Rest Haven Park, Glendale, Maricopa, Arizona.

This was from my mother Marie Damron Chisholm.

Early Days of Marie Damron Chisholm

After the death of their Father Edd, on November 8, 1904, who was only 33, the family went to the maternal grandparents, Wm. Dixon, in Dallas. Cooter, the youngest child, was born there on December 16, 1904. The family spent several years there. Think of the suffering of Mary (Maggie) the mother, to suddenly lose her husband, when she was within a month of having a baby. What our pioneer mothers went through to be with a wandering husband! They were on their way to the Oklahoma Territory in a covered wagon. It is hard to imagine them planning a trip to an unknown country with a child so close to being born. Cooter was born in Dallas December 16, 1904. Mom did not say why they were going to Oklahoma. She was probably too young to really care. Mom remembered the team that pulled their wagon was named Henry and Dora. They had three children, Marie the oldest was six, Thomas Roy (Jack) was five, and Laska Sewell (Dude) was two.

Mom's next thought to me was when she was ten or eleven, and going to live with a family in Buckholts to help them and to go to school. Marie was chased and threatened by the man of the household; so, she returned to her mother, Maggie. Mom remembered seeing her first car at Buckholts. Dude went to live with another family.

At the age of twelve, Mom went to spend the summer with her Aunt Maude. The next summer she went to Tom and Leila Tunstal at Center Hill. She enjoyed being there and talked very lovingly of them. I have a couple of post cards she received from them after leaving there; so, they must have appreciated her also. She went from Center Hill, to Thrall, to Palestine and at the age of thirteen to Crocket. She was probably with her family at this time. Even with all this moving around and helping other people, she was able to get her education.

The family was living in Pennington and moved from there to Cameron to help Uncle Sid and Aunt Ada Foster do their farming. It was there that a young neighbor girl became Mom's very good friend. Her name was Zenna Conn for whom I was named. The two corresponded after Mom left Uncle Sid's, I have a couple of post cards sent to her by Zenna Conn. There were other towns that Mom mentioned that they moved to in their desperate attempt to exist. It was about this time that Maggie met Emmett Moon and married him in June of 1911. Imagine all of those moves in seven years! From the Moon marriage, Mom was blessed with another half-sister, Fay.

I regret never asking Mom and Dad how they met. At the time the two families were living in Thrall, they got together and decided on another covered wagon trip, this time to Arizona. These were the Chisholm's, the Damron's and Mother Maggie Moon, now divorced. The families must have spent some time as neighbors in Thrall because Marie Damron and Tom Chisholm became close friends. It was not many days out on the trip when Mom and Dad decided to get married. They left Thrall October 31, 1916 and were married November 6, 1916 in the Lampasas, San Saba, Texas area. They were married standing beside a covered wagon with a stream nearby that was lined with cottonwood trees. Tom's father, George, was their best man. Mom was wearing two dresses (layered); it was cold in November.

The thing she remembered most about what Tom wore was he had a great big old safety pin in his lapel. She didn't remember just why. A minister came out from San Saba to perform the ceremony. Mom remembered just what he looked like. I have a post card that Mom wrote to her sister, Cora, in Dallas, telling her about her marriage and that it had taken place in San Saba. The reason I have the card was that she never had the chance to post it. She was probably in Arizona before her family in Dallas knew she was married or even knew they had traveled to Arizona. I think of my Mom's honeymoon in a covered wagon, in the middle of winter, with her family along on the trip.

God blessed our hearty pioneer relatives. They were happy with what they had and where they were. When they told the stories of their trips, they spoke more of the good times than the hardships. I will write more about the trip in the biography of my father, Tom Chisholm.

Zenna Chisholm Snowden
July 2007

Thomas and Marie had the following children:

+ 99 F i.   **Ruth Ester Chisholm** was born on 2 Dec 1917. She died on 13 Nov 1989.

  100 F ii. **Opal Marie Chisholm** was born on 23 Feb 1919 in Peoria, Maricopa, Arizona, USA. She died on 20 Apr 1919 in Peoria, Maricopa, Arizona, USA. She was buried in Rest Haven Park, Glendale, Maricopa, Arizona, USA.

+ 101 F iii. **Juanita Chisholm** was born on 14 Jul 1920. She died on 10 Mar 1967.

+ 102 F iv. **Zenna Chisholm** was born on 15 Sep 1921.

+ 103 F v. **Tommie Chisholm** was born on 23 Mar 1932.

+ 104 F vi.**Yvonne Chisholm** was born on 24 May 1940.

33. Calvin Alonzo Chisholm (George Langford, Glenn Thornton, Richard Henry) was born on 17 Feb 1895 in Bastrop, Texas, USA. He died on 6 Aug 1956 in Chowchilla, Madera, California, USA. He was buried on 8 Aug 1956 in Chowchilla District Cemetery, Chowchilla, Madera, California, USA.

Calvin married Jessie Marie Griffith daughter of Clark Griffith and Fannie Stitch on 11 Jul 1919 in Phoenix, Maricopa, AZ, USA. Jessie was born on 10 Feb 1901 in Ponca City, Oklahoma, USA. She died on 1 Aug 1979 in Yosemite Place Hospital, Fresno, Fresno, California, USA. She was buried on 6 Aug 1979 in Chowchilla District Cemetery, Chowchilla, , California, USA.

They had the following children:

+ 105 M i.**Ross Martin Chisholm** was born on 16 Jun 1920. He died on 20 Jul 2002.

+ 106 F ii.**Fannie Maude Chisholm** was born on 4 Jan 1923.

+ 107 M iii. **Daniel Webster Chisholm** was born on 18 Jan 1925. He died on 8 Dec 2006.

+ 108 M iv. **Chester Lee Chisholm** was born on 4 Nov 1926.

⟞⟝⟞⟝⟞━⟞⟝⟞⟝⟞

34. Jesse Chisholm (George Langford, Glenn Thornton, Richard Henry) was born on 9 Apr 1897 in , Bastrop, Texas, USA. He died on 13 Aug 1985 in Fresno, Fresno, California, USA. He was buried on 16 Aug 1985 in Washington Colony Cemetery, Easton, California, USA.

Jesse and Dena Chisholm

On May 18, 1978 Jesse and Dena celebrated their Sixtieth Wedding Anniversary. Their Granddaughter, Dena Pollard wrote the following paper:

"The Life and Times of Jesse and Dena Chisholm"

Jesse Chisholm was born April 9, 1897 in Bastrop, Texas. Dena Mae Kelso was born October 25, 1899 in Del Rio, Texas. They first met when Dena was 9 months old and Jess was 2 Years old. Their families were camped on the river near Del Rio, Texas.

In 1915 they became neighbors in Thrall, Texas when Dena was 16 and Jesse was 19.

In 1916 Jess decided to "Go West" and see the world. He traveled by train with his brother Calvin, Doc Jordan and Jack Damron. They went to Arizona then on to California and then back to Arizona. A few months later the rest of the Chisholm Family decided to move to Arizona and they asked Dena if she would like to come along. She said, "Yes" and so in the fall of 1916 they left Thrall, Texas and traveled by covered wagon for three months arriving in Glendale, Arizona in January 1917.

Eighteen months later on May 18, 1918 they were married in Glendale, Arizona by Rev. C. M. Northrup. Their witnesses were the minister's wife, Mrs. Northrup and Mr. R. Hoover who was the minister's mother-in-law. They settled in Peoria for a few years where their first daughter, Dorothy Flora, was born June 9, 1919.

During this time Jess spent a short term in the Army. He was in Company C. 81st Engineers. He was ready to ship overseas when World War I ended. He was discharged on December 13, 1918. He was given $60 travel pay which some of this was used to buy a new pair of boots.

57

The second daughter, Gladys Dena, was born Oct 1, 1920 in Peoria, Arizona.
From Peoria they moved to the area of Blythe, California, where their son, Robert (Bob), was born April 5, 1922.

In 1935 they moved to California where Dorothy, Gladys and Bob attended school.
In 1935 they moved to Caruthers where they bought and farmed an 80 acre ranch. From 1937 to 1941 they farmed on the West Side in the Five Points area. From 1941 to 1943 they had cattle ranches on the Bill Williams in Arizona and in Raymond, California and then returned to the ranch in Caruthers which they had bought in 1935.

Here in Caruthers they joined in the community belonging to the American Legion Auxiliary and the First Baptist Church.

From 1950 to 1958 they lived and farmed in various locations in and around the Fresno, Caruthers and Clovis areas.

In 1958 Jess and Dena moved to West Park School where Jess was Grounds Keeper and Dena helped out in the school cafeteria. Jess retired in April 1963 and they moved into the "Big City" of Caruthers where they lived for 13 years.

In 1976 they moved, where they presently reside, into a mobile home on their son Bob's ranch located in the Selma area.

During their 60 years together they have many memories to look back on and share with all of us. Their many camping trips, family reunion, bumps and bruises and all their ups and downs. Twenty-four grandchildren and 1 great-great grandchild.

Jess and Dena and all of their family wish to thank you for being here today to share this 60th wedding anniversary celebration.

Dena Mae Pollard
May 27, 1978

Jesse passed away August 13, 1985 in Fresno, California and Dena passed away February 27, 1992 in California.

Jesse married Dena Kelso daughter of William M Kelso and Mary Amanda Rustin on 18 May 1918 in Glendale, Maricopa, Arizona, USA. Dena was born on 25 Oct 1899 in Del Rio, Texas, USA. She died on 27 Feb 1992 in California, USA. She was buried on 2 Mar 1992 in Washington Colony Cemetery, Easton, California, USA.

Information from family and Funeral Service Brochure

Jesse and Dena had the following children:

+ 109 F i. **Dorothy Flora Chisholm** was born on 9 Jun 1919. She died in 1979.

+ 110 F ii. **Gladys Dena Chisholm** was born on 1 Oct 1920. She died on 10 Feb 2002.

+ 111 M iii. **Jesse Robert Chisholm** was born on 5 Apr 1922. He died on 29 Jan 2003.

35. **Virgie Eliza Chisholm** (George Langford, Glenn Thornton, Richard Henry) was born on 23 Sep 1899 in Geronimo, , Arizona, USA. She died on 6 Nov 1968 in Ceres, , California, USA. She was buried in Ceres, , California, USA.

Virgie Chisholm

Virgie Chisholm was born September 23,1899 in Geronimo, Arizona to George and Jennie Chisholm. They were on one of their trips to Arizona to visit Anne, George's sister, who lived there. It was sixteen years later when the family made their last trip to Arizona, to stay, that Virgie kept this diary. There is not much in her diary about the trip, but it is interesting to read what the younger generation of that time did for entertainment while traveling. Waving at the cowboys and solders lets you know they were not the only ones on the trail.

Diary of Virgie Chisholm
1916 - 1918

We left Thrall Texas Tuesday evening about 2 o'clock. There was papa's wagon leading the way. Next was my wagon. I was 16 years old and my 3rd cousin Dena Kelso also 16 years old rode with me. I drove the wagon and she applied the brakes.

It was quite a trip we were from the 31st of Oct 1916 till the 6 of Jan 1917. Papa had to keep a eye on us as we were daydreaming lots of times also lots of cowboys and soldiers along the way. We didn't dare let him see us wave at them. My Mother and Sister Totsie drove the Surrey which was the tail end.

My Bro. Tom drove the 3rd wagon and his girlfriend Marie Damron who later on the trip became his wife.

My Bro. Albert and Totsie got the measles. We had lots of cold weather along the way.

On the 31day of Oct we left Thrall Tex. Tue eve. 1916. There were 5 covered wagons - 1 Surry.

Got to Glendale 6 of Jan at 3 o'clock 1917. Marie and Tom were married Nov. 6 at 3:30 o'clock at Lampassas Texas.

G. L. Chisholm moved out on Holmes ranch Wed. Mar. 22, 1917. From Glendale, Ariz.

Tom came out to the Holme's ranch on the 25th of March Sunday 1917.

Tom Left for Greenhaw's the 20 day of April 1917.

On the 31st of Mar. Friday night we all went to our first dance at West End.

My Motto "Always were a sunny Smile - LOVE AND KISSES."

6 of Jan 1918 on Sun. Dena, Dock, and Virgia went to Phoenix.

Mon. Dec 24 = Dena and I went on the stage from Peoria to Glendale.

Tue Dec. 25, 1917--Charlie Tell - Georgia Evans - Dena Kelso - Jess Chisholm - Dock Jordan - Virgia Chisholm went to Phoenix. The lights on the car went out so we took the st car from Six points on to Phoenix.

Sun 3 of Feb 1918 - Dena, Jess, Dock, and Virgia went to Glendale, I got two letters from Jess.

Mon 4 went over on the desert. Gee But it is colds to night must retire.

Top and Lillie moved over from Agua Fria on Sat Feb 9, 1918. Dena is taking care of Dobboy.

On Sat Night Jess and Dena were married. Sat eve May 18, 1918 at Glendale.

Papa bought the Ford car on Tues May 22, 1918 at Glendale.

Albert and I are learning to drive the Ford we don't trust papa's driving.

Mon. the 18 of Feb 1918. Dena and I went to Phoenix to have Dena's eyes' s treated by Dr. Bakes.

Thur. Feb 21, 1918 Dena and I went back to Phoenix.

Sun. Feb 24. Dena, Jess, Dock, Virgia went to Phoenix to the show.

Mon. 25 Feb 1918 Dena and I went to Phoenix and Dena got her glasses from Dr. Bakes. Dena and I got our photograph album.

On Thur 28 Feb Dock and I went to Phoenix.

Sun 3 March. Flossie Ding came over and Sunday night Sam Griffinn and Sister came over.

Thur March 14, 1918 Papa killed a Mexican.

Friday March 22 Papa had his trial.

Wed 20 March 1918 Collie Died. This is a very cruel world and I would to god that I wasn't a girl.

April 10, 1918. A card from Jess and he was going to France.

Thur. April 11, 1918. Willie left home and came out here.

Sat night May 25, 1918. We went to a dance at Peoria at the home of Mrs. Pendergast.

Tues May 28, 1918. Went to Glendale to a dance.

Mon. 26, 1918 - 300 boys left Phoenix for Camp Cody Cody Dem, N. M.

Alice's calf Borned 1st June Sat.

Mother Left for Paducah Texas, the 14 day of May 1917 visiting Jennie.

Mother's death was Sept 15, 1917, on Saturday at five o'clock.

On Monday night the 18 of June Peoria burned down.

Papa went after Mama on the 2 of July on Monday.

On Friday night the 14 of July; Papa and Mama came in from Paducah Texas.

Jess left for Cal. the 7th of Sept.

On the 6th Calvin came home of a furlow, on the 17th of Aug he went back.

On July 27, 1917 a storm came and tore things up.

On the 15 Sept 1917 Mother died - Sunday 16, 1917 Calvin came in and we buried mother at the Glendale Cemetery - at 4:30 o'clock p.m. Calvin went back on Wed night the 19 of Sept 1917.

On the 14 day of Oct. Georgia Evans, Dena Kelso, Elsie Schindeler, Oswald Roach, Charlie, Jack Weaver and Virgia Chisholm went on a picnic the other side of Phoenix.

On the 24 of Sept Jennie arrived at Peoria.

Jess and Dock came in from Cal on Friday the 25 of Nov 1917.

Sunday night 1st of Dec. Jesse McCleskey and I went to phoenix got out of Gas-coming home.

On the 28 of Oct 1917 Elsie S. ,Bessie S., Georgia E., Eva A., Virgia C, Jess M., Charlie T., Duward R., Paul S., Rangy V., Mr. Schindeler all went on a picnic given to Jess M.

On the 8 of Dec. Sat night 1917. Jess M and I went to the show at Glendale.

Sunday Dec 9 ate dinner in Glendale.

On the 11 day of Den Tue 19 Jess M left.

On the 11 of Nov. Sam left for Camp Cody N.M. and returned that night. The war was over

Nov 11, 1918.

Virgie Chisholm
1916 to 1918

Virgie married Sam Griffith August 3, 1918. She tells in her diary about Sam and his sister visiting on the 3rd of March 1918. Five months later they married. You can trace their moves by where the children were born.

Their son, Buster, was born in Peoria; their daughter, Jewel, was born in Williams; then, daughters, Nellie and Violet, were born in Phoenix. Sam's dad and mother lived there. I can remember that Sam's dad had a Model T truck with the sides enclosed with canvas; there they placed vegetables and fruit and then went around the neighborhood selling it. They lived in town and had a flush toilet. It was still an outhouse but it was my first time to see one with the water closet up high on the wall with a long chain hanging down to flush it. Now, it may not have been so high on the wall and the chain may have not been so long, but I was very young and it seemed that way.

Virgie and family moved to northern California but I do not know the date. Since I do not have any memories of growing up around the family, they probably did not live in the Phoenix area long. Through the years we visited them occasionally in California. We spent more time with Virgie after we all retired.

Zenna Chisholm Snowden
June 2006

Virgie married Samuel Roberts Griffith son of Clark Griffith and Fannie Stitch on 3 Aug 1918 in Glendale, Maricopa, Arizona, USA. Samuel was born on 11 Aug 1897 in New Kirk, Oklahoma, USA. He died on 30 Nov 1973 in Ceres, California, USA. He was buried in Ceres, California, USA.

They had the following children:

+ 112 M i. **Milton Clark Griffith** was born on 31 May 1919. He died on 25 Aug 2003.

+ 113 F ii. **Leona Jewell Griffith** was born on 16 Aug 1922.

114 F iii. **Nellie June Griffith** was born on 28 Feb 1924 in Phoenix, Maricopa, Arizona, USA. She died on 5 May 2004 in Ceres, California, USA. The cause of death was

63

Throat Cancer. She was buried in Ceres, California, USA.

Nellie married **Paul Howard** on 19 Aug 1943 in Santa Rosa, , California, USA.

+ 115 F iv. **Violet Griffith** was born on 31 May 1927. She died on 28 Jul 1978.

36. **Albert Vivian Chisholm** (George Langford, Glenn Thornton, Richard Henry) was born on 12 Mar 1902. He died on 13 Dec 1971 in Hughson, California, USA.

Albert married Johnnie Lee Monteith daughter of John Bengamin Monteith and Etta Matilda Shell on 25 Jul 1925 in Phoenix, Maricopa, Arizona, USA. Johnnie was born on 4 Dec 1909 in Robert Lee, Texas, USA. She died on 7 Feb 1997 in Ceres, California, USA.

They had the following children:

+ 116 F i. **Jeannie May Chisholm** was born on 30 Apr 1926. She died in Apr 2007.
+ 117 M ii. **Randall Ray Chisholm** was born on 6 Sep 1936.

37. **Totsie Lee Chisholm** (George Langford, Glenn Thornton, Richard Henry) was born on 8 Mar 1905 in Bokist, Lee, Texas, USA.

A little tid-bit about why she was named Lee, because she was born in Lee County, Texas

Totsie married (1) John Clark Jr son of John Clark and Nora Michaelson in 1923 in Florence, Pinal, Arizona, USA. John was born on 3 May 1901 in Columbus, Kansas, USA.

They had the following children:

+ 118 M i.   **John Clark lll** was born on 27 Jun 1923. He died in 1997.

+ 119 M ii.   **Donald Clark** was born on 26 May 1926.

+ 120 M iii.   **Carroll Clark** was born on 4 Dec 1929. He died in 1996.

Totsie married (2) Alvin Burroughs .

38. **Mae Chisholm** (George Langford, Glenn Thornton, Richard Henry) was born on 8 Sep 1919 in Peoria, Maricopa, Arizona, USA. She died on 6 Dec 1977 in Nevada, Vernon, Missouri, USA. The cause of death was Cancer. She was buried on 9 Dec 1977 in Newton Burial Park, Nevada, Vernon, Missouri, USA.
Information from family and Funeral Service Brochure.

Mae married Alfred Fredrick Snowden son of Horace Frederick Snowden and Anna Kirchhofer on 7 Jun 1938 in Lordsburg, New Mexico, USA. Alfred was born on 26 Mar 1915 in Britt, Iowa, USA. He died on 29 Oct 1977 in New Orleans, Louisiana, USA. He was buried on 1 Nov 1977 in Newton Burial Park, Nevada, Vernon, Missouri, USA.

Information from family and Funeral Service Brochure.

Alfred and Mae had the following children:

+ 121 F i.   **Snowda Darlene Snowden** was born on 7 Apr 1939. She died on 11 Mar 2007.

  122 F ii.   **Alfreda Mae Snowden** was born on 12 Jan 1942 in Milo, Vernon, Missouri.
                She died on 26 Feb 1942 in Milo, Vernon, Missouri, USA. She was buried in Milo, Vernon, Missouri, USA.

+ 123 M iii.   **Alfred Dalton Snowden** was born on 16 Jan 1943.

+ 124 M iv.   **Harry Horace Snowden** was born on 27 Nov 1944. He died on 6 Jan 1999.

39. **Stanford Dalton Chisholm** (George Langford, Glenn Thornton, Richard Henry) was born on 21 Feb 1921 in Peoria, Maricopa, Arizona, USA. He died on 10 Jul 1958 in Phoenix, Maricopa, Arizona, USA. He was buried on 12 Jul 1958 in Rest Haven

Park, Glendale, Maricopa, Arizona, USA.

Stanford married Elizabeth Nadine Simmons daughter of Boyd Simmons and Bess Biggerstaff on 15 Sep 1941 in Wickenburg, Maricopa, Arizona, USA. Elizabeth was born on 25 Dec 1926 in Snowball, Arkansas, USA. She died on 6 Oct 2000 in Glendale, Maricopa, Arizona, USA. She was buried in Cremated.

They had the following children:

+ 125 M i. **Boyd Langford Chisholm** was born on 1 Jul 1942.

+ 126 M ii. **Ronald Lee Chisholm** was born on 14 Jul 1944. Died 7 March 2016 Phoenix, AZ

+ 127 F iii. **Karen Dudine Chisholm** was born on 21 Aug 1948 in Phoenix, Maricopa, Arizona. Karen died 17 April 2015. Karen married **Donald Bielfelt** (1), **O'Donnal** (2), singer **Dave Dudley** (3) and **Wright** and had a son, Preston Wright.

---

42. Frankie Middleton "Little Sister/Lupie" (Cora Chisholm, Glenn Thornton, Richard Henry).

Frankie had two boys Told to me by Marie Chisholm

Frankie married Martin Woods .

They had the following children:

128 M i. **Fred Woods**

129 M ii. **Cliff Woods**

---

45. Georgia Middleton (Cora Chisholm, Glenn Thornton, Richard Henry).

Georgia had two boys Wayne / Frank

This information given to me by Georgia.

Georgia married McAuley

They had the following children:

130 M i. **Wayne McAuley**

131 M ii. **Frank McAuley**

<hr />

54. Clara May Filleman (Annie Elizabeth Chisholm, Glenn Thornton, Richard Henry) was born on 20 Feb 1890 in Solomonville, Graham, Arizona, USA. She died on 10 Oct 1968 in Phoenix, Maricopa, Arizona, USA.

Clara married (1) **Claude Lexox Nichols** son of Nichols and Sarah Isabell Hudson on 18 Sep 1912 in Greenlee, Arizona, USA. Claude was born in Mar 1887 in Texas, USA. He died on 14 Oct 1941 in Greenlee, Arizona, USA.

They had the following children:

132 M i. **Herbert Nichols** was born on 30 Sep 1913. He died about 1966 in Greenlee, Arizona.

Herbert married **Judy Nichols**.

Clara married (2) **Davis**

<hr />

55. Effie Lucille Filleman (Annie Elizabeth Chisholm, Glenn Thornton, Richard Henry) was born on 17 Jul 1891 in Uvalde, Uvalde, Texas, USA. She died on 4 Jan 1961 in Morenci, Greenlee, Arizona, USA.

Effie married (1) **George Lumpkin Wyatt** son of George Washington Wyatt and Emma Eliza Bryan on 11 Oct 1909 in Safford, Graham, Arizona, USA. George was born on 20 May 1886 in Rose Hill, Covington, Alabama, USA. He died on 20 Apr 1942 in Mexia, Limestone, Texas, USA.

They had the following children:

+ 133 F i. **Geneva Arletta Wyatt** was born on 22 Apr 1910. She died on 9 May 1978.

Effie married (2) **Andrew Harrison Martin** on 6 Jul 1922 in Clifton, Greenlee, Arizona, USA.

They had the following children:

134 M ii. **Walter Raymond Martin** was born on 4 Jan 1926. He died in 1991.

<hr />

56. George Joseph Filleman (Annie Elizabeth Chisholm, Glenn Thornton, Richard

Henry) was born on 14 Oct 1893 in Solomonville, Graham, Arizona, USA. He died on 29 Aug 1960 in Eagle Creek, Greenlee, Arizona, USA.

George married Margaret Jane Trainor daughter of Patrick Trainor and Sarah Isabell Hudson on 15 Dec 1917 in Clifton, Greenlee, Arizona, USA. Margaret was born on 4 Feb 1898 in Nutrioso, Apache, Arizona, USA. She died on 14 Oct 1961 in Clifton, Greenlee, Arizona, USA.

They had the following children:

135 M i. **George Joseph Filleman** was born on 17 Dec 1920 in Greenlee, Arizona. He died in 2003 in Safford, Graham, Arizona, USA. George married **Barbara Ridlon**.

136 F ii. **Margaret Joyce Filleman** was born on 4 Apr 1922 in Greenlee, Arizona. She died in 2001 in Dallas, Dallas, Texas. Margaret married **Charles Brown**.

57. **William Howard Filleman** (Annie Elizabeth Chisholm, Glenn Thornton, Richard Henry) was born on 30 Jun 1895 in Solomonville, Graham, Arizona, USA. He died on 9 Feb 1973 in Phoenix, Maricopa, Arizona, USA.

William married Bessie Dow Cosper daughter of John C Cosper and Mary A Arhelger on 15 Dec 1917 in Clifton, Greenlee, Arizona. USA. Bessie was born about 1900 in Clifton, Greenlee, Arizona, USA. She died in Phoenix, Maricopa, Arizona, USA.

They had the following children:

137 M i. **John Joe DeWitt Filleman** was born on 6 Nov 1918 in Greenlee, Arizona, USA.

John married **Justine Filleman**

138 M ii. **Robert Harold Filleman** was born on 17 Jul 1920 in Greenlee, Arizona, USA.

Robert married (1) **Virginia Jones**

Robert married (2) **Jeanette Pace**

139 F iii. **Mildred Olive Filleman** was born about 1925 in Greenlee, Arizona, USA.

Mildred married (1) **Norman Mc Euen**

Mildred married (2) **Buddy Eldredge**

58. Coralea Filleman (Annie Elizabeth Chisholm, Glenn Thornton, Richard Henry) was born on 1 Aug 1897 in Geronimo, Graham, Arizona, USA. She died on 18 Mar 1981 in Morenci, Greenlee, Arizona, USA.

Coralea married William Clinton Edwards son of Thomas Clinton Edwards and Betty Ann Yarbrough on 18 Jun 1916 in Clifton, Greenlee, Arizona. USA. William was born on 14 Aug 1889 in Uvalde, Uvalde, Texas, USA. He died on 17 Jul 1945 in Morenci, Greenlee, Arizona, USA.

They had the following children:

140 F i.   **Elsie Lea Edwards** was born on 8 Mar 1917 in Metcalf, Greenlee, Arizona, USA. Elsie married **Robert Ford**.

141 M ii. **Jesse Clinton Edwards** was born on 30 Nov 1920 in Greenlee, Arizona, USA. He died on 30 Nov 1920 in Clifton, Greenlee, Arizona, USA.

142 F iii. **Irene Elizabeth Edwards** was born on 7 Dec 1921 in Clifton, Greenlee, Arizona, USA. Irene E. Wood died March 2017. Irene married **Stanley Wood**. They had a daughter Carol Wood Longstaff who died December 8, 2014. (from Will Bowen, son of Carol. Updated 12/29/18 from Facebook group)

143 M iv. **William Glenn Edwards** was born on 13 Apr 1926 in Greenlee, Arizona, USA. He died on 29 Apr 2004 in Greenlee, Arizona, USA.

William married (1) **Cecelia Jo Cox** .

William married (2) **Virginia Cox** .

59. Mary Annie Filleman (Annie Elizabeth Chisholm, Glenn Thornton, Richard Henry) was born on 15 Aug 1899 in Geronimo, Graham, Arizona, USA. She died on 13 Feb 1920 in Clifton, Greenlee, Arizona, USA.

Mary married John Cosper on 1 Nov 1917 in Clifton, Greenlee, Arizona. USA. John was born about 1896 in New Mexico, USA.

They had the following children:

> 144 M i. **Wilbert Cosper** was born about 1920 in Clifton, Greenlee, Arizona, USA. He died on 9 Mar 1988 in Clifton, Greenlee, Arizona, USA.

✳══✦══✦══✦══✳

61. Walter Jake Filleman "Mike" (Annie Elizabeth Chisholm, Glenn Thornton, Richard Henry) was born on 2 May 1904 in Geronimo, Graham, Arizona, USA. He died on 25 Apr 1947 in Prescott, Yavapai, Arizona, USA.

Walter married Ocie Marie Spence daughter of Richard Thaddeus Spence and Alve Belle Calahan on 28 Dec 1928 in Roswell, Eddy, New Mexico, USA. Ocie was born on 16 Aug 1910 in Tulia, Swisher, Texas, USA. She died on 1 Jul 1993 in Safford, Graham, Arizona, USA.

Walter and Ocie had the following children:

> 145 F i. **Mary Elizabeth Filleman** was born on 28 May 1929 in Arizona.
>
> Mary married **Richard Carpenter** .
>
> 146 M ii. **Spence Filleman** was born in Arizona.
>
> 147 M iii. **James Filleman** was born in 1936 in Arizona, USA.

✳══✦══✦══✦══✳

62. Nina Elsie Filleman (Annie Elizabeth Chisholm, Glenn Thornton, Richard Henry) was born on 13 Jan 1909 in Geronimo, Graham, Arizona, USA. She died on 23 Sep 1978 in Mesa, Maricopa, Arizona, USA.

Nina married William Arthur Griffiths son of Griffiths and Sparks on 1 Dec 1928 in , , Arizona, USA. William was born on 12 Nov 1904 in Oklahoma, USA. He died in Jan 1985 in Tempe, Maricopa, Arizona, USA.

They had the following children:

> 148 M i. **Harold Griffiths** was born about 1929 in Tempe, Maricopa, Arizona, USA. He died about 1997 in Tempe, Maricopa, Arizona, USA. Harold married **Sue Ann Sandoz** .

64. Addie Bell Chisholm (Daniel Fore, Glenn Thornton, Richard Henry) was born on 27 Jan 1890 in Goliad, Texas, USA. She died on 19 Mar 1968 in Twin Falls, Idaho, USA. She was buried in Twin Falls, Twin Falls, Idaho, USA.

Addie married (1) George Reinhart on 19 Mar 1968 in Twin Falls, Idaho, USA.

Addie married (2) Jesse Orin Smith son of William Henry Smith and Melissa Ellen Bowman on 29 Jan 1907 in Shoshore, Idaho, USA. Jesse was born on 5 Dec 1874 in Ridgeway, Missouri, USA. He died on 17 Mar 1955. **Pictured right.**

They had the following children:

  + 149 F i.   **Velma Vivian Smith** was born on 5 Nov 1907. She died on 22 Mar 1986.

  + 150 M ii. **Lawrence Elias Smith** was born on 20 Nov 1909. He died on 26 Feb 1980.

  + 151 F iii. **Rachel Alta Smith** was born on 2 Jan 1913. She died in Oct.

    152 M iv. **Norman Victor Smith** was born on 30 Oct 1915 in Picabo, Idaho, USA. He died on 18 May 1931 in Picabo, Idaho, USA. He was buried in Hailey, Idaho, USA. Norman and his father, Jesse, with a brother, Adrian, were working with cattle, when Norman was thrown or fell from his horse. He was kicked in the chest by his horse and did not survive the accident. Norman was a teen ager when this happened.

  + 153 M v.   **Adrian Aaron Smith** was born on 24 Sep 1919. He died on 27 Sep 1997.

    154 M vi. **Marne Smith** was born on 5 Jul 1922 in Picabo, Idaho, USA. He died on 14 Feb 1997 in Orofino, , Idaho, USA. He was buried in Twin Falls Cemetery, Idaho, USA.

  + 155 M vii. **Darrel Dalton Smith** was born on 21 Jul 1927.

  + 156 F viii. **Melissa Ellen Smith** was born on 21 Mar 1931.

74. **Winnie Mae Watson** (Nina Maud Chisholm, Bradford A, Richard Henry) was born in 1905. She died in 1989.

Winnie married Bobby Allen Christall

They had the following children:

    157 M i. **Bobby Christall Jr** .

HC

CHAPTER FIVE

FIFTH Generation

Ross and his brother Dan were two loving and caring cousins. There was never a death in the family in California or Arizona that they did not take time off to attend. Two cousins and their wives that I love dearly.
Zenna Chisholm Snowden

76. **Georgia Louise Evans** (Jennie Chisholm, George Langford, Glenn Thornton, Richard Henry) was born about 1902 in Junction City, Kimble, Texas, USA.

Georgia married Clinton Hawker .

They had the following children:

    158 F i.   **Louise Hawker** .

    159 M ii. **Robert Henry Hawker** was born on 28 Sep 1923 in Paducah, Texas, USA. He died on 11 Dec 1930 in Paducah, Texas, USA. He was buried in Paducah, Texas, USA. Robert was 7 years 2 months 13 days old when he died in Paducah Texas, Demount Route. This news was in a letter sent to Marie Chisholm.

78. **Oscar Tedford Evans** (Jennie Chisholm, George Langford, Glenn Thornton, Richard Henry) was born on 11 Jul 1905 in Junction City, Kimble, Texas, USA. He died on 15 Jun 1950 in Blythe, , California, USA. He was buried in Rest Haven Park, Glendale, Maricopa, Arizona, USA.

Ted had three Children: Joyce, Ted, Tommie.

Joyce said her Dad was born in Junction City, Texas

Oscar married Neomie Jesse Kincannon daughter of Thomas F Kincannon and Naome Estelle Drennan on 6 Nov 1923. Neomie was born on 12 Jan 1907 in Texas, USA. She died on 9 Feb 1989 in Riverside, Riverside, California, USA.

Naomi married five times before she married Tedford Evans. 1 Ed McClendon - 2 Al Aube - 3 Arliss Bradbury - 4 Paul Lewis - 5 Fletcher Collins.

Oscar and Neomie had the following children:

+ 160 F i.   **Joyce M Evans** was born on 9 Sep 1924. She died on 24 Mar 2002.

+ 161 M ii.   **Tedford Loren Evans** was born on 21 Aug 1926. He died on 21 Mar 1999.

+ 162 M iii.   **Thomas Leland Evans** was born on 30 Oct 1928. He died on 23 Jan 2004.

  163 M iv.   **Larry Walton Evans** was born on 25 Jan 1933. He died in Apr 1933.

79. **Vivian Mable Chisholm** (Martin Gaines, George Langford, Glenn Thornton, Richard Henry) was born in 1912.

Vivian married Lloyd Hindselman about 1931.

Lloyd and Vivian had the following children:

  164 F i.   **Wilma Hindselman** was born in 1932 in Safford, Graham, Arizona, USA. Wilma married **Unknown** in Chowchilla, California, USA.

  165 F ii.   **Inez Hindselman** was born in 1932 in Safford, Graham, Arizona, USA. Inez married **Robert Turner** in Chowchilla, California, USA.

  166 F iii. **Joyce Ann Hindselman** was born on 15 Dec 1934 in Chandler, Maricopa, Arizona. She died on 31 Aug 2004 in Fresno, California. Joyce married **William R Milton** .

  167 F iv.   **Billie Dean Hindselman** was born in Nov 1939 in Chowchilla, California. She died in 1986 in Fresno, California, USA. Billie married **Tom Violia** in Reno, Nevada.

80. **Vestal Chisholm** (Martin Gaines, George Langford, Glenn Thornton, Richard Henry) was born in 1914.

> Vita Records say she lived in Arilington, Arizona
>
> Her daughter Julia was by a second husband.

Vestal married Milton Arnold Moss son of Walter Moss and Lola M Willis. Milton was born in 1909. He died in 1970 in Fresno, Fresno, California, USA.

They had the following children:

    168 M i. **Conrad Arnell Moss** .

    169 F ii. **Julia Moss** .

81. **Bessie Loraine Chisholm** (Martin Gaines, George Langford, Glenn Thornton, Richard Henry) was born on 18 Jun 1917 in Granite, Oklahoma, USA. She died on 7 Oct 1988 in Roseburg, Oregon, USA. She was buried in Valley View Cemetery, Sutherlin, Oregon, USA.

Bessie married John Wm. Traylor son of John Thomas Traylor and Lucille Howard on 4 Nov 1933 in Safford, Arizona, USA. John was born on 18 May 1914 in Clifton, Greenlee, Arizona, USA. He died on 3 Dec 1999 in Sutherlin, Oregon, USA. He was buried in Sutherlin, Oregon, USA.

John worked as a miner in California, in the 50's he came to Sutherlin, Oregon and worked in a local mill. In the late 50's he went to Klamath, California and worked in a plywood mill until he retired in 1976. He and Bessie moved back to Sutherlin after retirement.

John and Bessie had the following children:

    + 170 F i. **Blanche Lucille Traylor** was born on 12 Aug 1934. She died on 8 Dec 2003.

    + 171 F ii. **Virginia May Traylor** was born on 22 Sep 1935. She died on 21 Sep 1993.

    + 172 F iii. **Joy Loraine Traylor** was born on 18 May 1937. She died on 22 Dec 1999.

    + 173 F iv. **Johnnie Louise Traylor** was born on 1 May 1939.

82. Thornton Dudley Chisholm (Richard Akley, George Langford, Glenn Thornton, Richard Henry) died on 15 Jun 1944.

In the Chisholm Trail Edition of the Old Trail Drivers magazine of 1956, Fannie G Chisholm writes about her brother, Thornton Dudley, who in 1939 entered in the Poney Express Race of a re-living of the old Pony Express days. There were thirty-four riders, including one girl, starting was made from Bastrop, Texas. Thornton held fifth place from Bastrop to Austin, and San Antonio, he took the lead through Seguin, Luling, Schulenburg, LaGrange, Smithville and into Bastrop. The only time he stopped was a few minutes to feed and water his mount. The ride was of 278 miles took 66 hours and six minutes, an average of one hour for 4.2 miles.

Thornton Dudley as killed in the Normandy Beach landing in France, June 15, 1944.

Thornton married Sunny Crabb.

They had the following children:

> 174 M i. **Gary Thornton Chisholm** was born on 23 Nov 1942 in Bastrop, Texas, USA.
>
> Gary served in the US Infantry.

> 175 M ii. **Richard Dudley Chisholm** was born on 15 May 1944.
>
> Richard Dudley served in the US Navy.
>
> Richard married (1) **Sandra G Crouse** on 10 Mar 1972 in Coryell, Texas, USA.
>
> Richard married (2) **Unknown** .

84. Fannie G Chisholm (Richard Akley, George Langford, Glenn Thornton, Richard Henry) was born on 16 May 1915 in Texas, USA. She died on 14 Dec 1973 in Stockton, Texas, USA. The cause of death was Heart Attack. She was buried in Clinton, Texas, USA.

Fannie G. Chisholm

Fannie G. was born in Texas on May 16, 1915 to Richard Akley and Narnie Bell Simmons Chisholm. She was the first of our Chisholm family to diligently research our family history and share it with others.

Living in Texas, she was able to get first-hand information from some of the old timers or from their close relations. Today we have access to the internet and history that is posted on it. Fannie had to spend many hours looking through census records and going through history books to get her information. Since I started collecting information in the 1950s, I have certainly done a lot of that myself.

In 1966, Fannie published her book, "The Four State Chisholm Trail." Many of us have her book and have appreciated learning about our family history through her writings. I have included many quotes from her book on this DVD.

My knowledge of our Chisholm history starts with Richard H. Chisholm, who in February of 1829 was granted land in DeWitt County, Texas where he started the Town of Clinton and lived out his life. There is no town there now. Fannie was able to acquire land on the old town site where she built a home. In the 1960s, I had the opportunity to visit the area and to get acquainted with her husband, Fred, and son, Thomas Dudley.

The Chisholm and Texas history was a big part of Fannie's life. In 1946, she became a member of the "Old Trail Drivers Assn. of Texas." She was also a charter member of the "Daughters and Wives of the Old Trail Drivers of Texas." She wrote, "That belonging to these organizations had been one of the most pleasurable experiences." In the "Battle of the Flowers Parade," on April 26, 1963, Fannie G. Chisholm was presented as 'Queen of the Chisholm Trail.' When I visited with her in the 1960s, I enjoyed attending one of those meetings with her. We were all dressed as old timers from the long dresses to the bonnets.

In December of 1973, Fannie G. and her husband, came to visit with us and some of her family that was living in Arizona. On their way home, Fannie had a heart attack in Stockton, Texas and passed away. It was a sad time and she was greatly missed.

Zenna Chisholm Snowden
July 2007

Fannie married Fred Hurst.

They had the following children:

    176 M   i.   **Thomas Dudley Hurst**.

85. Richard A Chisholm "Chick" (Richard Akley, George Langford, Glenn Thornton, Richard Henry) was born in 1918 in Thorndale, Texas, USA. He died on 2 Jan 1977 in Bouse, LaPaz, Arizona, USA.

Richard, son of Dick Chisholm, was called Chick. He served in World War ll and lost and eye in the service. He died at the age 59.

Richard married Faye Marie Menefee. Faye was born in 1927. She died in 1972 in Bouse, LaPaz, Arizona, USA.

Marie was 59 years old when she died. Information was given by Clarence Chambers.

Richard and Faye had the following children:

    177 F i. **Patsy Marie Chisholm** was born on 24 Nov 1947 in Bexar, Texas, USA.

    178 F ii. **Vivian Faye Chisholm** was born on 22 Oct 1949.

86. Beldon Hopkins Chisholm "Man and Hank" (Richard Akley, George Langford, Glenn Thornton, Richard Henry) was born on 7 Dec 1918 in Texas, USA. He died on 23 Apr 1972 in Texas, USA. He was buried in Texas, USA.

Death date from Clarence Chambers

Beldon married Fay Marie Chisholm . Fay was born in 1927. She died in 1952.

They had the following children:

    179 F i. **Doris May Chisholm**.

    180 F ii. **Janet Lucille Chisholm** was born on 24 Jan 1943 in Bastrop, Texas, USA.

    181 F iii. **Loretta Chisholm**.

88. Frances Charlene Chisholm (Richard Akley, George Langford, Glenn Thornton, Richard Henry) was born on 6 Sep 1928 in Williamson, Texas, USA.

Frances married (1) Oliver Eugene Balch son of Oliver Balch and Gertrude Matilda Allen on 2 Feb 1947 in Elgin, Texas. USA. Oliver was born on 24 Oct 1925 in Manard, Texas, USA. He died on 17 Dec 1992 in VA Hospital, Temple, Texas, USA. He was buried on 20 Dec 1992 in Youngs Prairie Cemetery, Texas, USA.

They had the following children:

+ 182M i. **Charlie Gene Balch** was born on 6 Jan 1948.

+ 183F ii. **Charlotte Jean Balch** was born on 6 Jan 1948.

+ 184M iii. **Terry Joe Balch** was born on 22 Mar 1949.

Frances married (2) Allen Marsh

---

92. Vernon Ansel Chisholm (Top, George Langford, Glenn Thornton, Richard Henry) was born on 26 Mar 1918 in Peoria, Maricopa, Arizona, USA. He died on 2 Dec 1995 in Pinole, California, USA. He was buried in California, USA.

Information from family and Funeral Service Brochure

Vernon married Ruth Brown on 3 Aug 1947. Ruth died in Apr 2005.

Vernon and Ruth had the following children:

185 F i. **Mary Ann Chisholm** was born on 8 Feb 1948. Mary married **Richard Peters**.

186 F ii. **Nina Chisholm** was born on 2 Apr 1949. Nina married **Michael Glenn**.

187 M iii. **Richard Chisholm**.

---

93. Oleta Chisholm "Sis" (Top, George Langford, Glenn Thornton, Richard Henry) was born on 20 May 1920 in Peoria, Maricopa, Arizona, USA.

Oleta married (1) Leyton Stuart Woolf Sr. son of John LeRoy Woolf and Anna Louise Stuart on 15 May 1948 in Presbyterian Church, Chowchilla, California, USA. Leyton was born on 6 Sep 1917 in Scottdale, Maricopa, Arizona, USA. He was christened in Presbyterian Church, Peoria, Maricopa, Arizona, USA. He died on 28 Mar 2001 in Glendale, Maricopa, Arizona, USA. He was buried on 2 Apr 2001 in Litchfield Park, Maricopa, Arizona, USA.

Leyton Sr had a twin brother.

Leyton and Oleta had the following children:

+ 188M i. **Leyton Stuart Woolf Jr** was born on 3 Apr 1949.

189 F ii. **Carol Lynn Woolf** was born on 6 Jul 1951. She was christened in Lutheran Church, Madera, Madera, California, USA. Carol married **Arthur Nonomura** son of Yuko Nonomura and Toshiko Kiyota. Arthur was born on 15 Dec 1950 in Washington District of Columbia, USA.

190 F iii. **Margaret Jo Woolf** "Jodie" was born on 11 Nov 1954 in St Joseph Hospital, Phoenix, Maricopa, Arizona, USA. She was christened in Luthern Church, Glendale, Maricopa, Arizona, USA. Margaret married **Jonathan Willis** son of Clifford Willis and Esther Willis in Wigwam Country Club, Litchfield Park, Maricopa, Arizona, USA. Jonathan was born on 6 Dec 1948.

Oleta married (2) Holland Kenny on 1 Jan 1938 in Dos Palos, California, USA.

94. **William Chisholm** "Bud" (Top, George Langford, Glenn Thornton, Richard Henry) was born on 10 Dec 1922 in Parker, LaPaz, Arizona, USA. He died on 4 Apr 2004 in Hanford, California, USA. He was buried in Pleasant Valley Cemetery, Coalinga, California, USA.

William married Billie Fay Williams daughter of Walter Williams and Velma Halbert on 25 Jan 1948 in Winton, California, USA. Billie was born on 2 Dec 1928 in Sudan, Texas, USA. She died on 19 Oct 2001 in Sacramento, California, USA. She was buried in Pleasant Valley Cemetery, Coalinga, California, USA.

They had the following children:

+ 191 F i. **Janice Ruth Chisholm** was born on 30 Aug 1950.

+ 192 F ii. **Jeanne Fay Chisholm** was born on 29 Sep 1951.

+ 193 M iii. **William Edward Chisholm** was born on 3 Dec 1952. He died on 21 Dec 2005.

194 F iv. **Mary Kathryn Chisholm** was born on 17 Jul 1954. She died on 4 Dec 1971 in Huron, California, USA. She was buried in Pleasant Valley Cemetery, Coalinga, California, USA.

95. Josephine May Chisholm "Jo" (Top, George Langford, Glenn Thornton, Richard Henry) was born on 17 Jan 1925 in Fig Farm, Maricopa, Arizona, USA. She died on 23 Feb 2001 in San Bernardino, California, USA. She was buried in Colton, California, USA.

The Fig Farm where Josephine was born was located about 8 miles north of Marinette on the Agua Fria River. There are no remains of the ranch anymore. Marinette was once located on Highway 60, Grand Ave and about 107th St. You can find a plaque on one of the side streets telling you about the town.

Zenna

Josephine married Ernest Irving Holober on 15 Apr 1946 in Nogales, Sonora, Mexico. Ernest was born on 29 Mar 1912 in St Louis, Missouri, USA. He died on 22 Aug 1994 in San Bernardino, San Bernardino, California, USA. He was buried on 25 Aug 1994 in Montecito Memorial Park, Colton, San Bernardino, California, USA.

Information from family and Funeral Service Brochure.

Ernest and Josephine had the following children:

195 F i. **Loreta Holober** was born on 17 Mar 1940.

196 F ii. **Geraldine Holober** was born 10 Jan 1947 in Walter Reed Hospital, Washington, DC.

197 F iii. **Lita Dell Holober** was born on 7 Apr 1956.

96. Douglas Fairbanks Chisholm (Top, George Langford, Glenn Thornton, Richard Henry) was born on 25 Oct 1926 in Fig Farm, Maricopa, Arizona, USA. He died on 13 Aug 1955 in Sutter, California, USA. He was buried in Merced, Merced, California, USA.

The Fig Farm where Douglas was born was located about eight miles north of Marinette on the Agua Fria River. There are no remains of the farm any more. The little town of Marinette was located on Highway 60, Grand Ave and about 107th Ave. There is not much left to remind you of Marinette today either. A plaque on a side street will tell you it was once there.

Douglas married Billie June Askew on 1 Nov 1946.

They had the following children:

    198 M i. **Roy Dean Chisholm** was born on 11 Jun 1948.

    199 F ii. **Sharon Chisholm** was born on 3 Apr 1953.

97. Lloyd Frances Chisholm "Pelone" (Top, George Langford, Glenn Thornton, Richard Henry) was born on 14 Oct 1928 in Fig Farm, Maricopa, Arizona. He died on 6 Dec 1959 in Chowchilla, California. He was buried in Chowchilla, California.

The Fig Farm where Lloyd was born was located about 8 miles north of Marinette on the Agua Fria River. There are no signs of where the Ranch once was. The town of Marinette was located on Highway 60, Grand Ave and about 107th Ave. About the only thing you can find of Marinette is a plaque located on a side street telling you about the town.

Zenna

Lloyd married Virgina Victoria Snyder daughter of Grant Theodore Snyder and Edna Larson on 6 Mar 1956. Virgina was born on 6 Apr 1928 in Grand Canyon, Coconio, Arizona, USA.

A Bit of History From Virginia Snyder Chisholm

In the 1920's, Edna Larson and a girlfriend were living in Elsmore, Kansas and decided to become Harvey Girls. (Harvey Girls were an elite group of ladies who were well educated, had good morals, manners, clear speech and neatness of appearance. The passengers of the Santa Fe Railroad were served first class meals by the Harvey Girls in first class restaurants located along the railroad. The Santa Fe Passengers were so impressed by the Harvey Girls that the Girls continued to serve them for three quarters of a century.)

Edna and her friend boarded a train in Kansas; their destination the El Tovar Hotel at the Grand Canyon National Park in Arizona. While working there, Edna met Grant Theodore Snyder who was working for the Bureau of Public Roads of Arizona. The Bureau was building the suspension bridge across the Colorado River at the bottom of the Grand Canyon.

In 1927 they were married at the Canyon where he offered her a tent for a home. It was in that tent that their only daughter, Virginia Victoria, was born on April 6, 1928. Virginia and her parents moved many times as her father helped to build roads throughout Arizona. Virginia remembers living in a tent in Oak Creek Canyon. A snow storm came up and the highway crew was snowbound on the job. They were building the winding road from Flagstaff to Sedona. Virginia's mom had to use a broom to keep the snow from crushing their tent during the night.

She has a vivid memory of her mother killing a sidewinder snake while walking her to school at Cave Creek one morning. Her favorite areas in Arizona were Flagstaff and Long Valley. In those days, the Navajo Indians came down to Flagstaff from the reservation to sell their beautiful hand woven rugs and jewelry. The family went up to the Hopi Mesas and were able to take pictures of the Hopis as they danced with live rattlesnakes in their mouths.

The family moved to California in 1937 so Virginia could finish her schooling in one place. It was there she met the love of her life, Lloyd Chisholm. Lloyd died of melanoma in 1959. They had two children, a daughter, Lorelei, and a son, Lance, who was born seven months after Lloyd's death.

In 2006, Virginia was living in California near her children, grandchildren and great-grandchildren.

Virginia Victoria Snyder Chisholm
Zenna Chisholm Snowden
August 2006

Lloyd and Virgina had the following children:

  + 200 F i. **Lorelei Francine Chisholm** was born on 5 Dec 1956.

  + 201 M ii. **Lance Lloyd Francis Chisholm** was born on 3 Jul 1960.

---

98. Toppy Monroe Chisholm (Top, George Langford, Glenn Thornton, Richard Henry) was born on 25 Jul 1931 in Colburn Place, Maricopa, Arizona, USA. He died 21 July 2009 in California.

Toppy was born on the Colburn Place, it was located about 8 miles north of Marinette on the Agua Fria River. There are no remains of the place anymore. Marinette was a little town located on Highway, Grand Ave and 107 Ave.

Zenna

Toppy married Mary Ann Alvaro daughter of Vincent Alvaro and Margaret Candela on 30 Apr 1955 in San Bernardino, San Bernardino, California, USA. Mary was born on 26 Jun 1928 in Olyphant, Lackawann, Pennsylvania, USA. She died July 17, 2018 in California.

They had the following children:

  +202 F i. **Mary Ellen Chisholm** was born on 22 Dec 1956.

  + 203 M ii. **Richard Chisholm** was born on 19 Mar 1957.

   204 F iii. **Lois Chisholm** was born on 14 Mar 1958 in San Bernardino, San Bernardino, California, USA.

  + 205 F iv. **Susan Chisholm** was born on 12 Jan 1965.

Obituary for Mary Ann Chisholm

Mary Ann Alvaro Chisholm was welcomed into Heaven on July 17, 2018 and waiting to embrace her once again were her loving husband, Toppy, parents, Vincent and Margaret Alvaro, siblings, Ellen Seymour, Rosemary Kamphaus, Anthony Alvaro and Rita Mikridge and her beloved grandson,

Alex Chisholm.

Mary left behind a grieving family, who remained by her side until it was time for her to leave. Her children, Mary Ellen Sexton, Richard & Viola Chisholm, Lois Chisholm, Susan & David Dillon were blessed to know her unconditional love and devotion. Her grandchildren, Christopher & Jenna Tourino, Daniel & Brianne Tourino, Nathan Chisholm, Nicholas & Annie Dillon knew, from the day they were born, that their grandmother adored them all and when her great-grandchildren, Mason Alexander Tourino and Makenna Rose Tourino were born in 2017 and early 2018, her heart burst with joy. Although she gave birth to only 4 children, she became a second mother to Carey Chenoski Wilson and Adele Calia Ray. Mary had a special relationship with all her nieces and nephews, near and far. A visit or phone call with "Auntie Mary" left each one with a smile on their face and love in their heart.

Mary was born in Olyphant, PA on January 26, 1928 and moved to Southern California in 1953, where she soon met the love of her life, Toppy Chisholm, who she married on April 30, 1955, and to whom she was devoted until his death on July 21, 2009. Mary moved to Highland in 1961 with her husband and children and remained there until her death.

Mary worked as a bookkeeper before starting a family. She enjoyed working, but her greatest love was her family.

A funeral mass will be held on Saturday, July 28, 2018 at 12:30 PM at St. Adelaide Catholic Church, 27487 Baseline St. Highland, and following the service, she will be laid to rest at Montecito 3520 E. Washington Street, Colton, Ca. To leave a condolence online please visit www.bobbittchapel.com. (added Dana S. Chisholm 2018)

99. **Ruth Ester Chisholm** (Thomas John, George Langford, Glenn Thornton, Richard Henry) was born on 2 Dec 1917 in Peoria, Maricopa, Arizona, USA. She died on 13 Nov 1989 in Cottonwood, Yavapai, Arizona, USA. The cause of death was Pancreatic Cancer. She was buried in Rest Haven Park, Glendale, Maricopa, Arizona.

Ruth married Thomas Lynn Mansfield son of Thomas Mansfield and Maude Mansfield on 27 Feb 1936 in Glendale, Maricopa, Arizona, USA. Thomas was born on 27 Feb 1916 in Hazelhearst, Mississippi, USA. He died on 30 Apr 2001 in Camarillo, California, USA. He was buried on 4 May

2001 in Rest Haven Cemetery, Glendale, Maricopa, Arizona, USA.

Information from family and Funeral Service Brochure

Thomas and Ruth had the following children:

+ 206 M i. **Thomas Gail Mansfield** was born on 1 Nov 1936.

+ 207 F ii. **Maudie Marie Mansfield** was born on 7 Mar 1938. She died on 24 Aug 2005.

101.   Juanita Chisholm (Thomas John, George Langford, Glenn Thornton, Richard Henry) was born on 14 Jul 1920 in Peoria, Maricopa, Arizona, USA. She died on 10 Mar 1967 in Glendale, Maricopa, Arizona, USA. The cause of death was Cancer. She was buried in Rest Haven Park, Glendale, Maricopa, Arizona, USA.

Juanita married (1) Joe Virgil Horton on 7 Aug 1937 in Phoenix, Maricopa, AZ, USA. Joe was born on 7 Sep 1919. He died in Jan 1985 in Peoria, Maricopa, Arizona, USA.

They had the following children:

+ 208 F i. **Janice Cliffine Horton** was born on 3 Jun 1938.

209 M ii. **Darryl Horton** was born on 16 Feb 1941 in Glendale, Maricopa, Arizona, USA. He died in May 1941 in Glendale, Maricopa, Arizona, USA. The cause of death was 3 months old. He was buried in Glendale Cemetery, Glendale, Maricopa, Arizona, USA.

Juanita married (2) Leroy K Shroeder on 12 Dec 1942 in Lordsburg, New Mexico, USA. Leroy was born on 18 Dec 1919 in Manitowoc, Wisconsin, USA.

102. **Zenna Chisholm** (Thomas John, George Langford, Glenn Thornton, Richard Henry) was born on 15 Sep 1921 in Peoria, Maricopa, Arizona, USA.

Zenna Chisholm

I was born in Peoria, Arizona September 15, 1921 on the old Sanderson Ranch where Daddy was farming. We did move some, but not as much as the older generations of Chisholm families.

In about 1927, I can remember living on the Fig Farm where Daddy farmed for a Mr. Ed Samuels. The farm was located north of Grand Avenue on the Agua Fria River. It was a real treat for Mr. Samuels to come to visit, and be invited to eat with the family. He loved Mom's biscuits and beans. He was from the 'City', and his wife didn't cook that poor folks food.

Uncle Top and his family lived a short distant from us. All of us kids walked across the desert to school which was about a mile away. I was in the first grade. I can remember the older kids loved to scare the younger ones, and that is how they got their highs without drugs. They would yell there is a skunk or snake and scare us to death. We had a fence to climb through and I remember losing my shoe, and afraid to go back to get it. Being without a shoe in the Arizona Desert was not good. Mother made my older sister, Ruth, go back for it. Ruth was one of the culprits who helped to scare us.

We attended a one room schoolhouse where all grades were taught by Mrs. McDonald. I can remember my first church service was at this little schoolhouse and the preacher was our Uncle Calvin.

There was a well and pump to irrigate the Fig Farm, and I remember the beautiful flowers Mom grew along the ditch bank. She also had a fantastic garden there, and at any other place we lived where water was available. The Fig Farm had ideal soil for her garden and flowers. I loved to go with Daddy when he irrigated or whatever he had to do. I would sit in his lap and drive the little work car we called the bug. I would sit for however long he had to do things so I could 'drive' the bug.

He was growing alfalfa on a farm in Blythe, and I went with him and drove the team while he loaded the bales of hay. I was real little so the horses probably moved when he talked to them. Daddy had spent most of his young life on a horse; so, he knew how to handle them.

Aunt Jennie lived in Blythe at the same time we did, and she came to visit often. She and Mom would take us swimming in the drainage ditch which was just across the road. Funny the little things you remember. Aunt Jennie dipped snuff. We probably wanted to try that; so, she took a little mesquite limb; fuzzed up the end; put the snuff on the end and gave it to us. That was the only time we tried dipping snuff.

In 1931 we moved to the "Olive Orchard" which was located north of Marinette on the Lake Pleasant Road. It was not a working orchard and since the house was unoccupied they let us live there for free.

Daddy worked at the Maricopa County Conservation District No.1 which is still the canal irrigation system from the Waddel Dam which holds Lake Pleasant. I have a check for $26.25 that Daddy was paid for two weeks of work. It was while we lived there that Dude and Ethel moved into a house that was nearby, and at that time in 1932 Tommie and Wanda were born. There was a house across the road that became empty, and Grandpa and Grandma Chisholm moved into it. Grandpa got a job with the Peoria School District to take us to Marinette to catch the school bus to Peoria. Grandpa had a four door open top Model T car. There was Ruth, Juanita, Zenna, Mae, Stanford and a couple of neighbor kids he transported, and that Model T was full. The highway was a divided dirt road with cottonwood trees lining the center.

I can remember when I was eleven I chopped cotton to get money for my first permanent. Mom and Dad took me to Phoenix to the beauty shop. It's a wonder I have any hair now as many perms as I have had over the years.

In 1935, we moved to Blythe where I spent my first year of high school, and then the next year we moved back to the Peoria School area.

I met my future husband in 1937 when he came to Arizona from California where he had been in the Civil Conservation Corp. His home was in Missouri but his brother, Alfred, had come to Arizona with some buddies; and he wanted Babe to come here where he could get him a job. Babe had the job of picking grapefruit at Citrus Park, which was a farm west of Cotton Lane about Bethany Home Road. He never moved back to Missouri. He was called to military service in 1941. I worked at the Litchfield Aircraft Plant until he came home in 1944 when we married. We were married in the Glendale Methodist Church. Babe was in the service another year in Texas, and after he was discharged we came home to Arizona. We lived in Phoenix for a while; then, we bought us a new home in Glendale with a big lot and 20 orange trees on it.

Babe worked for the Maricopa County road system until his county supervisor was defeated in an election. While he was working for the county, I worked for Safeway. In 1952 he started working with contractors on the State Highway System. We sold our home in Glendale and bought a little trailer. The jobs took us all over the state. It was at this time I joined the tradition of the ancestors of moving often.

We moved 64 times during the 26 years we were on highway construction. Every few years, we would get a bigger trailer and a bigger truck to move it. The truck held Babe's tools and my hobbies. We had a great time. Every time we moved to a new place the family would come to see us. They all got to enjoy beautiful Arizona with us. Job contracts became longer, and while we lived in Sierra Vista, I went to school and obtained a broker real estate license. I worked for McCulloch and flew to Elko, Nevada almost every week selling their property in Spring Creek. I had to quit when we moved to a different job.

Babe retired in 1978 and we moved to Cottonwood, Arizona.

In 1972 my sister, Ruth, and I went to Spain where her granddaughter, Sheryl, and husband, Rex, were stationed. From there Ruth and I took the train and visited France, Italy, Switzerland and Portugal. What a great trip for two women who didn't know their way around, but we made it and saw so much.

Since Babe and I had already been in almost every state including Alaska, in 1979 I was able to convince him to take a trip overseas. We flew to Tahiti where we both got sick; next on to New Zealand where we saw the beautiful mountains and the sheep shearing. Our next stop was Australia where we were taken into the Sydney Opera House, and then we were shown some of the outback. After that, on to Singapore with all the beautiful orchids and the Raffles Hotel that had a famous bar where the soldiers hung out during WWII. Singapore had very strict cleanliness laws and it showed. The streets and sidewalks were very clean. Thailand was interesting to see but rather dirty. Many people lived in house boats on very dirty water. Then we went to Macau, the gambling capital of the Pacific, and from there a short trip into China. In Japan we rode the Bullet Train to see Mt. Fiji, and later pushed our way through the crowded streets of Tokyo. On our trip home, we flew over the Aleutians Islands where Babe was stationed in the service. Going north over that part of the earth was our closest way home. That was a trip to remember.

After Babe passed away in 1986, I became interested in finding a church to attend. I started going to the Methodist Church but wasn't pleased with it. In watching TV, I became aware of the World Wide Church of God and they had a church in Cottonwood. I learned that the Bible said we were to keep all the commandments of God, and the fourth one was the one the Bible says, "Remember the Sabbath day to keep it holy. Six days you shall labor and do all your work but the seventh day is Sabbath of the Lord your God". I joined the Church and began keeping the Saturday Sabbath. While I was a member, every year we would make a trip arranged by the Church.

I was fortunate enough to go on a trip to Jordan and Israel. What a feeling, to walk the grounds that Jesus walked and to see the Jordon River where our Savior was baptized. The next trip we went on was to Spain, a cruise to Greece, and from there a cruise to Turkey. While in Turkey, we were able to visit three of the seven cities that are mentioned in the book of Revelation. We visited Ephesus, Smyrna and Pergamos. What a thrill to visit these ancient cities, and to behold one of the platforms where Paul spoke to his followers.

Remember the song, "On a Gondola love let us glide over a sleepy blue lagoon". I always enjoyed trying to sing that great love song. Well, here we were in Venice and there were the gondolas. I just had to ride in one. We were seated and gliding along when the Gondolier began to sing. This is the time you dream of a husband's loving arms around you. When the ride was over, we all gathered out in an open area to wait for our bus. Unfortunately, we had only a light rain coat and it began to rain. The bus didn't come and the rain began to really pour and no bus. We were sharing an umbrella and getting drenched and cold. Now all of the beautiful dreams on the gondola were forgotten and a different emotion swelled up inside. The warm bus finally came. We flew home from Spain. It was a wonderful trip with only this one uncomfortable incident.

I have always had a desire to go to Holland and see the tulips in bloom. My friend, Evelyn, and I arrived in Holland, and to our dismay one field of tulips was all that was in bloom since the rest had already been harvested. Our disappointment was short lived when we saw the beautiful yellow fields of mustard and the blue fields of lavender. It was interesting to see the dikes that were built to keep the ocean from the fields, and the unique large windmills. When we arrived in the Netherlands, we visited a cemetery where rows and rows of our WWII soldiers were buried. It was sad to think they were never brought home. Our trip took us to Germany where we cruised the Rhine and saw castles along the way. It was exciting to see the beautiful mountains of Austria where the Sound of Music was filmed. From our motel, we could hear the bells on the cattle as they grazed on the green hillsides. When we arrived in Switzerland, the country was so clean and towering mountains were all around us. It has a beauty that is hard to compare. After seeing the sights of Paris, we left our tour and went on our own to London.

We decided to take the train through the tunnel under the ocean. Later we regretted not taking a ship; so, we could have seen the White Cliffs of Dover. This was another great trip to reflect on.

My sis, Ruth, and I loved to travel; we were good traveling companions. Just before she became ill, we went to Mexico by train to see the Copper Canyon of Mexico. It was a beautiful trip, but it was Mexico and one of our motels had oil lamps for lights.

Babe and I had made several trips with my cousin, Ross, and his wife, Dorothy. When Babe passed away, Ross worried about me being alone; so, every year I was invited to spend a month traveling with them, until he was unable to make any more trips, due to his health. He passed away in 2002 and I have certainly missed being with them.

I moved from Cottonwood to Sun City West in 1995. While there, I joined the Seventh Day Adventist Church. I love my Church and keep very busy in it. In 1998 I moved to Wickenburg to be close to my sisters, Bonnie and Tommie. They are much younger than me and wanted me closer. If I had any problems, they wouldn't have so far to go if I needed help.

In 2000 my friend, Evelyn, and I took a cruise through the Panama Canal with several other stops along the way. It was exciting to see the canal and the locks. Our cabin, with a balcony, was located on the side of our ship where we could see a ship going out through the locks as we were coming in. That was my last long trip. I fell apart at eighty years and have had several health problems. In February of 2006, I fell and broke my leg, and I have had to have a lot of help. I have a dear friend who came to live with me until I was able to take care of myself. This last year I have spent many hours working on this DVD. Bonnie has helped me through the rough times. She is very knowledgeable about the computer.

Now life is good at eighty five. I hope all have as good a life as I have had.

Zenna Chisholm Snowden
November 2006

Zenna married Horace Pershing Snowden "Babe" son of Horace Frederick Snowden and Anna Kirchhofer on 9 Oct 1944 in Glendale, Maricopa, Arizona, USA. Horace was born on 9 Jan 1917 in

Charles City, Iowa, USA. He died on 8 Oct 1986 in Cottonwood, Arizona, USA. He was buried in Glendale Resthaven Cemetery, Glendale, Maricopa, Arizona, USA.

They had the following children:

210 F i. **My dog Cherie Snowden** was born in Jan 1963 in Congress, Yavapai, Arizona, USA.

My Dog Cherie

I bought Cherie in 1963 she was eight weeks old and a little bundle of fur. We were living at the foot of Yarnell Hill and Babe was working on the divided highway going up the hill. It was winter and not a good time to 'pottie' train a dog. When I brought her home, Babe was not very happy. He had never lived with a dog in the house, but it wasn't long until he learned to love her. She sat with him in his chair and they ate cheese together.

I groomed her often and bathed her weekly. We usually lived out in the country and when we went shopping Babe would stand outside of the store and wait for me with Cherie in his arms. He enjoyed the attention he got from everyone talking about the pretty little poodle. When she was almost ten years old and having her health problems, like we do, my sis, Ruth, and I made our trip to Europe. I emphatically told Babe, "don't you put 'my' dog to sleep, regardless of how sick she gets."

Babe was sent on a job out in the boonies near Buckeye. He was in the motorhome and decided he could see Cherie while he was working nearby; so, he put her outside on a rug and knew she would stay there. When he went to the motorhome, she was gone. No doubt a coyote got her.

Ruth's husband, Lynn, and Babe spent the weekend trying to find her or at least something to let them know what happened. Babe had a sad time until we came home, thinking about having to tell me he had let 'my' dog disappear. I was a sad, sad person, but I felt so sorry for Babe. He was as fond of her as I was and was upset that he had let it happen.

A cute thing happened one day when Mom came to see us. Cherie came to meet her and Mom didn't say hello to her; so, she scratched her on the foot until Mom said, "Well hi Cherie." Cherie turned and immediately went away. That's not the most dramatic thing a pet can do but it was pretty impressive. Cherie just needed some attention and wanted to say hello, and she didn't feel she had to bark to get it.

Everyone told me you don't want a poodle, she will destroy your house and you can never train her. When we would move our mobile home to a place that didn't have a fence, I would take her out in the yard and with a stick draw a line around our yard and tell her not to cross. I saw her chase a cat out of the area and stop right at the line.

Zenna Chisholm Snowden
September 2006

103.   Tommie Chisholm (Thomas John, George Langford, Glenn Thornton, Richard Henry) was born on 23 Mar 1932 in Marinette, Maricopa, Arizona, USA.

Tommie Chisholm

Tommie was born March 23,1932 at the "Old Olive Orchard" a couple of miles north of Marinette. Marinette was on about 107th Avenue and Grand Avenue. She was born at home and Daddy went to town to get the doctor. We kids were so worried about Mom that we did not want to go to school.

Grandma Maggie put us in the car and sent us away to a day of anguish. When we got home, there was a beautiful little sister. She was the fifth girl born to Tom and Marie. We had a sister, Opal Marie, born February 23, 1919 and she lived less than a month. Tommie was very ill shortly after she was born and there was concern whether she was going to live. She cried day and night and poor Mom got very little sleep. The doctor finally put her on rice water and she soon became a healthy child.

Mom's brother, Dude, and his wife, Ethel, moved next door and their daughter, Wanda Ruth, was born on October 22, 1932; so, the two little girls became great playmates until Daddy changed jobs and we moved away in 1937. Daddy went to work for Mr. Welborn in about 1939 and this job moved us several times until we finally settled at Bethany Home Road and Palm Lane in Glendale. There cattle feeding pens were put in and that was where Tommie learned to ride horses and she became an accomplished rider. We loved to see her riding in the parades.

It was always a great time when Daddy took the cattle to the Lakeside area for the summer. They could ride in the forest and enjoy the cool weather.

Tommie went to school in Glendale and graduated from Glendale High School. She attended Lamson Business College in Phoenix. During her high school years, she cashiered at the Glendale

Theater. She became acquainted with all the theater patrons and made many friends.

Tommie has a daughter, Velma Jean Grigsby, and a son, Charles Darren McCabe. After many years of working and being widowed, she married Floyd Howerton. They both retired from the FAA to a life of volunteering. Tommie has become an outstanding artist working in pastels and pencil. She has done custom work for several people and has won many ribbons for her art work.

In November of 2002, the Wickenburg Art Club named her "Artist of the Month." An article reads: "An example of Howerton's work, a painting entitled "Man On A Bench," is on display at the Willows Restaurant in the Americinn for public viewing. Howerton is an Arizona native, growing up on a ranch in the Glendale area. Her favorite subjects are animals, generally using her own pets as models, she works mostly with pencil and pastels, and often displays her work in local shows."

On December 17, 1999 Tommie wrote an article for the Arizona Republic and the headline was:

Rural living marked West Valley's early days: Times were simpler.

My parents came to the Valley by covered wagon from Texas in 1916. They settled in Glendale and my Dad worked for the Palo Verde Creamery where he hauled milk by horse drawn wagon.

I was born in 1932 in Marinette, which was at Grand Avenue and Lake Pleasant Road, now called Del Webb Boulevard. Our home was about a quarter-mile south of Bell Road on Lake Pleasant Road. My Dad worked as foreman on a large fig farm. An olive orchard was nearby. We had a garden but had to haul water from a nearby irrigation pump.

The house was heated by a fireplace and we cooked on a wood-burning stove. Saturday was bath day. The water was heated in a large pan on the old stove, and we bathed in a galvanized washtub. The order of bathing was the youngest first.

Saturday was a special day---that was when we went to town and to the show and the folks went grocery shopping. The movie was 10 cents, beans were 10 cents a pound; potatoes were 10 pounds for 10 cents; hamburger meat was 2 pounds for a quarter. That was one day a week we had meat. We had to eat it that night, or the next day, since we had no way of refrigerating it. The rest of the time, we ate pinto beans, corn bread, potatoes, noodles, rice and biscuits.

We could keep eggs and butter. We would place them in a wooden box that was covered with burlap, and on top of the box was a pan of water with strings running from the pan down to the burlap, thus by a wicking action, the burlap stayed damp.

When we had company and Mom happened to be cooking beans, it was really embarrassing.

That made us feel really poor. However a lot of people were eating beans during the Depression and glad to have them. My Sis devised a delicacy where she would pour bean juice over a slice of cake. She claims to this day she still likes it. I still love pinto beans and cornbread---must be a childhood memory thing.

I probably complain more than anyone about what progress has done to the Valley.

I can remember when it was safer to swim in the canals and ditches rather than in chlorinated pools, and when we never had to lock doors.

I remember being so upset in the '40s when the prefixes Yellowstone and Alpine were added to our three-digit phone numbers. I remember when the avenues were called laterals. Laterals carried the irrigation water and were bigger than ditches but smaller than canals.

Happily, I can remember when the sky was blue year 'round and there were no major traffic problems in the summer when the snowbirds would fly out of here.

Tommie Chisholm Howerton
1999 Wickenburg, Arizona

The family vacationed in Colorado for years and Tommie's dream was to someday live in Colorado. In 2004, the Howerton's moved to Colorado, in search of three digit phone numbers and no traffic. She did find blue skies, beautiful scenery and cooler weather. We are ever in pursuit of the American Dream, we were born with it. God Bless my Sister, she helped me through some trying health times before she moved away. By the way I am the one who likes pinto bean juice on cake.

Zenna Chisholm Snowden
June 2006

Tommie married (1) **Walter Otis Grigsby** on 1 Nov 1953 in Lordsburg, New Mexico, USA.

Walter was born on 21 Oct 1926 in Laveen, Maricopa, Arizona, USA.

They had the following children:

+ 211 F i. **Velma Jean Grigsby** was born on 16 Jul 1954.

Tommie married (2) Charles Lee McCabe "Chuck" on 7 Jun 1958 in Las Vegas, Nevada, USA. Charles was born on 28 Nov 1926 in Wichita, Kansas, USA. He died on 26 Jun 1980 in Phoenix, Maricopa, Arizona, USA. He was buried in Cremated.

Dates are from family and Funeral Service Brochure.

On February 19, 1945, Charles was among the first of the one hundred thousand soldiers to land on Iwo Jima, in the battle for the small island. The battle lasted 36 days. After the battle was won Charles was sent to Japan enroute home.

Charles and Tommie had the following children:

+ 212M ii.**Charles Darren McCabe** was born on 19 Nov 1959.

Tommie married (3) Floyd Howerton .

They had the following children:

213 F iii.**Gypsy Howerton My Dog**

104.   **Yvonne Chisholm** "Bonnie" (Thomas John, George Langford, Glenn Thornton, Richard Henry) was born on 24 May 1940 in Glendale, Maricopa, Arizona.

Yvonne (Bonnie) Chisholm

I was born on May 24, 1940 in Glendale, Arizona to Tom and Marie Chisholm. I was the youngest of six girls. Since there were quite a few years between us, it was almost as though I were an only child. I had two nieces and a nephew older than me.

I cannot remember a time that I didn't ride a horse. My childhood days seemed just about perfect. I was usually helping my dad work cattle or just riding and spending time outside with my four legged friends. I even raised and trained a Brahma bull, Blue. I was the talk of the town when I rode him in the rodeo parade in Glendale. Riding him was routine to me. When dad and I would go out to check on the cattle, Blue would load in the horse trailer right along with dad's horse. Sometimes dad's boss would go away for the summer and I would water his yard. He lived a couple of miles away and I would ride Blue over to his place. While I was watering the yard, Blue would lie down until we were ready to head for home. Dad use to say, he didn't need a boy he had Bonnie.

When I was about 10, the first horse that was actually mine, was given to me by neighbors, John and David Woods. Their father, Harry Woods, was a song writer and wrote "Four Leaf Clover",

"Side by Side" and more that I can't remember. I was thrilled to have my own horse and named him Sixguns.

I began entering gymkhanas and pretty soon our living room wall was filled with ribbons. Many years later, I helped start a therapeutic riding center for mentally and physically challenged youngsters. We put on a horse show for our riders and I donated my ribbons. After seeing the enjoyment of the kids receiving the ribbons, I felt they were more excited than I had been when I won them.

Our house was located on the corner of Palm Lane and L Av., that is now 63rd. Av. and Bethany Home Rd. It was a great place to grow up. In the 1950's, John F. Long changed all that when he bought the feed lot and started putting in subdivisions.

I went to Glendale Grammar School and then graduated from Glendale High School. I loved school and was in the National Honor Society and on the varsity tennis and softball teams. After graduation, I went to work for Mountain States Telephone and Telegraph Co. and retired after 32 yrs.

One event that stands out, when I was young, and that I think played an important part in later years was this: when five I started kindergarten, I knew it wasn't mandatory; so, after Christmas vacation I didn't want to go back to school. I wanted to stay home and ride. Well, when the school bus stopped to pick up my sister, Tommie, and me, I didn't want to get on it. Mom pulled a switch off an olive tree and switched the back of my legs all the way to the bus and as I was going up the steps. Needless to say, this embarrassed Tommie and after that she would never sit by me. I went on to have perfect attendance in grammar school, high school and at work.

One summer while I was in high school I spent some time with Zenna and Babe in Flagstaff. Everyday Zenna and I would go water skiing on Lake Mary. One time we loaded the boat on the trailer but could not get it out of the water. We decided to unload the boat and try another spot. In those days the little lakes did not have launching ramps, just mud banks. We finally got it loaded. As we were on the way home, we decided the trailer was not pulling straight and discovered we had bent the axle on the trailer. We unhooked the boat, leaving the boat and all the gear on the roadside. Babe went after work and straightened the axle and brought the boat home. Can you imagine in this day leaving a boat and gear along the side of the road? I don't think there would be anything left when you came back to pick it up.

I had many wonderful times visiting Zenna and Babe in the different places that they lived while he was working building some of our Arizona roads. They loved the outdoors as much as I did; so, we would travel the back roads and see some beautiful sights. If they were in the area for deer and javelina hunting , when season opened we were there. Zenna would usually scout the hunting area before we got there so we would know the best places to hunt.

I have always been active from waterskiing, riding motor cycles, riding horses, to hunting. In the 1970's, I was a licensed guide and guided bird hunters for Mearn's Quail in southeastern Arizona. I had several articles published in hunting magazines. When I started hunting, there weren't many women that hunted; so, hunting articles by a woman were unusual. I have since put away my gun and now my shooting is with a camera.

I have trained and shown horses but now trail riding is my passion. My home is adjacent to public lands so I am able ride out from my house. My friends and I have ridden most every trail in the surrounding area. We live close to the mountains so we have ridden some pretty narrow, steep trails. One was when my niece, Karol, and I rode to the top of Kendrick Peak near Flagstaff. The elevation at the top is 10,418ft. and we climbed over 3,000 ft. to get there. The views were breathtaking. We were able to see the north rim of the Grand Canyon. The trail down to Havasu Falls was steep but it was a good trail.

The real challenge, though, was riding a mule down to the bottom of the Grand Canyon on the Bright Angel Trail and out on the South Kaibab Trail. I would say it was breathtaking; I'm afraid of heights.

From the back of my beloved horse, Warrior, I saw beautiful country that I would not have been able to see if it weren't for him. He carried me down to the beautiful Havasu Falls in the western part of the Grand Canyon and along some awesome trails in the Colorado Rockies. He was my compadre for 20 years. Warrior crossed the Rainbow Bridge last year. After losing my buddy, I wasn't sure I wanted another horse, but then couldn't imagine life without one.

I have a dear friend who couldn't imagine we without a horse either; so, she gave me a beautiful 8 year old appaloosa, Mikey. He is turning into a great trail horse. Mikey and I are making some wonderful memories. There is nothing like sitting on a mountain side with just you, your horse and dog and seeing the beauty around you. That's my church.

I am a volunteer for "The Arizona Site Stewards." We adopt prehistoric and historic sites and monitor them for vandalism. It never ceases to amaze me at the disrespect people have for these wonderful sites and it is a challenge trying preserve these precious places.

I'm looking forward to seeing much more of this beautiful country that God created in the best possible way, from the back of a horse.

I currently live in Congress, Arizona with my husband, Richard, two dogs, Sackett and Levi, and a horse Mikey.

I feel blessed to have my sister, Zenna, living nearby in Wickenburg. I have a four wheel drive truck; so, the two of us sometimes travel the back roads. The lure of the wide open spaces is in both of us.

Tommie is in Colorado now, but when she lived near we all had some great times together.

My heroes were the "silver screen cowboys" and I guess just like the song says, " my heroes have always been cowboys and they still are."

Happy Trails,
Bonnie Chisholm Helten
June 2007

Yvonne married (1) Gerald Melvin Smith son of Melvin Vinson Smith and Dorothy Elain Percal on 11 Feb 1961 in Peoria, Maricopa, Az, USA. Gerald was born on 26 Feb 1941 in Rochester, Minnesota, USA.

Yvonne married (2) Richard E Helten son of Richard Leonard Helten and Emeline Janet Johnsgaard on 18 Nov 1981 in Sierra Vista, Arizona, USA. Richard was born on 10 Dec 1940 in Fairview, Montana, USA.

They had the following children:

214 M i. **My Horse Warrior Helten** was born on 5 May 1984 in Sierra Vista, Arizona, USA. He died on 4 Aug 2006 in Congress, Yavapai, Arizona, USA. The cause of death was Colic. He was buried in Congress, Yavapai, Arizona.

Warrior was born 5 Jan 1984. He was an Appaloose Gelding. I got him when he was two old and trained him to show in Western Pleasure, Western Trail and Western Riding. After tiring of the show circuit I rode him on many trails over the State of Arizona. We were living in Sierra Vista and he took me over many beautiful trails in that part of the state, then we moved to Congress and we trailed the Northern part of Arizona and also in Colorado. He was my faithful companion for Twenty years.

Bonnie Helton.

---

105.   **Ross Martin Chisholm** (Calvin Alonzo, George Langford, Glenn Thornton, Richard Henry) was born on 16 Jun 1920 in Peoria, Maricopa, Arizona, USA. He died on 20 Jul 2002 in Firebaugh, Fresno, California, USA. The cause of death was Prostate Cancer. He was buried on 24 Jul 2002 in Chowchilla District Cemetery, Firebaugh, , California, USA.

Ross Martin Chisholm

Ross was born June 16, 1920 to Calvin and Jessie Chisholm in Peoria, Arizona. He was the oldest of four children. It was rough times during his childhood and the kids took care of each other. If the food was in short supply, it was divided among all the siblings. The family moved around as most of the other Chisholm families did. They moved from Arizona to Blythe, California when Ross was ten years old. There he attended high school and was president of his class. He had worked and saved money for his class ring. His Dad spent the money and Ross was ashamed to be the only one without a ring; so, he left school without graduating.

He got wander-lust when a cousin, Richard A, nicknamed Chick, came with his father to spend time with some of the family that had moved from Texas. Chick soon got the urge to go home to Texas and wanted Ross to go with him. What could be more interesting than to hop a freight train and see the world. They found an empty train car and hopped aboard. Things went well until a 'railroad bull' came along and put them off in some little town along the way. With no money to buy food, it was time to become a hobo and go to a house along the tracks and ask for a handout. The people who lived along the tracks were use to that during the depression and were always willing to give a handout. The first time Ross went to a door to ask for food a pretty young girl came to the door, he was too embarrassed and did not ask for food, he did not want her to think he was a bum; so, Chick was the one to ask after that. One time when they were 'kicked off' the train, there was a hobo camp right next to the tracks where the hobos (they were not called homeless in those day) would congregate when thrown off the train. They were cooking a big pot of food and ask the youngsters to join them. What a treat for two hungry travelers. Being a hobo was a wild adventure. When they arrived in Texas, they went to stay with Chick's mom and then to his sister, Fannie G, in San Antonio. Ross's dad wanted him to come home; so, he sent him money for a ticket home.

The family moved to Chowchilla, California. It was while there, on February 18, 1941, that Ross enlisted for foreign duty in the US Army. He was assigned to Battery A 60th Coast Artillery Battalion as a Searchlight Crewman in the Philippines, and was stationed on the island of Corregidor when the Japanese attacked. Following is the speech that his daughter, Sharon, gave of his time as a POW.

Zenna Chisholm Snowden
March 2007

Sharon Wakefield
Speech 1
October 29, 2000
Title: **Guest to the Royal Emperor of Japan**
Central Idea: Because not too many World War II Prisoners of War (P.O.W) are left, I would like to
   share with you the dietary conditions that were endured during captivity.

Introduction: Who was GI Joe? GI Joe was the name used for the European soldier, the sailor, the airman, the marine and the Coast Guardsman of the 20th century. My father, Ross Chisholm, was not a GI Joe in Europe, but was a guest to the Royal Emperor of Japan during World War II as a Prisoner of War (P.O.W).

Growing up through the Depression, Ross said he joined the United States Army because he was hungry and wanted some adventure. His adventure would take him to Philippines to the island of Corregidor.

He said when the bombing started it was real exciting. But soon you found out what some of your fellow men were made of and you also had a keen since of using your hearing to know where the Japanese bullets and bombs were going to hit. One night in a Naval lookout, he used a huge telescope and reality hit him that the song Tokyo Rose sang, "Ships that Never Come In" was true, as before his eyes with the telescope facing the island of Bataan, he saw a huge group of American Soldiers captured. The Japanese forces had broken through the American defensive line.

I was positioned on the topside of the island, so all we could hear was the sound of a battle being waged. General MacArthur had indicated we were to fight to the death. Many things crossed his mind that night. He asked another soldier named, Cousin, if he would like to fight alongside of him. Cousin was grateful and eager to join him. My father said, he decided to himself, to fight to death like James Bowie had done in the picture the Alamo with his bowie knife.

They waited but the enemy never came, instead when they looked out the next morning, we saw Old Glory coming down, and a white flag going up. It was the saddest sight we ever saw. We could not believe General Wainwright had surrendered us. We had seen what the Japanese had done to the Chinese, and it was not pretty.

"While the white flag was still up, they still bombed us. The first time I saw the enemy was as they marched us down to the lower side of the island to camp that night. We were given no food, so a group of us went scavenging. The guards did not seem to mind. All we could find was a gallon of fig and strawberry preserves. I also found some sea rations and ate as many as possible. After a day or so they started moving us around Malinta Hill. When we had arrived to the other side of the island where the fighting had raged, what a scene. The smell choked you down. It was the most gruesome sights and smell one could imagine, I threw up whatever food I had in my stomach."

Feeding on all the dead, Big blue flies multiplied by the billions. Early in the morning it was like looking at a black screen that blocked out the sun. The flies would leave a live maggot on open wounds. If they landed on your lips, chances were you would get dysentery.

Going without food the Japanese finally let groups of us go out and look for food. I found a 50-pound bag of pinto beans, and a big can of chili powder. After the flies went to bed we cooked the beans during the night and ate them early in the morning before the flies woke up.

My buddy Cousin wanted me to escape with him in a boat. I asked him if he had any drugs to prevent malaria. He didn't so I didn't go, as the risk for tropical diseases was too great. He and another guy were caught and were shot.

The next time I was allowed to go out in search for food, I found a huge can a Vienna sausage. We noticed a small pinhole in the can so we scraped away the top layer of sausage and started eating the rest. Big mistake, the next day we all became ill with Ptomaine poisoning. (Food poisoning caused by bacteria or bacterial poisons. P834)

The only thing good about this experience was that you lost interest in food for a while.

One morning I woke up with a blister on my face. I broke the blister and as painful as it was, picked off the skin, exposing red flesh. The next morning whatever it was spread to more of my face. I pulled all the skin off again, but this time I looked for some type of medicine. A soldier gave me some powder he had and I put it on my face. By the next morning it had stopped spreading.

The Japanese were planning to parade us down MacArthur Boulevard, to show the Filipinos their victory. We were loaded on boats and then because the boats could not get close to the shore, we had to swim the rest of the way. We were lined up in parade fashion. The Japanese wanted Colonel Bunker to ride in a car with other imprisoned officers, but the old man refused. He expressed his wish to walk in front of his troops and they let him do so. It was hot and we had no water. Along the route, the Philippines cheered us, and whenever they could they gave us water. After we reached Bilibid Prison, the Old Colonel collapsed and I heard he died. He was like me and did not want to surrender. As a leader, he made me feel proud.

I was thrown into a dark room and dirt floor. My face was cracking and bleeding, my thoughts of making it out alive were at their lowest. Then we were loaded into some small boxcars, and were taken to Cabanatuan. We slept on the ground and no food was given. The next day we were marched up hills far into the mountains to Camp 3. It was such a long hot march some of men did not make it. We were assigned tent like barracks. No water or food supplies, just sleeping quarters. The next day we were fed rice and then made to dig latrine facilities. We bathed only when it rained. Sometimes the rain would stop, and there you were caught with all this soap on you. You would just wear it till it wore off, or the next rain came.

Every day your first priority was thinking about food. The Japanese came up with Sweet Potato Vine Soup. This was the ingredients: Take the vine of a sweet potato, throw it on the ground to decompose with many flies landing on it and then boil it in water.

Many prisoners developed beriberi. My dad stated that first your feet would swell and then your stomach. Your feet felt like they were asleep and they hurt to walk on. If it made to your stomach, you were dead. Grazing on grasses seemed to help; so, to keep from getting it, he started grazing too.

The flies were taking over the camp and the Japanese promised, that for every can filled with dead flies, we would be rewarded with a piece of bread. Everything was going ok, till they caught some of the guys putting straw in the bottom of the cans, so they cut the bread off.

One time a water buffalo fell in the urine pit and we dug him out and killed and butchered him in record time. We took him to the kitchen staff and everyone was excited because it had been a long time since we had meat. All we got was a big piece of gristle floating in water. The broth tasted good, but we figured the Japanese took the lion of the meat.

A group of us were given orders to start walking the long road back to Cabanatuan, where again we were loaded on boxcars with standing room only. During this journey I came down with a bad case of dysentery.

Arriving at Manila we were put on ships. They fed us fish cured with salt. The skin was coming off my mouth. It was hard to eat but I did, as you didn't know when you might eat again. On the boat citrus peelings were being given out for anyone with scurvy. I asked for some but was denied. The reason was lack of enthusiasm, you had to beg. Another buddy named, Cohen, went over and begged with enthusiasm so he could help me out.

These ships were also called "Hell Ships." Temperatures in the holds rose to more than 100 degrees; water was scarce; food was only a dream. Men died in their own filth. (Doyle, 40, 41). Dad said they named their ship the "Dysentery Maru." They could not throw waste over the side due to American submarines firing upon these ships. They did not mark them with P.O.W. Not knowing they contained captive human cargo, many ships were sunk and many men died, from being fired upon by American submarines.

After about 30 days the shipped docked in the port of Tywain because of a cyclone. When the cyclone was over we shipped out to Korea. A fever hit me before we reach Korea. We had come out of the tropics to a very cold climate. My buddies stripped me and put me in heavy clothing. It was about a mile to the train waiting to carry us to Mukden Manchuria. As we walked along, civilians would throw garbage at us. Sick and out my head, the thought came to me to grab one of my tormentors and kill him with what strength I had left, but this other sick little guy smiled at me and I said if he could make it, so can I. We both made it, but when I sat down my mind went blank. I woke up in bed with a burning fever.

I was in a shack for a hospital with a bunch of dying men. Dr. Brennan, an Australian doctor, looked after us. We were covered with lice, ticks, and fleas. My weight went to 104 pounds. My strength had diminished to a point where I could not lift my canteen to my mouth. We were fed blue maize, which is chicken feed. Dr. Brennan came by each day knowing he did not have medicine to cure us. He would ask me "How are you today Ross?" I guess I was just too dumb to know I was dying, and I would say fine. I was going to be moved to the room for the dying, but they took someone else instead. The doctor came by one day and gave me something that he thought would help me. He told me to hold onto my bread and he would come by and put something on it. It was cod liver oil and some type of medicine he had held out for himself.

I asked him why he did that for me, and he said because I never let him down when he asked how I was. I always said fine. You never once cursed me or told me it was my fault you were dying. He said he figured if I was so dumb not to know I was dying, he decided to save me.

As I lay there recuperating, I witnessed human misery. I watched men die in peaceful ways, and others fighting death with a bitterness that brought out all the hate they had inside them.

I met a 16 years old kid named Babe from North Carolina. We met facing each other nose to nose in the getting rid of some raw soybeans we had consumed. They were like shooting out bullets. Sounded like a machine gun. We had a good laugh. In the room where we lived, ice cycles had formed on the nails in the roof. We had a little stove, but it put off very little heat. We knew if we didn't do something soon a lot more of us were going to die from freezing to death. We took 7 dead men out of one wooden casket and burned the casket. The dead men were stacked along the wall. It was so cold in the barracks. One guy remarked that the dead men looked just as happy standing up as they did lying down. At least the men dying with pneumonia could go out warm.

I was placed into another miserable hospital around Thanksgiving time and by Christmas hundreds of men had died. I learned to count and talk some Japanese. A number had been given to me. It was Thirteen 0 Six (1306). We were not listed as POW's on the Geneva Convention. As long as we were guest of the Emperor of Japan, the Japanese did not have to account for any of us. I never worked in the factory but was used to work on different jobs at their beck and call.

One day some other men and myself were made to dig graves. The dead men were thawing out. It was a big day for the Japanese soldiers. The Japanese Lieutenant that had been educated in the United States, stood over the boxes of our dead and made this statement. "I want each of you to know, that these dead are what I call Good Americans." All I could see was men who died a horrible death because they were surrendered to a monster back stabbing traitor like Lt. Miki.

I found a job in the kitchen. One of the cooks liked to wrestle, so when we would wrestle, another guy would steal sugar from a sack. The guy stealing sugar got caught, and was beat real bad and put to work in the hyde factory.

On a 4th of July, Lt. Miki rounded us up. He was about to make a speech when he suddenly he asked if there were any men from Texas. So the Texas men raised their hands with great enthusiasm, yelling each one "I am from Texas." It was quite for a minute, and then Lt. Miki spoke and proclaimed that men from Texas were the Ass Holes of creation. From then on no one would tell where he was from. We made plans anyway for the 4th of July. A Marine had an American Flag, so we raised it high, and grabbed some pot and pans and started beating on them. We marched around the compound, whooping it up. But soon bayonets surrounded us and for a moment I thought we were going to be shot.

They took each of our numbers, confiscated the flag, the pots and pans. We were sent back to our barracks. The next day about 150 numbers were called out and to pack up we were moving to Japan. We were loaded back onto a ship and headed for somewhere in Japan. We were met by a mob when we left the ship. Cursing and throwing things at us again. The Japanese soldiers scared them back with gunshots. We were loaded on a train and made to hike into the mountains to our new camp in Kamioka.

We were made to work in the lead mines. Here we were fed a binto box once a day. It consisted of steamed rice, salted cherry, fish, and pickled vegetables. They also fed us crushed, dried grasshoppers and squid once in a while. You learned to swallow quickly.

When they were working them hard, the Japanese would feed them around a 1200-calorie diet. When not working, they fed them a 700-calorie diet.

I made some new friends here and some from my prior camp were with me also. These were the friends goods friends like the ones my dad told me about. "The men to ride the river with."(Dad's, 77)

As the bombing of Japan started, the people leaving their homes passed our camps and shook their fist and cursed us. We never heard the atomic bomb go off, but suddenly guards started disappearing. Fearing no reprisal against us, my buddies took off from camp. We walked to a farm about 15 miles and purchased a swayed back horse for 1,200 yen. Babe road the horse back to camp. He reminded me of a picture I saw once of Abraham Lincoln riding a horse.

We sold it when we got back to camp for 1,200 yens and provided we got the rump roast and some potatoes to go with it. The smell was wonderful. But there were so many men; we just enjoyed watching them enjoy it. We never had any of it. The war was over and I was happy.

No longer working in the mine, we just roamed around wondering how we were to be rescued. A plane made a pass one day over us and a parachute opened and the object came to the ground outside the camp. Myself and two other men were sent out to retrieve it. All around was penny chocolate bars lying on the ground. We started picking them up and cramming them into our mouths at the same time. I don't know how many we ate, but I started throwing them up. We also were dropped food and clothing. It was August when our troops came for us.

We marched out of the camp and caught the train that had brought us there. The Marine who had kept the flag placed her up high on the front of the train. We left the land of our confinement, with memories of those who were not coming with us.

We were taken to a medical compound and stripped of our clothes, and sprayed with DDT on all parts of our bodies. Then new clothes were given to us. At last we weren't infected with fleas or bed bugs.

One of my friends, Red Wade, wanted me to go on a cargo plane going back empty, but I did not go with him. A typhoon hit the island and I heard later Red died when the door on the cargo plane opened and dropped them into the ocean.

After the storm blew over, we were loaded into planes to Manila to tent like quarters. While waiting for orders a group of soldiers were escorting Japanese soldiers to some destination. But soon all hell broke loose and a mob of angry P.O.W.'s started doing what they had done to us. I did not join in as I remembered my feelings or rejection as I saw people that I had never harmed, yet was tired to such violence. I realized that most human beings were inflicted with the same emotions, outrage brought about by stirred up emotions.

We were put on a ship going to San Francisco. I became very sick and they had to give me glucose shots to keep me going. He spent 30 days in the hospital at San Francisco. They dewormed us of all parasites.

I asked my dad what was the one thing he remembered eating that taste so good when he arrived back to the United States, and he said it was a glass of cold chocolate milk.

Sharon Chisholm Wakefield

July 2007

Ross was liberated on September 6, 1945 and received an Honorable Discharge as a Sergeant on March 2, 1946. With a "little" worn Bible that his mom had given him when he left for the service, Ross returned home to a happy family and relatives. The pages of the "little" Bible were well worn by Ross and fellow prisoners seeking comfort.

Ross was living in Dos Palos, California when he meet a pretty little Oklahoma gal, Dorothy Garrett. They were married July 13, 1947 and were blessed with two children.

Their son, Gary Martin, was born October 8, 1950 and died December 20, 1969. Their daughter, Sharon Marie, was born January 4, 1954. Sharon has been a faithful, caring daughter helping her mom and dad through trying times in their later years.

Ross went to work for the Fresno County Public Works Road Division and retired from there after 36 ½ years. Ross was an avid golfer with a goal to see how many different courses he could play during his travels. He served as the President of the Whites Bridge Golf and Country Club and Men's Club. Ross was a member of the Madera Golf and Country Club.

Singing was one of his pleasures. At reunions, retirements, birthdays or at camp outs, Ross would usually write a poem and sing, of course, we would all sing along. Some of our best times were when his brother, Dan, was along. Dan would play the harmonica, pick his guitar and sing. Those are wonderful memories

Ross loved to travel and to have friends and family along. We crossed the United States with a caravan of five motor homes; Ross decided that was too many. After my husband passed away, Ross, Dorothy and I, took a trip together every year. What fun. We would stop by the side of the road to rest or eat and we might just have a game of cards to relax. Many miles of beautiful scenery and fun times.

When Ross became ill and Dorothy's back began to give her problems, life changed for all. Ross passed away July 20, 2002.

Ross and his brother Dan were two loving and caring cousins. There was never a death in the family in California or Arizona that they did not take time off to attend. Two cousins and their wives that I love dearly.

Zenna Chisholm Snowden
July 2007

Ross Martin Chisholm Written by Sharon his daughter

Hi Zenna: I am sending this story I wrote for a class project that dad told be about for my paper.

POW - 1306 is about my father, Ross Chisholm, who fought bravely against the Japanese on the island of Corregidor in the Philippines. Ordered to surrender to a vicious and violent enemy, over the next three and a half years, he would fight to survive the Japanese Death Camps.

Who was GI Joe? GI Joe was the name used for the soldier, the sailor, the airman, the marine and the Coast Guardsman of the 20th century during the World War II who stopped Hitler, Mussolini and Tojo from burning the world down (Ambrose, 14). My father, Ross Chisholm was not a GI Joe in Europe, but was a guest to the Royal Emperor of Japan during World War II for three and one-half years as a Prisoner of War (POW).

Growing up through the Depression, Ross said he joined the United States Army because he was hungry and wanted some adventure. His adventure would take him to Philippines to the island of Corregidor.

He said when the bombing started it was real exciting. But soon you found out what some of your fellow men were made of and you also had a keen since of using your hearing to know where the Japanese bullets and bombs were going to hit. One night in a Naval lookout, he used a huge telescope and reality hit him that the song Tokyo Rose sang, "Ships that Never Come In" was true, as before his eyes with the telescope facing the island of Bataan, he saw a huge group of American Soldiers captured. The Japanese forces had broken through the American defensive line.

I was positioned on the topside of the island, so all we could hear was the sound of a battle being waged. General Mac Arthur had indicated we were to fight to the death. Many things crossed his mine that night. He asked another soldier named, Cousin, if he would like to fight along side of him. Cousin was grateful and eager to join him. My father said he decided to himself to fight to death like James Bowie had done in the picture the Alamo with his bowie knife. They waited but the enemy never came, instead when they looked out the next morning, we saw Old Glory coming down, and a white flag going up. It was the saddest sight we ever saw. We could not believe General Wainwright had surrendered us. We had seen what the Japanese had done to the Chinese, and it was not pretty.

"While the white flag was still up, they still bombed us. The first time I saw the enemy was as they marched us down to the lower side of the island to camp that night. We were given no food, so a group of us went scavenging. The guards did not seem to mind. All we could find was a gallon of fig and strawberry preserves. I also found some sea rations and ate as many as possible. After a day or so they started moving us around Malinta Hill. When we had arrived to the other side of the island where the fighting had raged, what a scene. The smell choked you down. It was the most gruesome sights and smell one could imagine. I threw up whatever food I had in my stomach."

Feeding on all the dead, Big blue flies multiplied by the billions. Early in the morning it was like looking at a black screen that blocked out the sun. The flies would leave a live maggot on open wounds. If they landed on your lips, chances were you would get dysentery.

Going without food the Japanese finally let groups of us go out and look for food. I found a 50-pound bag of pinto beans, and a big can of chili powder. After the flies went to bed we cooked the beans during the night and ate them early in the morning before the flies woke up.

My buddy Cousin wanted me to escape with him in a boat. I asked him if he had any drugs to prevent malaria. He didn't so I didn't go, as the risk for tropical diseases was too great. He and another guy were caught and were shot.

The next time I was allowed to go out in search for food, I found a huge can a Vienna sausage. We noticed a small pinhole in the can so we scraped away the top layer of sausage and started eating the rest. Big mistake, the next day we all became ill with Ptomaine poisoning. (Food poisoning caused by bacteria or bacterial poisons. P834) The only thing good about this experience was that you lost interest in food for a while.

One morning I woke up with a blister on my face. I broke the blister an as painful as it was, picked off the skin, exposing red flesh. The next morning whatever it was spread to more of my face. I pulled all the skin off again, but this time I looked for some type of medicine. A soldier gave me some powder he had and I put it on my face. By the next morning it had stopped spreading.

The Japanese were planning to parade us down Mc Arthur Boulevard, to show the Phillipinos their victory. We were loaded on boats and then because the boats could not get close to the shore, we had to swim the rest of the way. We were lined up in parade fashion. The Japanese wanted Colonel Bunker to ride in a car with other imprisoned officers, but the old man refused. He expressed his wish to walk in front of his troops and they let him do so. It was hot and we had no water. Along the route, the Phillipinos cheered us, and whenever they could they gave us water. After we reached Bilibid Prison, the Old Colonel collapsed and I heard he died. He was like me and did not want to surrender. As a leader he made me feel proud.

I was thrown into a dark room and dirt floor. My face was cracking and bleeding. My thoughts of making it out alive were at their lowest. Then we were loaded into some small boxcars, and were taken to Cabanatuan. We slept on the ground and no food was given. The next day we were marched up hills far into the mountains to Camp 3. It was such a long hot march some of men did not make it. We were assigned tent like barracks. No water or food supplies, just sleeping quarters. The next day we were fed rice and then made to dig latrine facilities. We bathed only when it rained. Sometimes the rain would stop, and there you were caught with all this soap on you. You would just wear it till it wore off, or the next rain came.

Every day your first priority was thinking about food. The Japanese came up with Sweet Potato Vine Soup. This was the ingredients: Take the vine of a sweet potato, throw it on the ground to decompose with many flies landing on it and then boil it in water.

Many prisoners developed beriberi. My dad stated that first your feet would swell and then your stomach. Your feet felt like they were asleep and they hurt to walk on. If it made to your stomach, you were dead. Grazing on grasses seemed to help. So to keep from getting it, he started grazing too.

The flies were taking over the camp and the Japanese promised that for every can filled with dead flies, we would be rewarded with a piece of bread. Everything was going ok, till they caught some of the guys putting straw in the bottom of the cans, so they cut the bread off.

One time a water buffalo fell in the urine pit and we dug him out and killed and butchered him in record time. We took him to the kitchen staff and everyone was excited because it had been a long time since we had meat. All we got was a big piece of gristle floating in water. The broth tasted good, but we figured the Japanese took the lion of the meat.

A group of us were given orders to start walking the long road back to Cabanatuan, where again we were loaded on boxcars with standing room only. During this journey I came down with a bad case of dysentery.

Arriving at Manila we were put on ships. They fed us fish cured with salt. The skin was coming off my mouth. It was hard to eat but I did, as you didn't know when you might eat again. On the boat citrus peelings were being given out for anyone with scurvy. I asked for some but was denied. The reason was lack of enthusiasm. You had to beg. Another buddy named, Cohen, went over and begged with enthusiasm so he could help me out.

These ships were also called "Hell Ships." Temperatures in the holds rose to more than 100 degrees; water was scarce; food was only a dream. Men died in their own filth. (Doyle, 40, 41). Dad said they named their ship the "Dysentery Maru." They could not throw waste over the side due to American submarines firing upon these ships. They did not mark them with P.O.W. Not knowing they contained captive human cargo, many ships were sunk and many men died from being fired upon by American submarines.

After about 30 days the shipped docked in the port of Tywain because of a cyclone. When they cyclone was over we shipped out to Korea. A fever hit me before we reach Korea. We had come out of the tropics to a very cold climate. My buddies stripped me and put me in heavy clothing. It was about a mile to the train waiting to carry us to Mukden Manchuria. As we walked along, civilians would throw garbage at us. Sick and out my head, the thought came to me to grab one of my tormentors and kill him with what strength I had left. But this other sick little guy smiled at me and I said if he could make it, so can I.

We both made it, but when I sat down my mind went blank. I woke up in bed with a burning fever. I was in a shack for a hospital with a bunch of dying men. Dr. Brennan, an Australian doctor, looked after us. We were covered with lice, ticks, and fleas. My weight went to 104 pounds. My strength had diminished to a point where I could not lift my canteen to my mouth. We were fed blue maize, which is chicken feed.

Dr. Brennan came by each day knowing he did not have medicine to cure us. He would ask me "How are you today Ross?" I guess I was just too dumb to know I was dying, and I would say fine. I was going to be moved to the room for the dying, but they took someone else instead. The doctor came by one day and gave me something that he thought would help me. He told me to hold onto my bread and he would come by and put something on it. It was cod liver oil and some type of medicine he had held out for himself. I asked him why he did that for me, and he said because I never let him down when he asked how I was. I always said fine. You never once cursed me or told me it was my fault you were dying. He said he figured if I was so dumb not to know I was dying, he decided to save me. As I lay there recuperating, I witnessed human misery. I watched men die in peaceful ways, and others fighting death with a bitterness that brought out all the hate they had inside them.

I met a 16 years old kid named Babe from North Carolina. We met facing each other nose to nose in the getting rid of some raw soybeans we had consumed. They were like shooting out bullets. Sounded like a machine gun. We had a good laugh. In the room where we lived, ice cycles had formed on the nails in the roof. We had a little stove, but it put off very little heat. We knew if we didn't do something soon a lot more of us were going to die from freezing to death. We took 7 dead men out of one wooden casket and burned the casket. The dead men were stacked along the wall. It was so cold in the barracks.

One guy remarked that the dead men looked just as happy standing up as they did lying down. At least the men dying with pneumonia could go out warm. I was placed into another miserable hospital around Thanksgiving time and by Christmas hundreds of men had died. I learned to count and talk some Japanese. A number had been given to me. It was Thirteen 0 Six (1306). We were not listed as POW's on the Geneva Convention. As long as we were guest of the Emperor of Japan, the Japanese did not have to account for any of us. I never worked in the factory but was used to work on different jobs at their beck and call.

One day some other men and myself were made to dig graves. The dead men were thawing out. It was a big day for the Japanese soldiers The Japanese Lieutenant that had been educated in the United States, stood over the boxes of our dead and made this statement. "I want each of you to know, that these dead are what I call Good Americans." All I could see was men who died a horrible death because they were surrendered to a monster back stabbing traitor like Lt. Miki.

I found a job in the kitchen. One of the cooks liked to wrestle, so when we would wrestle, another guy would steal sugar from a sack. The guy stealing sugar got caught, and was beat real bad and put to work in the hyde factory.

On a 4th of July, Lt. Miki rounded us up. He was about to make a speech when he suddenly he asked if there were any men from Texas. So the Texas men raised their hands with great enthusiasm, yelling each one "I am from Texas." It was quite for a minute, and then Lt. Miki spoke and proclaimed that men from Texas were the Ass Holes of creation. From then on no one would tell where he was from. We made plans anyway for the 4th of July. A Marine had an American Flag, so we raised it high, and grabbed some pot and pans and started beating on them. We marched around the compound, whooping it up. But soon bayonets surrounded us and for a moment I thought we were going to be shot. They took each of our numbers, confiscated the flag, the pots and pans. We were sent back to our barracks. The next day about 150 numbers were called out and to pack up we were moving to Japan.

We were loaded back onto a ship and headed for somewhere in Japan. We were met by a mob when we left the ship. Cursing and throwing things at us began. The Japanese soldiers scared them back with gunshots. We were loaded on a train and made to hike into the mountains to our new camp in Kamioka.

We were made to work in the lead mines. Here we were fed a binto box once a day. It consisted of steamed rice, salted cherry, fish, and pickled vegetables. They also fed us crushed, dried grasshoppers and squid once in a while. You learned to swallow quickly.
When they were working them hard, the Japanese would feed them around a 1200-calorie diet. When not working, they fed them a 700-calorie diet.

I made some new friends here and some from my prior camp were with me also. These were the friends goods friends like the ones my dad told me about. "The men to ride the river with."(Dad's, 77)

As the bombing of Japan started, the people leaving their homes passed our camps and shook their fist and cursed us. We never heard the atomic bomb go off, but suddenly guards started disappearing. Fearing no reprisal against us, my buddies took off from camp. We walked to a farm about 15 miles and purchased a swayed back horse for 1,200 yen. Babe road the horse back to camp. He reminded me of a picture I saw once of Abraham Lincoln riding a horse.

We sold it when we got back to camp for 1,200 yens and provided we got the rump roast and some potatoes to go with it. The smell was wonderful. But there were so many men; we just enjoyed watching them enjoy it. We never had any of it. The war was over and I was happy.

No longer working in the mine, we just roamed around wondering how we were to be rescued. A plane made a pass one day over us and a parachute opened and the object came to the ground outside the camp. Myself and two other men were sent out to retrieve it. All around was penny chocolate bars lying on the ground. We started picking them up and cramming them into our mouths at the same time. I don't know how many we ate, but I started throwing them up.

111

We also were dropped food and clothing. It was August when our troops came for us. We marched out of the camp and caught the train that had brought us there. The Marine who had kept the flag placed her up high on the front of the train. With left the land of our confinement, with memories of those who were not coming with us.

We were taken to a medical compound and stripped of our clothes, and sprayed with DDT on all parts of our bodies. Then new clothes were given to us. At last we weren't infected with fleas or bed bugs.

One of my friends, Red Wade, wanted me to go on a cargo plane going back empty, but I did not go with him. A typhoon hit the island and I heard later Red died when the door on the cargo plane opened and dropped them into the ocean.

After the storm blew over, we were loaded into planes to Manila to tent like quarters. While waiting for orders a group of soldiers were escorting Japanese soldiers to some destination. But soon all hell broke loose and a mob of angry P.O.W.'s started doing what they had done to us. I did not join in as I remembered my feelings or rejection as I saw people that I had never harmed, yet was tired to such violence. I realized that most human beings were inflicted with the same emotions, outrage brought about by stirred up emotions.

We were put on a ship going to San Francisco. I became very sick and they had to give me glucose shots to keep me going. He spent 30 days in the hospital at San Francisco. They dewormed us of all parasites.

I asked my dad what was the one thing he remembered eating that taste so good when he arrived back to the United States, and he said it was a glass of cold chocolate milk.

Ross married Dorothy Christine Garrett daughter of Valde Garrett and Lillie Zinger on 13 Jul 1947 in Reno, Nevada, USA. Dorothy was born on 17 Sep 1929 in Hydro, Oklahoma, USA.

They had the following children:

> 215 M i. **Gary Martin Chisholm** was born on 8 Aug 1950 in Dos Palos, California, USA. He died on 20 Dec 1969 in Valley Children Hospital, Fresno, Fresno, California, USA. He was buried on 23 Dec 1969 in Chowchilla Cemetery, Chowchilla, Madera, California, USA.

> + 216 F ii. **Sharon Chisholm** was born on 4 Jan 1954.

106.   **Fannie Maude Chisholm** "Faye" (Calvin Alonzo, George Langford, Glenn Thornton, Richard Henry) was born on 4 Jan 1923 in Blythe, California, USA.

Fannie married (1) **Phillip Harding Chambers** son of Phillip Hooper Chambers and Lorna Elizabeth Klaholtz on 21 Sep 1941 in Reno, Nevada, USA. Phillip was born on 2 Aug 1922 in Williams, California, USA. He died on 20 Jan 1990 in Phoenix, Maricopa, Arizona, USA. He was buried in Twenty Nine Palms, California, USA .

Philip Harding Chambers was cremated

Phillip and Fannie had the following children:

+ 217M i. **Phillip Alonzo Chambers** was born on 16 Jun 1942.

+ 218F ii. **Phyllis Marie Chambers** was born on 18 Jul 1942.

+ 219M iii. **Clarence Lester Chambers** was born on 25 Aug 1946.

+ 220F iv. **Trudy Ann Chambers** was born on 22 Nov 1949.

Fannie married (2) Bill Avedisian.

Fannie married (3) Dan Robert Thatcher on 29 Jul 1972. Dan was born on 6 Mar 1920.

107. **Daniel Webster Chisholm** (Calvin Alonzo, George Langford, Glenn Thornton, Richard Henry) was born on 18 Jan 1925 in Marinette, Maricopa, Arizona, USA. He died on 8 Dec 2006 in Coalinga, , California, USA. He was buried on 14 Dec 2006 in Coalinga, California, USA.

Dates from funeral service brochure and Family Group Records sent to be by Bernice Chisholm in 2006.

Dan attended grade school in Arizona and graduated from Chowchilla High School. Shortly after graduating, Dan enlisted in the US Navy and proudly served during WWII. He served on a Mine sweeper in the Pacific.

Dan lived in Coalinga 48 years and worked for the Fresno County Department of Public Works 35 years, 25 Years as Road Foreman. He loved music and played the guitar and harmonica.

He was active in the First Southern Baptist Church where he served as Song Leader and Deacon for many years. He also taught Sunday School.

He was rather quiet and a loving person and fun to know. I loved him dearly.

Zenna Chisholm Snowden

Daniel married Joy Bernice Curry daughter of George Curry and Bessie Batey on 21 Jun 1948 in Dos Palos, California, USA. Joy was born on 2 Mar 1929 in Hinton, Oklahoma.

Family Group Records sent to be by Bernice Chisholm in 2006.

Daniel and Joy had the following children:

+ 221 F i. **Rita Marlene Chisholm** was born on 12 Apr 1949.

+ 222 F ii. **Sandra Eva Chisholm** was born on 18 Mar 1957. She died on 21 Mar 2003.

+ 223 F iii. **Karen Marie Chisholm** was born on 7 Dec 1960.

108.   **Chester Lee Chisholm** "Chet" (Calvin Alonzo, George Langford, Glenn Thornton, Richard Henry) was born on 4 Nov 1926 in Phoenix, Maricopa, Arizona.

Chester served in the US Army during World War 2 in the occupation of Japan.

Chester married (1) Joan Greene daughter of Eleswood Greene and Dorothy Rust on 29 Dec 1946. Joan was born on 22 Oct 1929 in Ponca City, Oklahoma, USA.

They had the following children:

224 M i. **Steven L Chisholm** was born on 1 Feb 1948 in Dos Palos, ,California, USA.

Steven married **Shirley Chisholm** in 1973.

+ 225 F ii. **Linda Sue Chisholm** was born on 12 Apr 1949.

Chester married (2) Denise Chisholm.

109.   **Dorothy Flora Chisholm** (Jesse, George Langford, Glenn Thornton, Richard Henry) was born on 9 Jun 1919 in Peoria, Maricopa, Arizona. She died in 1979.

Dorothy married (1) **Jimmy Frye** on 17 Dec 1934 in Yuma, Yuma, Arizona, USA.

They had the following children:

+ 226 F i. **Dena Mae Frye** was born on 16 Feb 1936.

Dorothy married (2) **George Cline** in 1938. George was born on 20 Apr 1917.

They had the following children:

+ 227 M ii. **David Cline** was born on 15 May 1946.

+ 228 F iii. **Donna Cline** was born on 31 Jul 1948.

110.   **Gladys Dena Chisholm** (Jesse, George Langford, Glenn Thornton, Richard Henry) was born on 1 Oct 1920 in Peoria, Maricopa, Arizona, USA. She died on 10 Feb 2002 in Selma, Fresno, California, USA. She was buried on 15 Feb 2002 in Washington Colony Cemetery, Easton, California, USA.

Information from family and Funeral Service Brochure.

Gladys married **James Harold Bachar** on 7 Nov 1937 in Caruthers, California, USA. James was born on 19 Oct 1915 in Marmaduke, Arkansas, USA. He died on 10 Dec 1984 in Fresno, Fresno, California, USA. He was buried on 12 Dec 1984 in Washington Colony Cemetery, Easton, California, USA.

Information from family and Funeral Service Brochure

James and Gladys had the following children:

+ 229 M i. **Roger Eugene Bachar** was born on 14 Feb 1942.

111.   **Jesse Robert "Bob" Chisholm** (Jesse, George Langford, Glenn Thornton, Richard Henry) was born on 5 Apr 1922 in Blythe, Riverside, California, USA. He died on 29 Jan 2003 in Selma, Fresno, California, USA. He was buried on 4 Feb 2003

in Washington Colony Cemetery, Easton, California, USA.

Information from family and Funeral Service Brochure

Jesse "Bob" married (1) Delsie Blackwell on 18 Mar 1941 in Riverside, California, USA. Delsie was born on 21 Aug 1922 in Riverdale, California, USA.

They had the following children:

+ 230 F i. **Patricia Ruth Chisholm** was born on 5 Feb 1942.

+ 231 F ii. **Verna Jean Chisholm** was born on 29 Aug 1943.

    232 F iii.**Jennifer Lee Chisholm** was born on 25 Oct 1949 in Selma, Fresno, California, USA. Jennifer married **Robert Adamson** .

Jesse "Bob" married (2) Adaline Borges on 11 Apr 1962. Adaline was born 28 Aug 1938 and died 12 Feb 2018 in Hanford, California.

Obituary Adeline C. Chisholm

August 28, 1938 – February 12, 2018

Adeline C. Chisholm, a resident of Hanford, passed away Monday, February 12, 2018. She was 79 years old. Adeline was born on August 28, 1938 to Tony and Adeline Borges. She married Bob Chisholm and they were married for 40 years. Adeline was a licensed insurance agent for many years, helping clients with auto and homeowner's insurance as well as serving commercial and farming accounts with their insurance needs. She retired from Jackson & Associates in Kingsburg.

After retiring Adeline and Bob enjoyed traveling to Hawaii and England and going RV camping with their family. Whenever you walked in the door she would say "Hello, let's play cards." She was a favorite Aunt and she would always say," How's my babies?" Adeline loved her sweets, romance novels and the Hallmark Channel.

112.   **Milton Clark Griffith** (Virgie Eliza Chisholm, George Langford, Glenn Thornton, Richard Henry) was born on 31 May 1919 in Peoria, Maricopa, Arizona, USA. He died on 25 Aug 2003 in Ceres, , California, USA. The cause of death was Prostate Cancer. He was buried in Ceres, California, USA.

Milton married Crystal Kathleen Monteith daughter of John Bengamin Monteith and Etta Matilda Shell on 16 May 1945 in Santa Rosa, California, USA. Crystal was born on 10 Mar 1927 in Hot Springs, California, USA.

The Griffith family history was sent to me by Crystal Kathleen Montieth, Wife of Milton Clark Griffith. The information was sent on Family Group Records that I sent to her. I received them 21 Aug 2006.

Milton and Crystal had the following children:
+ 233 M i. **Larry Craig Griffith** was born on 20 Mar 1946. He died on 24 Feb 1988.
+ 234 M ii. **David Clark Griffith** was born on 1 Sep 1950.

113.   **Leona Jewell Griffith** (Virgie Eliza Chisholm, George Langford, Glenn Thornton, Richard Henry) was born on 16 Aug 1922 in Williams, Coconino, Arizona. She died in McKinleyville, California. She was buried in McKinleyville, California.

Leona married Louis Magliano on 22 Jul 1939 in Merced, California. Louis was born about 1912.
They had the following children:
235 M i. **Sammy Magliano**
236 F ii. **Carol Magliano**
237 F iii. **Susan Maglaino**
238 M iv. **Phillip Magliano**

115.   **Violet Griffith** (Virgie Eliza Chisholm, George Langford, Glenn Thornton, Richard Henry) was born on 31 May 1927 in Phoenix, Maricopa, Arizona, USA. She died on 28 Jul 1978. The cause of death was Breast Cancer. She was buried in Cremated, Ashes Scattered at Sea.

Violet married LLoyd Whitcomb on 17 Sep 1945 in Santa Rosa, , California, USA.

They had the following children:

    239 M i. **Daniel Whitcomb**

    240 F ii. **Cynthia Whitcomb**

116.   **Jeannie May Chisholm** (Albert Vivian, George Langford, Glenn Thornton, Richard Henry) was born on 30 Apr 1926 in Phoenix, Maricopa, Arizona, USA. She died in Apr 2007. She was buried Cremation.

Jeannie married Plunket Weaver on 30 May 1948 in California, USA.

They had the following children:

    241 F i.   **Sheila Weaver** was born on 23 Jan 1949.

  + 242 M ii. **Plunkett Allen Weaver** was born on 3 Oct 1950.

    243 M iii. **Eric Albert Weaver** was born on 11 Mar 1966.

117.   **Randall Ray Chisholm** (Albert Vivian, George Langford, Glenn Thornton, Richard Henry) was born on 6 Sep 1936 in Madera, Madera, California, USA.

Randall served in the Navy from 30 Sept 1951 to 12 Sept 1955.

Randall married Vera Mae Alora daughter of Prydenclo Villa Blonco Alora and Edna Hopple on 21 Dec 1957 in Eureka, California, USA. Vera was born on 26 May 1936 in Eureka, Humboldt, California, USA.

They had the following children:

    244 M i. **Keith Randall Chisholm** was born on 17 Dec 1960 in Eureka, Humboldt, California.

  + 245 M ii. **Steven Ray Chisholm** was born on 6 Jul 1963.

118.   John Clark III (Totsie Lee Chisholm, George Langford, Glenn Thornton, Richard Henry) was born on 27 Jun 1923 in Phoenix, Maricopa, Arizona, USA. He died in 1997.

John married Barbara Snow.

They had the following children:

    246 F i. **Linda Clark** was born on 18 Mar 1951.

            Linda married **Scott Norman McArthur.**

    247 F ii. **Nancy Clark** was born on 15 Jan 1954 in Oakland, California, USA.

119.   Donald Clark (Totsie Lee Chisholm, George Langford, Glenn Thornton, Richard Henry) was born on 26 May 1926 in Tempe, Maricopa, Arizona, USA.

Donald married Patricia Daniels on 24 Oct 1954. Patricia was born on 1 Feb 1930 in Worthington, Minnesota, USA. She died on 3 Oct 2006 in Green Valley, Pima, Arizona, USA.

They had the following children:

    248 F i.   **Vickie Clark** was born in Jun 1947. Vickie was adopted

  + 249 F ii.   **Kathy Clark** was born on 18 Aug 1948.

    250 M iii. **Nathanial Clark**

    251 F iv.   **Jean Clark.** Jean married **William Benevides**

    252 F v.   **Sheryl Clark** was born on 1 Jan 1965. Sheryl was adopted

120.   Carroll Clark (Totsie Lee Chisholm, George Langford, Glenn Thornton, Richard Henry) was born on 4 Dec 1929 in Modesto, Modesto, California, USA. He died in 1996.

Carroll married Gloria Valla.

They had the following children:

253 F i. **Susan Clark** was born on 25 Sep 1964.

254 F ii. **Stacy Clark** was born in 1974.

121.   **Snowda Darlene Snowden** "Tootie" (Mae Chisholm, George Langford, Glenn Thornton, Richard Henry) was born on 7 Apr 1939 in Milo, Vernon, Missouri, USA. She died on 11 Mar 2007 in Commerice, Texas, USA. She was buried in Fairley Cemetery, Fairley, Texas, USA.

Snowda married (1) Walter Burton Milam son of Paul B Milam and Viola Barker on 5 Oct 1963 in Missouri, USA. Walter was born on 8 Jun 1927 in Newburn, Dyer, Texas, USA.

They had the following children:

255 M i.   **Ricky Lynne Milam** was born on 24 Oct 1957 in Nevada, Vernon, Missouri. Ricky was adopted by Burton Milam.

+ 256 F ii.   **Rhonda Lea Milam** was born on 7 May 1959.

257 M iii.   **Randall Milam** "Randy" was born on 1 Mar 1966 in Nevada, Vernon, Missouri. Randy was born at the Nevada, Missouri Hospital.

+ 258 F iv.   **Rita Mae Milam** was born on 14 Oct 1968.

Snowda married (2) Ova Roselle Wooldridge son of Floyd Wooldridge and Beulah Kirksey on 29 Jan 1957 in Bentonville, Benton, Arkansas, USA. The marriage ended in divorce. Ova was born in Greenfield, Missouri, USA.

123.   **Alfred Dalton Snowden** (Mae Chisholm, George Langford, Glenn Thornton, Richard Henry) was born on 16 Jan 1943 in Sheldon, Vernon, Missouri.

Alfred married (1) Janice Hargrove in 1959. The marriage ended in divorce.

They had the following children:

+259 F i. **Gloria Mae Snowden** was born in Feb 1960.

Alfred married (2) Danna Lee Smith "Dee Ann" daughter of Dan Smith and Jackie Smith. Danna was born on 31 Oct in Nevada, Vernon, Missouri, USA.

Alfred married (3) Kay Parry daughter of Ira Parry Jr and Ruth Head in 1966 in Las Vegas, Nevada, USA. Kay was born on 2 Jul 1943 in Rolla, Phelps, Missouri, USA.

They had the following children:

+260 F ii. **Carrie Snowden** was born in Jul 1967.

+261 F iii. **Emily Snowden** was born in Jun 1974.

124.   **Harry Horace Snowden** (Mae Chisholm, George Langford, Glenn Thornton, Richard Henry) was born on 27 Nov 1944 in Nevada, Vernon, Missouri, USA. He died on 6 Jan 1999. The cause of death was Diabeties. He was buried in Newton Burial Park, Nevada, Vernon, Missouri, USA.

Harry married (1) Gloria Jean Farmer daughter of Dorothy Farmer in Jul 1967 in Nevada, Vernon, Missouri, USA.

They had the following children:

262 M i. **Alfred Duane Snowden** was born on 20 Jun 1968 in Nevada, Vernon, Missouri.

Harry married (2) Sherlyn Baker "Sherry" on 15 Mar 1985.

125.   **Boyd Langford Chisholm** (Stanford Dalton, George Langford, Glenn Thornton, Richard Henry) was born on 1 Jul 1942 in Litchfield Park, Maricopa, Arizona, USA.

Boyd Langford Chisholm

Boyd Langford Chisholm, oldest son of Stanford and Nadine Chisholm, was born at home in a farmhouse in Litchfield, Arizona on July 1, 1942. He attended various schools in the valley as the family moved where jobs were available. The family spent many hours at the home of his Uncle Dude and Aunt Ethel who lived in the Waddell area.

In 1957 while living in the Williams area, Stanford's health began to fail; he was diagnosed with cancer. He had to quit his job of driving a truck for Safeway. Boyd said there wasn't much to do in Williams, and he was glad to move but not under those circumstances. The family saw their father struggle a long hard time before his death.

Stanford had a very generous and loving cousin, Oleta, and her husband, Leyton Woolf. They offered them a home to live in on their farm, out in the country, on 59th Avenue and Bell Road. Boyd's maternal grandparents, Boyd and Bess Simmons, moved a small trailer next to their home and saw their family through this trying time.

Life changed for Boyd. This was a working farm and he was sixteen years old; he was old enough to work. Oleta's brother was working there and became Boyd's teacher and mentor. He taught him to run the tractor and to plow a straight row, and when he turned around at the end of the field to get close to the ditch but not in it. It wasn't long until he was in the ditch. Dobboy came to his rescue and pulled him and the tractor out of this predicament. Many such mishaps helped to mold him into the person he has become.

His father died July 10, 1958 and left three children for their mother to raise. In 1959 Boyd joined the US Air Force, he trained to be a parachute rigger. While in the service, he married Anita Jean Ewing on August 20, 1960, both were the young age of eighteen. After his discharge from the Air Force, they moved to Bakersfield, California.

In July 1964, he enlisted in the US Navy where he served for sixteen years. He had three combat tours to Viet Nam aboard aircraft carriers. He retired from the US Navy in December of 1979. He was still a young man of 37 years and decided to go to work again, and this time for the Aerospace Industry where he worked for 20 years. He retired in April 2004.

In 1988, a large multi-national sea exercise was held off the shores of southern California. In the mock battles to be fought, Firebees were used to simulate "enemy" aircraft and missiles. Part of the exercise, transporting and firing of the Firebees, was under the management of Boyd Chisholm and his crew.

Since 1985, the team had air-launched 184 Firebees into flight beneath the wings of the transports. Nine times, including the RIMPAC 1988 exercise, Boyd had assembled his team for Firebee operations.

A former Navy drone control operator with NAS, Boyd had grown-accustomed to prolonged, over-water flights in vintage "Hercs".

In Sept 1983 Boyd, as the senior direct control officer in Dept. 1-462 Lockheed-Ontario, had become a member of a very exclusive 1000 hour flying fraternity. As a matter of fact, he was the only member. A certificate was given to him for reaching the 1000 flight-hour level in C-130 drone-launch aircraft as DCO (direct control officer) of the flight crew; he was the person who actually launched the drones. He is the only civilian DCO to achieve this distinction.

In addition to serving as DCO while flying missions for the Navy, Boyd also trained 10 flight crew members to the DCO position. He noted that he had been flying with the same pilot, Dave Ellefson, for nearly 75% of the time for the last 8 ½ years, both in the navy and as a civilian.

Even though he was 'completely' retired, he was called by his fellow workers to go to New Orleans after Katrina to help set up their offices.

Boyd and Anita raised three children and have seven grandchildren. They are living in Valley Center, California at this time in 2007.

Boyd Langford Chisholm
Zenna Chisholm Snowden
January 2007

Boyd married Anita Jean Ewing daughter of Miles Richard Ewing and Mary Imogene Harlan on 20 Aug 1960 in Glendale, Maricopa, Arizona, USA. Anita was born on 2 Feb 1942 in Chicago, Illinois, USA. Anita died March 4, 2013 of a stroke in Escondido, CA at Palomar Hospital. She was a great woman of faith and touched many lives – her celebration of life was attended by 400 people remembering the impact she had on their lives and sharing her love of the Lord. (Dana S. Chisholm)
They had the following children:

+263 F i.   **Dawn "Dondi" Annette Chisholm** was born on 11 Jul 1962.

+ 264F ii.   **Dana Suzanne Chisholm** was born on 18 Jul 1967.

+ 265M iii. **Christopher Boyd "Bo" Chisholm** was born on Oct 1970.

Obituary Anita Jean (Ewing) Chisholm

Chisholm, Anita Jean 02/02/1942 ~ 03/04/2013 ESCONDIDO -- Anita married her high school sweetheart, Boyd Chisholm, and they were married 52 years, moving to Escondido in 1968. She was a dedicated Navy wife, and mother of three. Anita's life revolved around her savior, Jesus, and was involved in her church touching lives; Lincoln Avenue Baptist Church and Emmanuel Faith Community Church. She worked 22 years at Union Bank in Escondido and will be missed by many. Anita is survived by her loving husband, Boyd Chisholm; and three children: Dawn and Rich Bell, Dana S. Chisholm, and Christopher and Laura Chisholm; seven grandchildren: Josh and Brittany, Jake, Chris John and Savannah, Emily, Nathan, Luke and Zachary; and by her two sisters, Diana "Jane" Peaker and Margaret Burnes. You are invited to join the family in celebrating her life on Saturday, March 16, 2013 at 10am at Emmanuel Faith Community Church, 639 E. Felicita Ave., Escondido, CA 92025.

Published in The San Diego Union Tribune on Mar. 10, 2013 (added by Dana S. Chisholm 2018)

126.   **Ronald Lee Chisholm** (Stanford Dalton, George Langford, Glenn Thornton, Richard Henry) was born on 14 Jul 1944 in Phoenix, Maricopa, Arizona. Ronnie died March 7, 2016 in Arizona.

Ronald married Becky Chisholm on 6 Sep 1963 in Phoenix, Maricopa, Arizona, USA.
They had the following children:

266 M i. **Ronald Lee Chisholm Jr** was born on 15 Dec 1964 in Phoenix, Maricopa, Arizona.

   "Little Ronnie" Ronald married Kathy Chisholm on 20 Feb 1995. Kathy was born in Kansas, USA.

+ 267F ii.   **Rene Inez Chisholm** was born on 18 May 1967.

+ 268 M iii.   **Robert Chisholm** was born on 24 Jul 1969.

269 M iv.   **Rick Stanford Chisholm** was born on 20 Sep 1985 in Phoenix, Arizona.

133.   Geneva Arletta Wyatt (Effie Lucille Filleman, Annie Elizabeth Chisholm, Glenn Thornton, Richard Henry) was born on 22 Apr 1910 in Geronimo, Graham, Arizona, USA. She died on 9 May 1978 in Alpine, Apache, Arizona, USA.

Geneva Arletta Wyatt

Geneva was eighteen years old when she married Mid Charles Gatlin. Mid owned a ranch on the Blue River in Greenlee County in eastern Arizona. In the early spring of 1929, right after they were married Mid became very ill. They were at the ranch and Geneva did everything she could to help him, but he kept getting worse. She saddled two horses, and got Mid on one of them. Together they rode all day and into the evening to get to Clifton and a doctor. Mid lived several days, but later died of meningitis; so, Geneva was a 19 year old widow.

A short time after Mid died, she realized she was pregnant with his son. Marvin Clifford Gatlin was born December 28th, 1929. The depression had begun, and Geneva could hardly make ends meet. She had to sell the ranch and got very little for it, but she was able to move to Clifton, and with the support of her extended family she made out ok.

On January 17, 1932, Geneva married Oscar Brice Willis in Lordsburg, New Mexico. Oscar hauled freight and mail to the ranches on Blue River and Eagle Creek. Oscar raised Geneva's son, Clifford, as his own. Clifford later changed his name to Willis.

Brice Willis
August 2007

Geneva married (1) Mid Charles Gatlin about 1928 in Lordsburg, New Mexico. Mid died in 1929. **They had the following children:**

270 M i. **Marvin Clifford Gatlin** was born on 28 Dec 1929.

Geneva married (2) Oscar Brice Willis son of Mather L. Willis and Mrs. Mather Willis on 17 Jan 1932 in Lordsburg, Hidalgo, New Mexico, USA.

They had the following children:

   271 F ii. **Geneva Mae Willis** was born in 1932. She died about 1933. Cause of death

        was Pneumonia.

   272 F iii.**Patricia Anne Willis** was born on 27 Nov 1933 in Greenlee, Arizona, USA.

  +273M iv.**Brice Willis** was born on 15 Mar 1944.

149.   Velma Vivian Smith (Addie Bell Chisholm, Daniel Fore, Glenn Thornton, Richard Henry) was born on 5 Nov 1907 in Picabo, Idaho, USA. She died on 22 Mar 1986 in Yoncalla, Oregon, USA. She was buried in Newport, Oregon, USA.

Velma married (1) Arthur E. Brown on 3 Jul 1928 in Jerome, Idaho.USA.

They had the following children:

   274 M i.   **Farrell Brown** was born on 27 Jun 1929.

   275 F ii.   **Nellie Darlene Brown** was born on 28 Mar 1934.

   276 M iii.   **Eudell Reece Brown** was born on 5 Feb 1936.

Velma married (2) Clarence Bodenstab in Twin Falls, Idaho, USA.

Velma married (3) Jay Traylor in Twin Falls, Idaho, USA.

150.   Lawrence Elias Smith (Addie Bell Chisholm, Daniel Fore, Glenn Thornton, Richard Henry) was born on 20 Nov 1909 in Picabo, Idaho, USA. He died on 26 Feb 1980 in SunValley, Idaho. He was buried on 29 Feb 1980 in Carey, Idaho.

Lawrence married Emily May Wilde daughter of James Henry Wilde and Ida Lucile Clark on 5 Dec 1931. Emily was born on 6 Oct 1907 in Carey, Idaho, USA. She died on 30 Sep 1994 in Lewiston, Idaho, USA. She was buried on 5 Oct 1994 in Carey, Idaho, USA.

They had the following children:

  + 277M i. **Lennis Dean Smith** was born on 28 Mar 1932. He died on 1 Apr 2002.

+ 278 F ii. **Helen Erlene Smith** was born on 8 Aug 1934.

+ 279 F iii. **Sharon June Smith** was born on 5 Jun 1943. She died on 11 Oct 1980.

+ 280 F iv. **Merla Joyce Smith** was born on 23 Apr 1947.

281 F v. **Rayda La Dell Smith** was born on 12 Jan 1949 in Carey, Idaho, USA. She died on 12 Jan 1949 in Carey, Idaho, USA. She was buried in Carey, Idaho, USA.

---

151. **Rachel Alta Smith** (Addie Bell Chisholm, Daniel Fore, Glenn Thornton, Richard Henry) was born on 2 Jan 1913 in Picabo, Idaho, USA. She died in Oct in Lewiston, Idaho, USA. She was buried in Hailey, Idaho, USA.

Rachel married (1) William Chese on 7 Jun 1930 in Jerome, Idaho. USA. The marriage ended in divorce.

They had the following children:

282 F i. **Dollie Joy Chese** was born on 6 Apr 1931.

283 F ii. **Ruth Alta Chese** was born on 31 Mar 1933.

284 F iii. **Donna Bell Chese** was born on 31 Mar 1935.

285 M iv. **Billie Chese Jr** was born on 6 Jun 1938.

Rachel married (2) Robert Eskridge. The marriage ended in divorce.

They had the following children:

286 M v. **Robert Eskridge** "Bob" was born on 23 Dec 1944.

---

153. **Adrian Aaron Smith** (Addie Bell Chisholm, Daniel Fore, Glenn Thornton, Richard Henry) was born on 24 Sep 1919 in Picabo, Idaho, USA. He died on 27 Sep 1997 in Twin Falls, , Idaho, USA. He was buried in Twin Falls, Idaho, USA.

Adrian married Lavone Beth Doggett on 18 Nov 1945 in Cassia, Idaho. Lavone was born on 1 Jan 1927 in Heyburn, Idaho.

They had the following children:

+ 287 M i. **Adrian Randall Smith** was born on 8 Oct 1946.

+288 F ii. **Bonnie Luann Smith** was born on 10 May 1954.

<hr>

155.   **Darrel Dalton Smith** (Addie Bell Chisholm, Daniel Fore, Glenn Thornton, Richard Henry) was born on 21 Jul 1927 in Carey, Idaho, USA.

Darrel married Nancy Broner. Nancy was born in Twin Falls, Twin Falls, Idaho, USA. She died in Twin Falls, Twin Falls, Idaho, USA. She was buried in Twin Falls Cemetery, Idaho, USA.

They had the following children:

289 F i. **Gloria Jean Smith.**

290 F ii. **Joyce Marie Smith.**

<hr>

156.   **Melissa Ellen Smith** (Addie Bell Chisholm, Daniel Fore, Glenn Thornton, Richard Henry) was born on 21 Mar 1931 in Picabo, Idaho, USA.

Melissa married John West Jr on 16 Nov in Elko, Nevada, USA. John was born on 26 Jun 1930 in Hazelton, Idaho, USA.

They had the following children:

+291 F i. **Linda R West** was born on 23 Jun 1951.

292 F ii. **Connie F West** was born on 4 Sep 1952 in Twin Falls, Twin Falls, Idaho. She died on 12 May 1973 in Lewiston, Idaho. She was buried in Normal Hill Cemetery, Lewiston , Idaho, USA.

293 F iii. **Vickie K West** was born on 16 Aug 1953 in Lewiston, Idaho, USA.

+294 M iv. **John Larry West** was born on 2 Apr 1956.

+ 295 M v. **Thomas Orin West** was born on 28 Oct 1957.

CHAPTER SIX

SIXTH Generation

God Bless my Sister, she helped me through some trying health times before she moved away.
By the way I am the one who likes pinto bean juice on cake.
Zenna Chisholm Snowden

160.   **Joyce M Evans** (Oscar Tedford Evans, Jennie Chisholm, George Langford, Glenn Thornton, Richard Henry) was born on 9 Sep 1924 in Blythe, Riverside, California, USA. She died on 24 Mar 2002 in Corona, California, USA.

Joyce married Jack Pershing Farnham son of Jack McCarty Farnham and Stella Webb on 17 Nov 1939 in Phoenix, Maricopa, Arizona, USA. Jack was born on 2 Apr 1922 in Bethal, New Mexio, USA.

They had the following children:

+ 296 M i.   **Jerry Lee Farnham** was born on 25 Nov 1940. He died on 2 Nov 1995.

+ 297 M ii.   **Earl Wayne Farnham** was born on 3 Jan 1943.

+ 298 M iii.   **Jack p Farnham Jr** was born on 23 Jan 1946.

+ 299 M iv.   **Timothy Farnham** was born on 1 Mar 1947.

161.   **Tedford Loren Evans** (Oscar Tedford Evans, Jennie Chisholm, George Langford, Glenn Thornton, Richard Henry) was born on 21 Aug 1926. He died on 21 Mar 1999.

Tedford was in the Military at Fort Mac Arthur, San Pedro California.

Tedford married (1) Mary Jane Bridenbaker .

They had the following children:

    300 M i. **Larry Evans** was born in 1949.

Tedford married (2) Beverly Evans

162.   **Thomas Leland Evans** (Oscar Tedford Evans, Jennie Chisholm, George Langford, Glenn Thornton, Richard Henry) was born on 30 Oct 1928. He died on 23 Jan 2004 in Corona, , California, USA.

Thomas married Roberta Muriel Lane daughter of Henry Edward Lane and Roberta Ely. Roberta was born on 11 Nov 1933.

They had the following children:

    + 301 F i. **Laural Ann Evans** was born on 18 Dec 1953.

    + 302 M ii. **Thomas Evans** was born on 29 Mar 1955.

    + 303 F iii. **Kemberly Evans** was born on 7 Apr 1959.

170.   **Blanche Lucille Traylor** (Bessie Loraine Chisholm, Martin Gaines, George Langford, Glenn Thornton, Richard Henry) was born on 12 Aug 1934 in Chowchilla, Fresno, California, USA. She died on 8 Dec 2003 in Mercy Hospital, Roseburg, Oregon, USA. She was buried in Cremated.

Blanche married Clarence J Hedgecock on 23 Nov 1951 in Roseburg, Oregon, USA.

They had the following children:

    + 304 F i. **Betty Lorene Hedgecock** was born on 18 Jun 1953.

    + 305 F ii. **Kathy Lynn Hedgecock** was born on 7 Apr 1958.

    + 306 F iii. **Ladina Hedgecock** was born on 3 Aug 1963.

171.　**Virginia May Traylor**　(Bessie Loraine Chisholm, Martin Gaines, George Langford, Glenn Thornton, Richard Henry) was born on 22 Sep 1935 in Madera, Medera, California, USA. She died on 21 Sep 1993 in Newport Hospital, Newport, , Oregon, USA. She was buried in Cremated.

Virginia married Thomas C Dodson on 28 Jan 1955 in Sutherland,,Oregon,USA.

They had the following children:

　　307　F　i.　**Linda Dodson** .

　　308　F　ii.　**Tressa Dodson** .

　　309　F　iii.**Gloria Dodson** was born in Mar 1960.

　　　　　　　Gloria married **Unknown**　Never Married.

　　310　M　iv.　**Joe Dodson** .

　　311　M　v.**Sam Dodson** .

　　　　　　　Sam married **Unknown** Never Married.

172.　**Joy Loraine Traylor**　(Bessie Loraine Chisholm, Martin Gaines, George Langford, Glenn Thornton, Richard Henry) was born on 18 May 1937 in Safford, Graham, Arizona, USA. She died on 22 Dec 1999 in Oakland, Oregon, USA. She was buried in Cremated.

Joy married Jerry Williams　son of John Williams and Mildred Williams on 18 May 1957.

They had the following children:

　　312　F　i.　**Inez Williams** was born on 14 Apr 1958 in Washington, USA.

　　313　M　ii.**Doug Williams** was born in 1961 in Kellogg, Idaho, USA.

　　　　　　　Doug married **Carolyn Cross**

173.　**Johnnie Louise Traylor** (Bessie Loraine Chisholm, Martin Gaines, George Langford, Glenn Thornton, Richard Henry) was born on 1 May 1939 in Solomonville, Arizona, USA.

Johnnie married Delbert Glendon Upton on 11 Jun 1955 in Oakland, Oregon, USA. Delbert was born on 10 Jan 1934 in Atoka, , Oklahoma, USA. He died on 19 Oct 2002 in Mercy Hospital, Roseburg, Oregon, USA. He was buried in Cremated.

They had the following children:

+ 314F i. **Debra Upton** was born on 16 Apr 1957.

+ 315F ii. **Karen Upton** was born on 22 Jan 1959.

+ 316M iii. **John Upton** was born on 4 Aug 1960.

<hr>

182. **Charlie Gene Balch** (Frances Charlene Chisholm, Richard Akley, George Langford, Glenn Thornton, Richard Henry) was born on 6 Jan 1948 in Elgin, Bastrop, Texas, USA.

Charlie and Charlotte are twins.

Born at Fleming Hospital.

Charlie married Kathy Laffere on 10 Aug 1968 in Rockdale, , Texas, USA.

They had the following children:

317 M i. **Eric Balch** .

318 F ii. **Wendy Balch** .

<hr>

183. **Charlotte Jean Balch** (Frances Charlene Chisholm, Richard Akley, George Langford, Glenn Thornton, Richard Henry) was born on 6 Jan 1948 in Elgin, Bastrop, Texas, USA.

Born at Fleming Hospital In Elgin, Texas.

Charlotte married Michael Verne Rogers on 17 Feb 1968 in Stockdale, , Texas, USA.

They had the following children:

319 M i. **Eugene Griffin Rogers**

320 F ii. **Leslie Lynn Rogers**

184. **Terry Joe Balch** (Frances Charlene Chisholm, Richard Akley, George Langford, Glenn Thornton, Richard Henry) was born on 22 Mar 1949 in Bastrop, Texas, USA.

Terry married Candy June Ford on 4 May 1968 in Harris, Texas, USA.

They had the following children:

321 F i. **Shanna Balch**

322 M ii . **Jason Balch**

323 M iii. **Jim Bob Balch**

324 F iv. **Jo Hanna Balch**

325 F v. **Rebeca Balch**

188. **Leyton Stuart Woolf Jr** (Oleta Chisholm, Top, George Langford, Glenn Thornton, Richard Henry) was born on 3 Apr 1949 in Madera Sanitarium, Madera, Madera, California. He was christened in Presbyterian Church, Chowchilla, California.

Leyton married (1) Maria Gonzales . Maria was born in Mexico.

They had the following children:

326 M i. **Leyton Stuart Woolf lll** was born on 19 Jan 1977 in Maryvale Hospital, Maricopa, Arizona, USA. He was christened in Church of Litchfield Park, Litchfield Park, Maricopa, Arizona.

327 F ii. **Stephanie Lynn Woolf** was born on 24 Dec 1984 in Thunderbird Hospital, Phoenix, Maricopa, Arizona.

328 Miii.**Matthew Doboy Woolf** was born on 28 Jun 1989 in Thunderbird Hospital, Phoenix, Maricopa, Arizona, USA.

Leyton married (2) Kathy Heivelin .

They had the following children:

329 Fiv. **Melissa Ann Woolf** was born on 7 Oct 1970 in Tucson, Pima, Arizona, USA.

191.   **Janice Ruth Chisholm** (William, Top, George Langford, Glenn Thornton, Richard Henry) was born on 30 Aug 1950 in Madera, Madera, California, USA.

Janice married (1) Danny Ernest Parolini son of Ernest Parolini and Lillian Lundquist on 12 Mar 1976 in Coalinga, California. Danny was born on 10 Feb 1947 in Hanford, California.

They had the following children:

330 Fi.   **Jennifer Fay Parolini** was born on 27 Jan 1981 in Fresno, Fresno, California, USA.

Janice married (2) Gary Lee Hawk son of Paul Hawk and Wanda Hawk on 26 Jun 1970 in Huron, California. The marriage ended in divorce. Gary was born on 17 Apr 1947. He died on 4 Apr 1976. He was buried in Madera, California, USA.

They had the following children:

+ 331 F ii. **Amanda Lee Hawk** was born on 10 Aug 1971.

192.   **Jeanne Fay Chisholm** (William, Top, George Langford, Glenn Thornton, Richard Henry) was born on 29 Sep 1951 in Coalinga, California, USA.

Jeanne married Edward Louis Paroline son of Emilo Paroline and Christina Ramos on 1 Jun 1973 in Coalinga, California, USA. Edward was born on 30 Mar 1950 in Hanford, California, USA.

They had the following children:

+ 332 F i. **Erica Marie Paroline** was born on 19 Apr 1977.

333 M ii. **Michael Edward Paroline** was born on 18 Sep 1979 in Fresno, Fresno, California. Michael married **Kelsey Ann Deering** daughter of Robert Deering and Sue Starbuck on 9 Nov 2003 in San Luis Obispo, California. Kelsey was born on 27 Nov 1979.

193. William Edward Chisholm (William, Top, George Langford, Glenn Thornton, Richard Henry) was born on 3 Dec 1952 in Coalinga, California, USA. He died on 21 Dec 2005 in Visalia, California, USA. He was buried in Coalinga, California, USA.

William married (1) Teresa Luann Trent daughter of A J Trent and Twila Trent on 30 Aug 1972 in Coalinga, California, USA. The marriage ended in divorce. Teresa was born on 10 Dec 1954.

They had the following children:

   + 334M i. **William Robert Chisholm** was born on 24 Jan 1973.

   335 M ii. **Andrew Edward Chisholm** was born on 6 Jan 1979 in Santa Maria, Santa Maria, California. Andrew married **Unknown** on 24 Apr 1993 in Reno, Wasade, Nevada.

William married (2) Sandra Lynn Gobel on 24 Apr 1993 in Rena, Nevada. Sandra was born on 24 Apr 1951 in Reno, Nevada, USA.

200. Lorelei Francine Chisholm (Lloyd Frances, Top, George Langford, Glenn Thornton, Richard Henry) was born on 5 Dec 1956 in , , California, USA.

Lorelei married Gary Curtis Preciado . Gary was born in Madera, Medera, California, USA.

They had the following children:

   336 M i.   **Ryan Preciado** was born on 15 Aug 1978 in Madera, Madera, California, USA.

   + 337 F ii.   **Lindsey Victoria Preciado** was born on 2 Jun 1980.

   338 M iii.   **Colton Preciado** was born on 16 Sep 1983 in Fresno, Fresno, California, USA.

201. Lance Lloyd Francis Chisholm (Lloyd Frances, Top, George Langford, Glenn Thornton, Richard Henry) was born on 3 Jul 1960 in Chowchilla, California.

Lance married Janet Sue Womack on 26 Jan 1979 in Madera, California, USA. Janet was born on

15 Apr 1960 in Glendale, California, USA.

They had the following children:

+ 339 F i. **Taryn Kathrine Chisholm** was born on 7 Aug 1979.

+ 340 F ii. **Stacy Les-Lea Chisholm** was born on 20 Aug 1981.

---

202.   **Mary Ellen Chisholm** (Toppy Monroe, Top, George Langford, Glenn Thornton, Richard Henry) was born on 22 Dec 1956 in San Bernardino, San Bernardino, California, USA.

Mary married Johnny Tourino on 2 Feb 1980 in San Bernadina, San Bernadina, California, USA.

They had the following children:

341 M i. **Christopher Tourino** was born on 5 Aug 1985 in San Bernardino, CA.

342 M ii. **Daniel Tourino** was born on 2 Jan 1988.

---

203.   **Richard Chisholm** (Toppy Monroe, Top, George Langford, Glenn Thornton, Richard Henry) was born on 19 Mar 1957 in San Bernardino, San Bernardino, California, USA.

Richard married Viola Blau on 6 Apr 1991 in Highland, San Bernardino, California, USA.

They had the following children:

343 M i. **Nathan Chisholm** was born on 30 Jul 1994 in San Bernardino, California.

344 M ii. **Alex Jason Chisholm** was born on 15 Oct 1996 in San Bernardino, California. Died 29 December 2013 in Palm Springs, California in a motorcycle accident.

Obituary Alex Jason Chisholm

Alex Jason Chisholm was born in Newport Beach, CA and was called to his Heavenly Father December 29, 2013 in Palm Springs, CA at the age of 17.

Alex was an energetic child, who had many passions, including high school wrestling, motorcycle

riding, hunting and weight training.

Alex attended Our Lady Queen of Angels Catholic School for 8 years and was a junior at Corona Del Mar High School at the time of his passing.

He is survived by his devoted mother, Viola, adoring father, Richard and older brother and best friend, Nathan.

Funeral mass will be held at Our Lady Queen of Angels Catholic Church, 2046 Mar Vista Drive, Newport Beach on Saturday, January 4 at 11:00AM. Reception immediately following in parish hall.

In lieu of flowers, donations may be made in Alex's memory to Cradle to Career Kenya (C2Ckenya.org). (add by Dana S. Chisholm 2018)

205.   **Susan Chisholm** (Toppy Monroe, Top, George Langford, Glenn Thornton, Richard Henry) was born on 12 Jan 1965 in San Bernardino, San Bernardino, California, USA.

Susan married David Dillon on 19 Apr 1985 in San Bernardino, San Bernardino, California, USA.

David and Susan had the following children:

345 M i. **Nicholas Dillon** was born on 28 Apr 1993 in San Bernardino, California, USA.

346 F ii. **Ann Marie Dillon** was born on 14 Mar 1997 in San Bernardino, California, USA.

206. **Thomas Gail Mansfield** (Ruth Ester Chisholm, Thomas John, George Langford, Glenn Thornton, Richard Henry) was born on 1 Nov 1936 in Glendale, Maricopa, Arizona, USA.

Thomas married Lois Mansfield on 31 Dec 1958 in „North Carolina, USA.

They had the following children:

347 F i. **Linda Mansfield.** Linda married **Sid Leibovitch** .

348 F ii. **Lisa Dawn Mansfield.** Lisa married **Robert Eugene Waldo Dr.** on 13 Oct 1993 in Las Posas Country Club, Camarillo, California, USA.

207.   Maudie Marie Mansfield "Sis" (Ruth Ester Chisholm, Thomas John, George Langford, Glenn Thornton, Richard Henry) was born on 7 Mar 1938 in Glendale, Maricopa, Arizona. She died on 24 Aug 2005 in Sierra Vista, Arizona.

Maudie married (1) Newel Spence Shumway Jr about 1956. Newel was born on 5 Dec 1934.

They had the following children:

> + 349 F i. **Sheryl Lynn Shumway** was born on 18 Aug 1957.

> + 350 F ii. **Terry Sue Shumway** was born on 18 Aug 1959.

Maudie married (2) Richard Bouilly.

208.   Janice Cliffine Horton "Cliff" (Juanita Chisholm, Thomas John, George Langford, Glenn Thornton, Richard Henry) was born on 3 Jun 1938 in Glendale, Maricopa, Arizona, USA.

Janice married (1) Robert Mendenhall on 7 Feb 1958.

They had the following children:

> + 351 M i. **Robert Wayne Mendenhall** was born on 17 Apr 1959.

Janice married (2) Edward Kernan.

211. **Velma Jean Grigsby** "Jeannie" (Tommie Chisholm, Thomas John, George Langford, Glenn Thornton, Richard Henry) was born on 16 Jul 1954 in Phoenix, Maricopa, Arizona, USA.

Velma married (1) Rick Brooks about 1973.

They had the following children:

> + 352 F i. **Cheyanne Brooks** was born on 22 Feb 1974.

> + 353 F ii. **Autumn Rene Brooks** was born on 12 Feb 1977.

Velma married (2) Jim Ledy.

212. **Charles Darren McCabe** (Tommie Chisholm, Thomas John, George Langford, Glenn Thornton, Richard Henry) was born on 19 Nov 1959 in Phoenix, Maricopa, Arizona.

Charles married **Karol West** daughter of Donald Dade West and Luella Coleman on 19 Nov 1980. Karol was born on 30 Apr 1962 in Tucson, Pima, Arizona, USA.

They had the following children:

   354Mi **Charles Kristopher McCabe** was born on 17 Aug 1984 in Phoenix, Arizona.

216. **Sharon Chisholm** (Ross Martin, Calvin Alonzo, George Langford, Glenn Thornton, Richard Henry) was born on 4 Jan 1954 in Dos Palos, California, USA.

Sharon married **David Wakefield** son of Alvin Earl Wakefield and Elva Edith Jesse on 22 Apr 1977 in South LakeTahoe, Nevada, USA. David was born on 31 Jan 1939 in Gustav Jesse Home, Grandfather Wray, Colorado, USA.

They had the following children:

   +355 M i. **Justin Chisholm Wakefield** was born on 7 Apr 1978.

   356 F ii. **Leanne Marie Wakefield** was born on 12 Apr 1980.

217. **Phillip Alonzo Chambers** (Fannie Maude Chisholm, Calvin Alonzo, George Langford, Glenn Thornton, Richard Henry) was born on 16 Jun 1942 in Dos Palos, California, USA.

Phillip married (1) **Cynthia Coxsey** daughter of Patrick Pusly Coxsey and Stella Marion Hall on 18 Jun 1966. Cynthia was born on 26 Dec 1946 in Fort Sill, Oklahoma, USA.
They had the following children:

   357 M i. **Matthew Phillip Chambers** was born on 25 Dec 1974 in Lompoc, , California, USA. Matthew married **Stella Marian Hall**.

Phillip married (2) **Mei Chu**.

218.   **Phyllis Marie Chambers** (Fannie Maude Chisholm, Calvin Alonzo, George Langford, Glenn Thornton, Richard Henry) was born on 18 Jul 1942 in Dos Palos, California, USA.

Phyllis married (1) Wendell Kirkpatrick on 24 Apr 1973 in Reno,Wasade,Nevada,USA.

They had the following children:

  +358 M i. **Brad Kirkpatrick**.

  359 M ii.**Kelly Alan Kirkpatrick** was born on 3 Jul 1973.

  360 M iii. **Ryan Neal Kirkpatrick** was born on 9 Dec 1994.

Phyllis married (2) John Lawless on 11 Sep 1964.

219.   **Clarence Lester Chambers** (Fannie Maude Chisholm, Calvin Alonzo, George Langford, Glenn Thornton, Richard Henry) was born on 25 Aug 1946 in Dos Palos, Merced, California, USA.

Clarence married (1) Geradine Mae Glidden daughter of Le Roy Maurice Glidden and Eva Dorothy Fallis on 22 May 1971 in Virginia City, Nevada, USA. Geradine was born on 19 Oct 1944 in Los Banos, Merced, California, USA.

They had the following children:

  +361 F i. **Leslie Elizabeth Chambers** was born on 18 Nov 1971.

  +362 F ii. **Amy Ann Chambers**.

Clarence married (2) Denice Arline Bronson on 30 Aug 1983 in Dawson City, , Yukon Territory. Denice was born on 10 Feb 1959 in Dos Palos, California, USA.

They had the following children:

  363M iii.**Chancey Levy Chambers** was born on 12 Jan 1984 in Los Banos, Merced, California.

220.   **Trudy Ann Chambers** (Fannie Maude Chisholm, Calvin Alonzo, George Langford, Glenn Thornton, Richard Henry) was born on 22 Nov 1949 in Dos Palos, California, USA.

Trudy married (1) James Darrel Bronson in Dos Palos, California, USA. James was born on 17 Oct 1944 in Bakersfield, California, USA.

They had the following children:

    +364 F i.   **Shannon Lorene Bronson** was born on 7 Mar 1968.

    +365 M ii. **Duane Edward Bronson** was born on 6 Oct 1969.

    +366 Miii. **Bryan Darrel Bronson** was born on 16 Mar 1977.

     367 Miv.   **Shawn Bronson** was born on 21 May 1979 in Los Banos, Merced, California, USA.

Trudy married (2) Jim Hodson on 22 Aug 1966.

221.   **Rita Marlene Chisholm** (Daniel Webster, Calvin Alonzo, George Langford, Glenn Thornton, Richard Henry) was born on 12 Apr 1949 in Dos Palos, California.
    Family Group Records sent to be by Bernice Chisholm in 2006.

Rita married Keith Scrivner son of P M Scrivner and Mary Barns on 28 Dec 1968 in Coalinga, California, USA. Keith was born on 15 Sep 1949. He died on 5 May 1998 in California, USA. He was buried on 8 May 1998 in Pleasant Valley Cemetery, Coalinga, California, USA.

    Family Group Records sent to be by Bernice Chisholm in 2006.

Keith and Rita had the following children:

     368 F i.   **Robin Scrivner** was born on 9 Jan 1971 in Hardford, California, USA.

    +369 F ii. **Rhonda Scrivner** was born on 10 Jun 1973.

    +370 F iii. **Rhoda Scrivner** was born on 23 Dec 1974.

    +371 F iv. **Reggan Scrivner** was born on 7 Apr 1978.

222.   Sandra Eva Chisholm (Daniel Webster, Calvin Alonzo, George Langford, Glenn Thornton, Richard Henry) was born on 18 Mar 1957 in Dos Palos, California, USA. She died on 21 Mar 2003 in San Francisco, California, USA. She was buried on 26 Mar 2003 in Pleasant Valley Cemetery, Coalinga, California, USA.

Family Group Records sent to be by Bernice Chisholm in 2006.

Sandra married Ted W Den Hartog son of John Den Hartog and Verna Kreyenhagen on 13 May 1974 in Fort Lewis, Washington, USA. Ted was born on 25 Nov 1953.

Ted and Sandra had the following children:

372 M i. **John Daniel Den Hartog** was born on 27 Sep 1974 in Hanford, California, USA. He died on 12 Nov 1982 in California, USA. He was buried on 15 Nov 1982 in Pleasant Valley Cemetery, Coalinga, California, USA.

373 M ii.**Joshua Den Hartog** was born on 8 Feb 1977 in Hanford, California, USA. He died on 2 Nov 1983 in California, USA. He was buried on 5 Nov 1983 in Pleasant Valley Cemetery, Coalinga, California, USA.

+374 F iii.**Christen Den Hartog** was born on 10 Oct 1978.

223.   Karen Marie Chisholm (Daniel Webster, Calvin Alonzo, George Langford, Glenn Thornton, Richard Henry) was born on 7 Dec 1960 in Fresno, California.

Family Group Records sent to be by Bernice Chisholm in 2006.

Karen married Craig Young son of Edward Young and Wanda Hamner on 17 Jul 1982 in Coalinga, California, USA. Craig was born on 28 Dec 1953 in California, USA.

Craig and Karen had the following children:

375 M i. **Derrick William Young** was born on 5 Sep 1986 in Fresno, California, USA.

376 M ii.**Dustin Allen Young** was born on 15 Jun 1993 in Fresno, California, USA.

Family Group Records sent to be by Bernice Chisholm in 2006.

225.   **Linda Sue Chisholm** (Chester Lee, Calvin Alonzo, George Langford, Glenn Thornton, Richard Henry) was born on 12 Apr 1949 in Dos Palos, California, USA.

Linda married Robert G Endera on 3 May 1969.

They had the following children:

377 M i. **Robert Gongals Endera III** was born on 30 Oct 1969 in Fresno, California, USA.

378 M ii. **Skye Endera** was born in 1983.

226.   **Dena Mae Frye** "Tootie" (Dorothy Flora Chisholm, Jesse, George Langford, Glenn Thornton, Richard Henry) was born on 16 Feb 1936 in Merced, Merced, California, USA.

Dena was adopted by George Cline, her step father, when she was 12 years old.

Dena married Robert Pollard on 12 Oct 1955. Robert was born on 10 Jul 1935 in Fresno, Fresno, California, USA.

They had the following children:

+379 F i. **Ellen Pollard** was born on 20 Oct 1956.

+380 F ii. **Sue Carol Pollard** was born on 22 Sep 1958.

227.   **David Cline** (Dorothy Flora Chisholm, Jesse, George Langford, Glenn Thornton, Richard Henry) was born on 15 May 1946 in Selma, Fresno, California.

David married Kathy Jaco on 24 Mar 1967.

They had the following children:

381 M i. **Brian Cline** was born on 16 Jan 1969 in California, USA.

382 M ii. **Vince Cline** was born on 4 May 1973 in California, USA.

383 F iii.**Kristi Cline** "Kris" was born on 29 May 1975 in California, USA. She died in 1978 in California, USA.

228.   Donna Cline (Dorothy Flora Chisholm, Jesse, George Langford, Glenn Thornton, Richard Henry) was born on 31 Jul 1948 in Selma, Fresno, California.

Donna married Lloyd Sullivan on 29 Jan 1966. Lloyd was born on 20 Jan 1949.

They had the following children:

384 F i. **Gaylene Sullivan** was born on 4 Jul 1972.

Gaylene married **Ryan Sullivan s**on of Lloyd Sullivan and Donna Cline. Ryan was born on 19 Feb 1974.

385 M ii.**Ryan Sullivan** was born on 19 Feb 1974. Ryan married **Gaylene Sullivan** daughter of Lloyd Sullivan and Donna Cline. Gaylene was born on 4 Jul 1972.

229.   Roger Eugene Bachar (Gladys Dena Chisholm, Jesse, George Langford, Glenn Thornton, Richard Henry) was born on 14 Feb 1942 in Los Angeles, Los Angeles, California, USA.

Roger married Lettie Stone daughter of Claude Winston Stone and Margaret Hales on 16 Jul 1965 in Fresno, Fresno, California, USA. Lettie was born on 27 Dec 1942 in Perryville, Arkansas.

They had the following children:

+ 386M i. **James Winston Bachar** was born on 23 Dec 1970.

230. **Patricia Ruth Chisholm** (Jesse Robert, Jesse, George Langford, Glenn Thornton, Richard Henry) was born on 5 Feb 1942 in Selma, Fresno, California.

Patricia married Raymond Wilson.

They had the following children:

    387 F i. **Tracy Louise Wilson** was born on 26 Aug 1961.

    388 M ii.**Raymond Wilson Jr** was born on 28 Aug.

    389 F iii.**Barbara Wilson** was born on 16 Oct 1970.

---

231. **Verna Jean Chisholm** (Jesse Robert, Jesse, George Langford, Glenn Thornton, Richard Henry) was born on 29 Aug 1943 in Selma, Fresno, California.

Verna married Alton Powell on 29 Dec 1961. Alton was born on 19 May 1942 in Paula Valley, Oklahoma, USA.

They had the following children:

    390 M i. **Michael Powell** was born on 10 Oct 1963 in Fresno, Fresno, California, USA.

    391 M ii.**Scott Powell** was born on 21 May 1966 in Fresno, Fresno, California, USA.

---

233. **Larry Craig Griffith** (Milton Clark Griffith, Virgie Eliza Chisholm, George Langford, Glenn Thornton, Richard Henry) was born on 20 Mar 1946 in Santa Rosa, California, USA. He died on 24 Feb 1988 in Ceres, California, USA. He was buried in Ceres, California, USA.

Larry married Shelly Burdick daughter of Wendall Burdick and Gladys Burdick in Ceres, , California, USA. Shelly was born in Wisconsin, USA.

They had the following children:

    +392 M i. **Jonathan Craig Griffith** was born on 26 Jan 1973.

    +393 M ii.**Samuel Roberts Griffith III** was born on 11 May 1978.

234.   **David Clark Griffith** (Milton Clark Griffith, Virgie Eliza Chisholm, George Langford, Glenn Thornton, Richard Henry) was born on 1 Sep 1950 in Eureka, Humboldt, California, USA.

David married Denice Kaye Achterberg daughter of Frank Royce Achterberg and Mable Catherine Foster on 3 Jul 1971 in Reno, Nevada, USA. Denice was born on 18 Sep 1951 in Modesto, Stanislaus, California, USA.

This Griffith family information was sent to me by Crystal Monteith Griffith. I received it 21 Aug 2006. They were sent on Family Group Records Papers that I sent to her.

David and Denice had the following children:

+394 F i.   **Aimee Lynne Griffith** was born on 23 Feb 1972.

+395 M ii. **Joshua David Griffith** was born on 20 Jan 1979.

242.   **Plunkett Allen Weaver** (Jeannie May Chisholm, Albert Vivian, George Langford, Glenn Thornton, Richard Henry) was born on 3 Oct 1950.

Plunkett married Ms P A Weaver.

They had the following children:

396 M i.   **Christopher Teala Weaver** was born on 14 Apr 1978.

245.   **Steven Ray Chisholm** (Randall Ray, Albert Vivian, George Langford, Glenn Thornton, Richard Henry) was born on 6 Jul 1963 in Eureka, Humboldt, California.

Steven married Alanna Moses daughter of Wayne Moses and Eva Solgodo on 27 Aug 1986 in Carson City, Nevada, USA. Alanna was born on 6 Jun 1964 in Richmond, California, USA.

They had the following children:

    397 F i. **Jennifer Michelle Chisholm** was born on 28 Oct 1987 in Modesto, Stanislaus, CA.

    398 M ii. **Shaun Chisholm** was born on 1 Jul 1992 in Eureka, California, USA.

---

249.   **Kathy Clark** (Donald Clark, Totsie Lee Chisholm, George Langford, Glenn Thornton, Richard Henry) was born on 18 Aug 1948.

Kathy married Ron Bataya.

They had the following children:

    399 M i. **Rath Bataya**

    400 F ii. **Ronnie Bataya**

---

256.   **Rhonda Lea Milam** (Snowda Darlene Snowden, Mae Chisholm, George Langford, Glenn Thornton, Richard Henry) was born on 7 May 1959 in Nevada, Vernon, Missouri, USA.

Ronda was adopted by Burton Milam.

Rhonda married unmarried.

They had the following children:

    401 M i. **Daniel Steven Milam** was born on 3 Oct 1977 in New Orleans, Louisiana.

        Daniel was born in the Louisiana Baptist hospital.

    402 M ii.**Joshua Lynne Milam** was born on 15 May 1980 in New Orleans, Louisiana, USA.

        He died in Jan 1981 in Gretna, Louisiana, USA. He was buried in Gretna Baby Land Restlawn, Louisiana, USA.

    403 M iii. **Dustin James Milam** was born on 14 Feb 1985 in Gretna, Louisiana, USA.

        Dustin was born at the Meadow Crest Hospital in Gretna, Louisiana

258.   **Rita Mae Milam** (Snowda Darlene Snowden, Mae Chisholm, George Langford, Glenn Thornton, Richard Henry) was born on 14 Oct 1968 in Monroe, Jefferson, Louisiana, USA.

Rita married (1) Bryan Heath Brown on 16 Jan 1987 in Fairlie Baptist Church Fairlie, Texas, USA. The marriage ended in divorce.

They had the following children:

   404 M i. **Brandon Heath Brown** was born on 6 Aug 1987 in Sulpher Springs, Texas, USA.

   405 M ii. **Burton Thomas Brown** was born on 18 Oct 1989 in Sulpher Springs, Texas, USA.

Rita married (2) Robert Kodle on 16 Mar 2001.

259.   **Gloria Mae Snowden** (Alfred Dalton Snowden, Mae Chisholm, George Langford, Glenn Thornton, Richard Henry) was born in Feb 1960 in Nevada, Vernon, Missouri, USA.

Gloria married David Duane Cullison son of Geraldine McWilliams on 28 Jun 1984 in Missouri.

They had the following children:

   406 M i. **Zachary Cade Cullison** was born on 6 Apr 1998 in Nevada, Vernon, Missouri, USA.

   407 F ii. **Alexa Janae Cullison** was born on 28 Aug 2000 in Nevada, Vernon, Missouri, USA

260.   **Carrie Snowden** (Alfred Dalton Snowden, Mae Chisholm, George Langford, Glenn Thornton, Richard Henry) was born in Jul 1967 in Greenville, Mississippi.

Carrie married Todd Williams in 1995 in Springfield, Missouri, USA.

Todd and Carrie had the following children:

   408 M i. **Wesley Alexander Williams** was born on 8 Nov 2003 in Rolla, Phelps, Missouri.

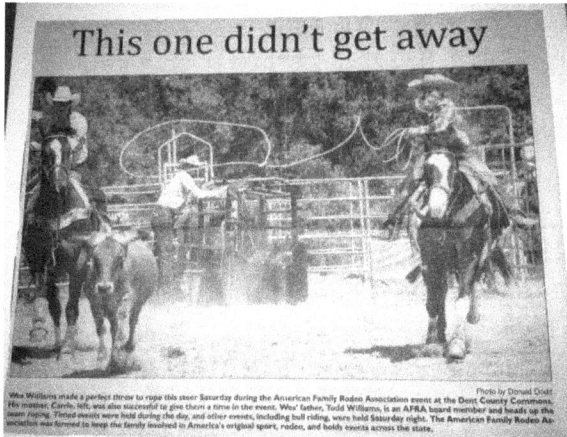

This one didn't get away

RIGHT: Wesley Williams roping in Chisholm tradition

Carrie Snowden Williams & son, Wesley keeping the traditions alive!

261.   **Emily Snowden** (Alfred Dalton Snowden, Mae Chisholm, George Langford, Glenn Thornton, Richard Henry) was born in Jun 1974 in Rolla, Phelps, Missouri, USA.

Emily married Brad Turner in 1998 in Salem, Missouri, USA.

They had the following children:

409 M i. **Cade Dalton Turner** was born in Jun 2003 in Rolla, Phelps, Missouri, USA.

263.   **Dawn Annetta Chisholm** (Boyd Langford, Stanford Dalton, George Langford, Glenn Thornton, Richard Henry) was born on 11 Jul 1962 in Glendale, Maricopa, Arizona, USA.

Dawn married Richard James Bell son of James Bell and Sharlene Pagel on 18 Jun 1983 in Escondido, , California, USA. Richard was born on 27 Dec 1960.

They had the following children:

410 M i. **Joshua Richard Bell** was born on 23 Mar 1987 in ST Paul, Minneapolis, Minnesota.

Married 2 kids

411 M ii.**Jacob Andrew Bell** was born on 3 Nov 1990 in Escondido, San Diego, California.

Married

412 F iii.**Emily Kathryn Bell** was born on 30 Dec 1992 in Escondido, San Diego, California.

Married

264.   Dana Suzanne Chisholm   (Boyd Langford, Stanford Dalton, George Langford, Glenn Thornton, Richard Henry) was born on 18 Jul 1967 in Lemoore, California, USA.

Dana S. Chisholm – Good News, Etc. San Diego newspaper story 2006

Ms. Dana Serrano Chisholm was named 2006 Woman of the Year by California Assemblyman Ray Haynes, 66th District. The ceremony was conducted on March 20, 2006 in Sacramento with a presentation by California First Lady Maria Shriver. This was the 20th Anniversary of the Woman of the Year presentations for California.

Dana was recognized for outstanding service and dedication to the people of the State of California. This past year her projects have included work with offering alternatives to abortion for women in unplanned pregnancy, promoting abstinence in California and the nation, providing resources for single moms, working to change the legislative process for specialty plates so that "Choose Life" plates are available in California to raise millions of dollars for crisis pregnancy centers throughout the state, and working with Assemblyman Ray Haynes and the Governor's office so California will accept its $14 million in federal funding for abstinence education for the first time.

Dana also coordinated efforts in San Diego to take relief supplies and funding to the pregnancy centers in Louisiana and Mississippi after Hurricanes Katrina and Rita and worked on site for a week. She herself a single mother of two boys, is the author of, "Single Moms Raising Sons" published by Beacon Hill Press.

Dana is the Founder of a non-profit organization that coordinates the efforts of organizations across the state and nation addressing women's issues that relate to abortion and adoption bringing together diverse groups, crossing political lines, and overcoming barriers that would otherwise keep free services from under-served women.

Dana has won numerous awards for her fulltime work and for her volunteer efforts on behalf of women and children. Ms. Chisholm was also named Woman of the Year in 2000 by then Assemblyman Howard Kaloogian, a distinction few women hold having been named twice for her accomplishments. Lt Gov. Cruz Bustamante (D) wrote in 2000, " I would like to commend you for your outstanding efforts, exceptional service to your community, and for serving as a positive role model for all women. Women in today's hectic world have so many responsibilities that it is truly remarkable that you have managed not only to meet all of the demands on your time, but have even found the time and energy to excel in many additional areas. Through your hard work, you have demonstrated the importance and the positive impact of dedication, enthusiasm and perseverance"

Ms. Chisholm holds a Bachelor of Arts in Communication Studies from the University of California, Santa Barbara; a certificate in Non-Profit Management from California State University, San Marcos; and a Masters of Arts in Organizational Leadership from Biola University.

She says, "of all my goals and accomplishments, the most important one is being a mom and raising two Godly men to love the Lord. In 2000 I was able to take my oldest son to Sacramento. The Lord was kind enough to bless me yet a second time, enabling me to bring my youngest son, Nathan. The highlight of that day for me was seeing him as 'King for a Day', meeting some of our strong Christian leaders who are serving each and every day in the face of adversity in Sacramento. I was honored to introduce my son to these fine men and women, who then escorted my son down to the House Floor to sit right beside me! I am so thankful both my boys have had these wonderful experiences that will help shape the men of God they are becoming."

Zenna Chisholm Snowden
April 2007

Dana married Johnny Serrano Jr on 1 Jun 1991 in Newburgh, New York, USA. The marriage ended in divorce in 1996. Johnny was born 15 0ct 1970 in Newburgh, New York, USA. Dana kept the name Serrano so the names would "match" for the boys, until CJ got to middle school and wanted to change his name to Chisholm to match the family he was close to in San Diego. Johnny was not involved in the boys' lives. So, the courageous young man went before a judge and asked for his name to be changed, and Dana then went back to her maiden name to match. Nathan was still too young (I thought at the time) to make that decision for him, so when we changed the names, Nathan's kept both names so he could decide later which one he wanted. He always says we should have dropped the "Serrano" name at the same time since it is just too long. The name "Antonio" is from Johnny's brother and I (Dana) chose it. (Dana S. Chisholm, 2018 notes)

They had the following children:

413 M i. **Christopher John "CJ" Chisholm** was born on 20 Dec 1991 in Escondido, San Diego, California, USA. Married **Savannah Alexander** 21 November 2012. **Adalynn Grace** born 25 August 2014 and **Elodie Jean** born 7 May 2017.

414 M ii. **Nathan Antonio Serrano Chisholm** was born on 11 Nov 1995 in Escondido, San Diego, California, USA.

265. **Christopher Boyd Chisholm** (Boyd Langford, Stanford Dalton, George Langford, Glenn Thornton, Richard Henry) was born on Oct 1970 in Escondido, San Diego, California, USA.

Christopher married Laura Ann Wallace daughter of Nathan Wallace and Janet Hentine on 12 Dec 1998 in San Diego, San Diego, California, USA. Laura was born on 19 Sep 1971 in San Diego, San Diego, California, USA.

They had the following children:

    415 M i. **Luke Wallace Chisholm** was born on 30 Aug 2003 in San Diego, California.

    416 M ii. **Zachary Christopher Chisholm** was born on 6 Jan 2006 in Guam.

---

267.   **Rene Inez Chisholm** (Ronald Lee, Stanford Dalton, George Langford, Glenn Thornton, Richard Henry) was born on 18 May 1967 in Scottdale, Maricopa, Arizona, USA.

Jacob Mueller, son of Rene Chisholm, helped to bring a great- granddaughter to his Grandparents, Ronald Lee and Becky Chisholm. The child was named Kayla Rene Mueller, born in Aug 2005.

Jessica Muller, daughter of Rene Chisholm, also helped to bring a great granddaughter to her Grandparents, Ronald and Becky Chisholm. The girl was named AALayah Muller and was born 3 Sept 2006.

Rene married (1) Mueller.

They had the following children:

   + 417M i. **Jacob Mueller** was born on 27 Nov 1989.

   + 418 F ii.**Jessica Mueller** was born on 15 Jun.

Rene married (2) Chris Murdie in May 1992. Chris was born on 6 Feb 1971 in Saratoga Springs, New York.

They had the following children:

    419 M iii. **Justin Murdie** was born on 23 Dec 1993 in Phoenix, Maricopa, Arizona, USA.

---

268.   **Robert Chisholm** (Ronald Lee, Stanford Dalton, George Langford, Glenn Thornton, Richard Henry) was born on 24 Jul 1969 in Phoenix, Maricopa, Arizona.

Robert married Lisa Maria Booth on 22 Feb 1991 in Phoenix, Maricopa, Arizona, USA. Lisa was born on 23 Oct 1968 in Phoenix, Maricopa, Arizona, USA.

They had the following children:

420 F i. **Alyssa Chisholm** was born on 15 Dec 1998 in Scottdale, Maricopa, Arizona, USA.

273.   Brice Willis (Geneva Arletta Wyatt, Effie Lucille Filleman, Annie Elizabeth Chisholm, Glenn Thornton, Richard Henry) was born on 15 Mar 1944 in Morenci, Greenlee, Arizona, USA.

Brice Willis

I spent my early working days as a classroom teacher, but most of my career was as an elementary principal. My wife, Carol, and I have three children and each have given us a grand-child.

Today we enjoy our grand-children, country living, and family history. We own the Old West Trading Post, in Safford, which is an antique mall and gift shop. We have a good manager and the store does not take much of our time.

Brice Willis
August 2007

Brice married Carol Lynn Piercefield daughter of Marshall A. Piercefield and Dorothy Day. Carol was born in Phoenix, Maricopa, Arizona, USA.

Carol Lynn Piercefield

Carol Lynn Piecefield, the wife of Brice Willis, spent her first working days as a teacher and later as the County Director of Extention for the University of Arizona. Carol is the great grand-daughter of Warren E. Day. An early physician who came to Arizona in 1872, to work at Fort Verde. He was notorious in Yavapai County and a book could be written about his escapades.

Brice Willis
Aug 2007

Brice and Carol had the following children:

    421 M i. **Eric Willis**

    422 M ii.**Christopher Mather Willis**

    423 F iii.**Emily Day Willis**

277.   **Lennis Dean Smith** (Lawrence Elias Smith, Addie Bell Chisholm, Daniel Fore, Glenn Thornton, Richard Henry) was born on 28 Mar 1932 in Picabo, Idaho, USA. He died on 1 Apr 2002 in Tukwila, Washing, USA. He was buried in Cremated.

Lennis married Barbara Belbeck on 23 Aug 1957 in Seattle, Washington, USA.

They had the following children:

    424 M i. **Wade Doyle Smith** was born on 5 Dec 1958.

    425 M ii.**Adrian Randall Smith** was born on 9 Jul.

    426 M iii. **Lawrence Rupert Smith** was born on 5 Mar 1965.

    427 M iv. **Jesse Dean Smith** was born on 4 Apr 1969.

278.   **Helen Erlene Smith** (Lawrence Elias Smith, Addie Bell Chisholm, Daniel Fore, Glenn Thornton, Richard Henry) was born on 8 Aug 1934 in Picabo, Idaho.

Helen married Verlon Ray Hobdey on 3 Apr 1954 in Twin Falls, Idaho, USA.

They had the following children:

    428 M i. **Alan Arthur Hobdey** was born on 5 Jan 1957 in Twin Falls, Twin Falls, Idaho, USA.

    429 F ii. **Karen Kaye Hobdey** was born on 21 May 1958 in Twin Falls, Twin Falls, Idaho.

279.   **Sharon June Smith** (Lawrence Elias Smith, Addie Bell Chisholm, Daniel Fore, Glenn Thornton, Richard Henry) was born on 5 Jun 1943 in Hailey, Idaho, USA. She died on 11 Oct 1980 in Hailey, Idaho, USA. She was buried on 14 Oct 1980 in Bellevue, Idaho, USA.

Sharon married Martin Gutches on 15 Jul 1960.

Martin and Sharon had the following children:

430 F i. **Lisa Kaye Gutches** was born on 21 Aug 1960.

431 M ii.**Mitchell Troy Gutches** was born on 22 Dec 1963.

280.   **Merla Joyce Smith** (Lawrence Elias Smith, Addie Bell Chisholm, Daniel Fore, Glenn Thornton, Richard Henry) was born on 23 Apr 1947 in Hailey, Idaho, USA.

Merla married Jack C Powell on 24 Jan 1969 in Spokane, Washington, USA.

They had the following children:

432 F i. **Michelle Lynn Powell** was born on 16 Feb 1978.

433 F ii. **Stacy Emily Powell** was born on 21 Nov 1979.

287.**Adrian Randall Smith** (Adrian Aaron Smith, Addie Bell Chisholm, Daniel Fore, Glenn Thornton, Richard Henry) was born on 8 Oct 1946 in Burley, Idaho, USA.

Adrian married Susan Storer.

They had the following children:

+ 434F i. **Mary Ann Smith** was born on 14 Sep 1963.

+ 435F ii. **Mary Lou Smith** was born on 13 Feb 1966.

436 F iii.**Shannon Smith** was born on 17 Nov 1973 in Idaho Falls, , Idaho, .

288.**Bonnie Luann Smith** (Adrian Aaron Smith, Addie Bell Chisholm, Daniel Fore, Glenn

Thornton, Richard Henry) was born on 10 May 1954 in Burley, Idaho, USA.

Bonnie married (1) David Nylander. David was born on 25 Jan 1952. He died on 18 Jan 1979 in Idaho, USA.

They had the following children:

  + 437 F i. **Angella Gail Nylander** was born on 12 Aug 1977.

Bonnie married (2) Michael Rowland. Michael was born on 24 Aug 1945 in Boise, Idaho, USA.

They had the following children:

  438 M ii. **Phillip Rowland** was born on 15 Aug 1978 in Idaho, USA.

291.   **Linda R West** (Melissa Ellen Smith, Addie Bell Chisholm, Daniel Fore, Glenn Thornton, Richard Henry) was born on 23 Jun 1951 in Twin Falls, Twin Falls, Idaho, USA.

Linda married (1) Scott Platt in Lewiston, Idaho, USA. The marriage ended in divorce.

They had the following children:

  439 M i. **John Ryan Platt** was born on 15 Jan 1972 in Myrtle Beach, Idaho, USA.

  440 F ii. **Connie Michelle Platt** was born on 18 Nov 1974 in Clarkston, Washington, USA.

Linda married (2) JIm Whitney on 27 Jun 1992. Jim was born on 27 Jun 1959.

294. **John Larry West** (Melissa Ellen Smith, Addie Bell Chisholm, Daniel Fore, Glenn Thornton, Richard Henry) was born on 2 Apr 1956 in Clarkston, , Washington, USA.

John married (1) Tammy Brown in Lewiston, Idaho, USA. The marriage ended in divorce.

They had the following children:

  +441 F i. **Brandi L West** was born on 14 Nov 1983.

  442 M ii. **Sean D West** was born on 4 May 1988 in Lewiston, Idaho, USA.

John married (2) Millie Reisenauer on 17 Dec 2004 in Lewiston, Idaho,USA.

295.   **Thomas Orin West** (Melissa Ellen Smith, Addie Bell Chisholm, Daniel Fore, Glenn Thornton, Richard Henry) was born on 28 Oct 1957 in Nampa, Idaho, USA.

Thomas married Teri Stephens on 31 Dec 1979 in Pierce,,Idaho,USA.

They had the following children:

443 F i. **Brittine N West** was born on 30 Nov 1983 in Lewiston, Idaho, USA.

Brittine married **Adam Purington** on 18 Jul 2006 in Lewiston,, Idaho,USA.

444 F ii. **Kelly R West** was born on 1 Aug 1986 in Lewiston, Idaho, USA.

HC

CHAPTER SEVEN

SEVENTH Generation

They might be rich and have lots to donate to a museum and fight over a name,
but we have our stories. That's all that's important.

Zenna Chisholm Snowden email to Dana S. Chisholm
August 1, 2011

296.   **Jerry Lee Farnham**   (Joyce M Evans, Oscar Tedford Evans, Jennie Chisholm, George Langford, Glenn Thornton, Richard Henry) was born on 25 Nov 1940. He died on 2 Nov 1995 in Corona, Riverside, California, USA.

Jerry married Eleanor Louise McKinnis on 19 Dec 1964. Eleanor was born on 30 Dec 1945.

They had the following children:

   + 445 F i. **Jessie Robin Lynn Farnham** was born on 23 Apr 1966.

   446 M ii. **Scott Joseph Lee Farnham** was born on 6 May 1970.

297. **Earl Wayne Farnham** (Joyce M Evans, Oscar Tedford Evans, Jennie Chisholm, George Langford, Glenn Thornton, Richard Henry) was born on 3 Jan 1943 in Riverside, California, USA.

Earl married (1) Catherine Myrtle Moffiet on 11 Jan 1964.

Earl married (2) Cynthia Ann Wales daughter of Richard Wales and Leona Kerner on 30 Jun 1979 in Utica, Michigan, USA. Cynthia was born on 2 Nov 1944 in Mt Clemens, Michigan, USA.

They had the following children:

   + 447 F i. **Diann Marie Farnham** was born on 19 Nov 1968.

448 M ii.**David Wayne Farnham** was born on 3 May 1971 in San Diego, San Diego, California, USA. David married **Angela Louise Saporito** daughter of Albert Joseph Saporito and Angel Rose Magliocco. Angela was born on 28 Nov 1972.

298. **Jack p Farnham Jr** (Joyce M Evans, Oscar Tedford Evans, Jennie Chisholm, George Langford, Glenn Thornton, Richard Henry) was born on 23 Jan 1946 in Arlington, California, USA.

Jack married Mary Fretias Souza daughter of Joseph Anthony Souza and Fhilomena Chaves Fretias on 9 May 1969 in Corona, Riverside, California, USA. Mary was born on 19 May 1950.

They had the following children:

+449 M i. **Jeffery Keith Farnham** was born on 3 May 1971.

450 M ii.**Jeremy Jason Farnham** was born on 20 Jan 1975.

451 F iii.**Jeana Marie Farnham** was born on 8 Oct 1980.

452 F iv.**Janna Farnham** was born on 25 Jan 1985.

299. **Timothy Farnham** (Joyce M Evans, Oscar Tedford Evans, Jennie Chisholm, George Langford, Glenn Thornton, Richard Henry) was born on 1 Mar 1947 in Arlington, California, USA.

Timothy married (1) Sue Ann Newton daughter of William Henry Newton and Gladys Darleen Bryant on 25 Oct 1969 in Corona, California,USA. Sue was born on 15 Jun 1952 in Illinois, USA.

They had the following children:

+ 453M i. **Kevin Lee Farnham** was born on 31 Mar 1972.

454 F ii. **Kara Deann Farnham** was born on 25 Oct 1974 in Riverside, Riverside, California.

Kara married (1) **Mike Rene Nabarrete** son of Miguel Alejandro Nabarrete and Patricia Catherine McQuade. Mike was born on 2 May 1972.

Kara married (2) **Sandor Wade Sklar** son of Kenneth Joseph Sklar and Linda Ginger on 25 Jul 1998 in Las Vegas, Nevada, USA. Sandor was born on 18 May 1972 in Queens, New

York, USA.

Timothy married (2) Paula Eleen Kerner daughter of Elmer Kerner and Bonnie Pauline Palmer on 29 Nov 1978 in Utica, Michigan. Paula was born on 5 Jun 1955 in Macomb, Michigan, USA.

They had the following children:

    455 F iii. **Melinda Dawn Farnham** was born on 8 Mar 1981 in San Diego, California.

    456 F iv. **Elyse Pamela Farnham** was born on 17 Nov 1983 in San Diego, California.

---

301.   **Laural Ann Evans** (Thomas Leland Evans, Oscar Tedford Evans, Jennie Chisholm, George Langford, Glenn Thornton, Richard Henry) was born on 18 Dec 1953.

Laural married John Klausing .

They had the following children:

    457 F i. **Marie Klausing**.

    458 M ii. **John Henry Klausing**.

---

302.   **Thomas Evans** (Thomas Leland Evans, Oscar Tedford Evans, Jennie Chisholm, George Langford, Glenn Thornton, Richard Henry) was born on 29 Mar 1955.

Thomas married (2) Kelly Evans

They had the following children:

    459 F   i.   **Katie Evans** .

    460 F   ii.   **Kala Rene Evans** .

---

303.   **Kemberly Evans** (Thomas Leland Evans, Oscar Tedford Evans, Jennie Chisholm, George Langford, Glenn Thornton, Richard Henry) was born on 7 Apr 1959.

Kemberly married Paul Buzza

They had the following children:

    461 M i.   **Charly Buzza** was born on 29 Jul 1982.

    462 F ii.   **Jenna Buzza** was born on 7 Jul 1984.

304.   **Betty Lorene Hedgecock** (Blanche Lucille Traylor, Bessie Loraine Chisholm, Martin Gaines, George Langford, Glenn Thornton, Richard Henry) was born on 18 Jun 1953 in Sacramento, Sacramento, California, USA.

Betty married Martin in Roseburg,,Oregon,USA.

They had the following children:

    463 M i.   **Bruce Martin** was born on 24 Jan 1977.

  + 464F ii.   **Lislie Martin** was born on 7 Jul 1979.

305. **Kathy Lynn Hedgecock** (Blanche Lucille Traylor, Bessie Loraine Chisholm, Martin Gaines, George Langford, Glenn Thornton, Richard Henry) was born on 7 Apr 1958.

    Katky had a Foster son, Kevin.

Kathy married John Cox .

They had the following children:

  +465 F i.   **Juanita Hedgecock**

    466 M ii.   **Kevin Foster**

306.   **Ladina Hedgecock** (Blanche Lucille Traylor, Bessie Loraine Chisholm, Martin Gaines, George Langford, Glenn Thornton, Richard Henry) was born on 3

Aug 1963.

Ladina married Tony Schindler . Tony was born on 13 Sep 1968.

Tony and Ladina had the following children:

    467 M   i.   **Raymond Hedgecock**

    468 F   ii.   **Rena Hedgecock**

314.   Debra Upton (Johnnie Louise Traylor, Bessie Loraine Chisholm, Martin Gaines, George Langford, Glenn Thornton, Richard Henry) was born on 16 Apr 1957 in Sutter Memorial Hospital, Sacramento, Sacramento, California, USA.

Debra married Brian Greenwalt in Roseburg, Oregon, USA.

They had the following children:

    469 F   i.   **Briannia Greenwalt** was born on 9 Aug 1989.

315.   Karen Upton (Johnnie Louise Traylor, Bessie Loraine Chisholm, Martin Gaines, George Langford, Glenn Thornton, Richard Henry) was born on 22 Jan 1959 in Sutter Memorial Hospital, Sacramento, Sacramento, California, USA.

Karen married Monty Rondeau in „Oregon,USA.

They had the following children:

    470 F   i.   **Keisha F Rondeau** was born on 5 Jun.

  +471 F   ii.   **Ashley Rose Rondeau** was born in Jul.

    472 F   iii. **Savanna Lynn Rondeau**

316.   John Upton (Johnnie Louise Traylor, Bessie Loraine Chisholm, Martin Gaines, George Langford, Glenn Thornton, Richard Henry) was born on 4 Aug 1960 in Douglas Community Hospital, Roseburg, Oregon, USA.

John married Nancy Beabeau in Rangley,,Colorado,USA.

They had the following children:

473 F i. **Amber Daun Upton** died on 22 May 2004 and buried in Oregon.

474 M ii. **Dillon Scott Upton**

331.   **Amanda Lee Hawk** (Janice Ruth Chisholm, William, Top, George Langford, Glenn Thornton, Richard Henry) was born on 10 Aug 1971 in Fresno, Fresno, CA.

Amanda married Rodney Allen Brumit son of Allen Brumit and Sharolyn Boyles on 7 Jan 1995 in Shell Beach, California, USA. Rodney was born on 18 Aug 1967 in San Jose, California, USA.

Rodney and Amanda had the following children:

475 M i.   **Nathan Allen Brumit** was born on 22 Sep 1998 in Hanford, , California, USA.

476 F ii.   **Madelyn Fay Brumit** was born on 24 Apr 2002 in Hanford, , California, USA.

332.   **Erica Marie Paroline** (Jeanne Fay Chisholm, William, Top, George Langford, Glenn Thornton, Richard Henry) was born on 19 Apr 1977 in Salinas, CA.

Erica married John Houston Schlosser son of John Schlosser and Mary Polden on 28 Jul 2000 in Modesto, Stanislaus, California, USA. John was born on 21 Feb 1977 in Carmel, California, USA.

They had the following children:

477 M i. **Luke Huston Schlosser** was born on 27 May 2005 in Bakersfield, California, USA.

334.   **William Robert Chisholm** (William Edward, William, Top, George Langford, Glenn Thornton, Richard Henry) was born on 24 Jan 1973 in Coalinga, Fresno, California, USA.

William married Courtney Ann Allen daughter of John Allen and Robyn Allen on 10 Aug 2001 in Aloha, Oregon, USA. Courtney was born on 12 Nov 1976 in Corvallis, Oregon, USA.

They had the following children:

478 M i. **William Ryan Chisholm** was born on 3 Dec 2005 in Portland, Oregon, USA.

---

337. **Lindsey Victoria Preciado** (Lorelei Francine Chisholm, Lloyd Frances, Top, George Langford, Glenn Thornton, Richard Henry) was born on 2 Jun 1980 in Madera, Madera, California.

Lindsey married Jon Howard Peltier on 14 Jul 2001 in Bass Lake, California, USA.

They had the following children:

479 M i. **Baelin Henley Peltier** was born on 10 Oct 2003 in Clovis, Fresno, California, USA.

---

339. **Taryn Kathrine Chisholm** (Lance Lloyd Francis, Lloyd Frances, Top, George Langford, Glenn Thornton, Richard Henry) was born on 7 Aug 1979 in Madera, Madera, California, USA.

Taryn married Dustin Wayne Freeman on 20 Oct 2001 in Coarsegold, California, USA. Dustin was born on 29 Apr 1981 in Fresno, Fresno, California, USA.

Dustin and Taryn had the following children:

480 M i. **Alexander Lance Freeman** was born on 8 Dec 2005 in California, USA.

He died on 8 Dec 2005 in California, USA.

481 F ii. **Alexandria Hope Freeman** was born in 2007 in , , California, USA.

---

340. **Stacy Les-Lea Chisholm** (Lance Lloyd Francis, Lloyd Frances, Top, George Langford, Glenn Thornton, Richard Henry) was born on 20 Aug 1981 in Fresno, CA.

Stacy married Ryan Joseph Hansen on 2 Jun 2001 in Wawona, California, USA. Ryan was born on 13 Apr 1979 in Monterey, California, USA.

They had the following children:

482 F i. **Grace Kathrine Hansen** was born on 17 Jun 2003 in Fresno, California.

483 F ii. **Leah Amanda Hansen** was born on 13 May 2005 in Fresno, California.

349.   **Sheryl Lynn Shumway** (Maudie Marie Mansfield, Ruth Ester Chisholm, Thomas John, George Langford, Glenn Thornton, Richard Henry) was born on 18 Aug 1957 in Phoenix, Maricopa, Arizona.

Sheryl married Rex Sistek on 4 Jul 1975 in Phoenix, Maricopa, Arizona, USA. Rex was born on 14 May 1955 in Madison, Wisconsin, USA.

They had the following children:

484 F i. **Nicole Sistek** was born on 9 Mar 1981 in Phoenix, Maricopa, Arizona, USA.

485 F ii. **Samantha Sistek** was born on 7 Nov 1983 in Phoenix, Maricopa, Arizona, USA.

350.   **Terry Sue Shumway** (Maudie Marie Mansfield, Ruth Ester Chisholm, Thomas John, George Langford, Glenn Thornton, Richard Henry) was born on 18 Aug 1959 in Phoenix, Maricopa, Arizona, USA.

Terry married Wendell Wayne Hargis on 2 Jul 1982 in Phoenix, Maricopa, Arizona, USA.

They had the following children:

486 M i. **Brandon Wayne Hargis** was born on 2 Apr 1984 in Mesa, Maricopa, Arizona, USA.

487 M ii. **Shea Spencer Hargis** was born on 2 Apr 1987 in Mesa, Maricopa, Arizona, USA.

488 F iii. **Brianna Lynn Hargis** was born on 29 Jul 1988 in Mesa, Maricopa, Arizona, USA.

351.   **Robert Wayne Mendenhall** (Janice Cliffine Horton, Juanita Chisholm, Thomas John, George Langford, Glenn Thornton, Richard Henry) was born on 17 Apr 1959 in California, USA.

Robert married Mrs. Robert Wayne Mendenhall

They had the following children:

489 M i. **Joshua Caine Mendenhall** was born in 1980 in Glendale, Maricopa, Arizona, USA.

490 F ii. **Sara Rose Mendenhall** was born in 1982.

352.　**Cheyanne Brooks** "Chi" (Velma Jean Grigsby, Tommie Chisholm, Thomas John, George Langford, Glenn Thornton, Richard Henry) was born on 22 Feb 1974 in Phoenix, Maricopa, Arizona, USA.

Cheyanne married (1) Brad Rains

Cheyanne married (2) George

They had the following children:

491 F i. **Makaela George** was born on 26 Jun 1998 in Phoenix, Maricopa, Arizona, USA.

353.　**Autumn Rene Brooks** (Velma Jean Grigsby, Tommie Chisholm, Thomas John, George Langford, Glenn Thornton, Richard Henry) was born on 12 Feb 1977 in Glendale, Maricopa, Arizona, USA.

Autumn married Tomlinson unmarried.

They had the following children:

492 M i. **Skylar Tomlinson** was born on 8 Aug 1998 in Phoenix, Maricopa, Arizona, USA.

355.　**Justin Chisholm Wakefield** (Sharon Chisholm, Ross Martin, Calvin Alonzo, George Langford, Glenn Thornton, Richard Henry) was born on 7 Apr 1978 in Fresno, Fresno, California, USA.

Justin married Mishia Rivas daughter of Michael Anthony Rivas and Soccorro Penny Martinez on 14 Jan 1997 in Firebaugh, California. Mishia was born on 24 Jan 1978 in Fresno, California, USA.

Justin and Mishia had the following children:

    493 M i. **Julian Michael Wakefield** was born on 30 Jun 1997 in Merced, California, USA.

    494 M ii. **Sean Ross Wakefield** was born on 31 Aug 2001 in Fresno, Fresno, California, USA.

358.   **Brad Kirkpatrick** (Phyllis Marie Chambers, Fannie Maude Chisholm, Calvin Alonzo, George Langford, Glenn Thornton, Richard Henry).

Brad married Polly Kirkpatrick on 29 Apr 1993 in Redmond, Washington, USA.

They had the following children:

    495 M i. **Rorey Kirkpatrick** was born on 16 Aug 1996 in Redmond, Washington, USA.

    496 F ii. **Tessa Kirkpatrick** was born on 18 Oct 1999 in Redmond, Washington, USA.

361.   **Leslie Elizabeth Chambers** (Clarence Lester Chambers, Fannie Maude Chisholm, Calvin Alonzo, George Langford, Glenn Thornton, Richard Henry) was born on 18 Nov 1971 in Merced, Merced, California, USA.

Leslie married (1) Matthew Wayne Hurt

They had the following children:

    497 M i. **Cody Matthew Hurt** was born on 22 Dec 1995 in Palm Springs, Riverside, CA.

    498 F ii. **Summer Ann Hurt** was born on 22 Apr 1997 in Rancho Mirage, Riverside, CA.

Leslie married (2) Jeramy Lee Fisher .

They had the following children:

    499 F iii. **Rebekah Lee Fisher** was born on 3 Apr 1903 in Hicksville, Defiance, Ohio, USA.

        Rebekah was born one minute before her twin sister, Kirsten

    500 F iv. **Kirsten Elizabeth Fisher** was born on 3 Apr 1903 in Hicksville, Defiance, Ohio.

        Kirsten was born one minute after Rebekah, her twin.

362. Amy Ann Chambers (Clarence Lester Chambers, Fannie Maude Chisholm, Calvin Alonzo, George Langford, Glenn Thornton, Richard Henry) was born in Merced, Merced, California, USA.

Amy married Richard Sequeira

They had the following children:

501 M i. **Gavan Sequeira**

364. Shannon Lorene Bronson (Trudy Ann Chambers, Fannie Maude Chisholm, Calvin Alonzo, George Langford, Glenn Thornton, Richard Henry) was born on 7 Mar 1968 in Las Vegas, , Nevada, USA.

Shannon married Michael Tarissus Beaber on 15 Oct 1994. Michael was born on 3 Mar 1964 in Nancy, France, Europe.

They had the following children:

502 F i. **Fallon Faye Beaber** was born on 5 Jun 1997 in Turlock, , California, USA.

365. Duane Edward Bronson (Trudy Ann Chambers, Fannie Maude Chisholm, Calvin Alonzo, George Langford, Glenn Thornton, Richard Henry) was born on 6 Oct 1969 in Las Vegas, Nevada, USA.

Duane married Shannel Silva . Shannel was born in Los Banos, , California, USA.

They had the following children:

503 M i. **Joshua Michael Bronson** was born on 28 Oct 1990 in Los Banos, Merced, CA.

504 F ii. **Jacqueline Macy Bronson** was born on 20 Dec 1991 in Los Banos, Merced, CA.

366.   **Bryan Darrel Bronson** (Trudy Ann Chambers, Fannie Maude Chisholm, Calvin Alonzo, George Langford, Glenn Thornton, Richard Henry) was born on 16 Mar 1977 in Los Banos, Merced, California, USA.

Bryan married (1) Merrick Carter .

They had the following children:

> 505 M i. **Maize Justice Bronson** was born on 17 Jul 1993 in Los Banos, California, USA.

Bryan married (2) Krystal Duarte in Nov 1998.

Bryan and Krystal had the following children:

> 506 M   ii.   **Brayden Darrel Bronson** was born on 2 Mar 1999.

369.   **Rhonda Scrivner** (Rita Marlene Chisholm, Daniel Webster, Calvin Alonzo, George Langford, Glenn Thornton, Richard Henry) was born on 10 Jun 1973 in Hanford, California, USA.

Family Group Records sent to be by Bernice Chisholm in 2006.

Rhonda married Randy Hendrix on 15 Apr 2000 in Coalinga, , California, USA.

They had the following children:

> 507 M i. **Christopher Scrivner** was born on 29 Oct 1990.
>
> 508 F ii. **Kabella Marie Hendrix** was born on 6 Feb 2004.

370.   **Rhoda Scrivner** (Rita Marlene Chisholm, Daniel Webster, Calvin Alonzo, George Langford, Glenn Thornton, Richard Henry) was born on 23 Dec 1974 in Hanford, California, USA.

Rhoda married Albert Linch on 2 Mar 2002 in Bakersfield, , California, USA.

They had the following children:

> 509 M i. **Hunter Kaden Linch** was born on 4 Apr 2006.

371. **Reggan Scrivner** (Rita Marlene Chisholm, Daniel Webster, Calvin Alonzo, George Langford, Glenn Thornton, Richard Henry) was born on 7 Apr 1978 in Hanford, California, USA.

Family Group Records sent to be by Bernice Chisholm in 2006.

Reggan had the following children:

510 F i. **Raine Marlene Scrivner** was born on 4 Dec 2001.

511 M ii. **Ryan Edd Maylin** was born on 24 Apr 2006.

374. **Christen Den Hartog** (Sandra Eva Chisholm, Daniel Webster, Calvin Alonzo, George Langford, Glenn Thornton, Richard Henry) was born on 10 Oct 1978 in Hanford, California, USA.

Family Group Records sent to me by Bernice Chisholm in 2006. (Zenna)

Christen Roping with Dad January 2018

Christen married Venton Shoemaker on 2 Jun 2001 in Cambria, California, USA.

Venton and Christen had the following children:

512 F i. **Tyler Joy Shoemaker** was born on 10 Jul 2003.

513 F ii. **Cassie Diane Shoemaker** was born on 6 Mar 2006.

Girls "Then and Now" (2018)

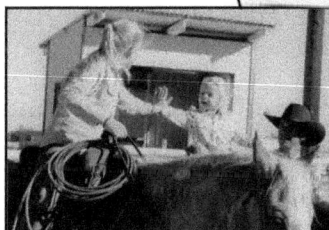

Christen married Paul Morris on August 20, 2010

379.   **Ellen Pollard** (Dena Mae Frye, Dorothy Flora Chisholm, Jesse, George Langford, Glenn Thornton, Richard Henry) was born on 20 Oct 1956 in Selma, Fresno, California, USA.

Ellen married Baxley.

They had the following children:

514 F i.   **Jessica Pollard**

515 M ii. **Robbie Baxley**

516 F iii. **Nikki Baxley**

517 M iv. **Brad Baxley**

380.   **Sue Carol Pollard** (Dena Mae Frye, Dorothy Flora Chisholm, Jesse, George Langford, Glenn Thornton, Richard Henry) was born on 22 Sep 1958 in Fresno, Fresno, California, USA.

Sue married Hagopjan

They had the following children:

518 F i.   **Erin Elizabeth Hagopjan** Erin married **Christopher Richard Merrin** on

17 Mar 2007 in California, USA.

386.   **James Winston Bachar** (Roger Eugene Bachar, Gladys Dena Chisholm, Jesse, George Langford, Glenn Thornton, Richard Henry) was born on 23 Dec 1970.

James married Charlotte Ann Edwards daughter of James T Edwards and Mrs James T Edwards on 12 Mar 1994 in Easton, California, USA.

They had the following children:

519 M i.   **Jonah Caleb Bachar** was born on 31 Aug 2002 in Fresno, Fresno, California, USA.

392.   Jonathan Craig Griffith (Larry Craig Griffith, Milton Clark Griffith, Virgie Eliza Chisholm, George Langford, Glenn Thornton, Richard Henry) was born on 26 Jan 1973 in Modesto, Stanislaus, California, USA.

Jonathan married **Tamara Danelle Downs** on 21 Feb 1998 in Modesto, Stanislaus, California.

They had the following children:

    520 M i. **Connor Craig Griffith** was born on 3 Dec 2004 in Modesto, Stanislaus, CA.

393.   Samuel Roberts Griffith lll (Larry Craig Griffith, Milton Clark Griffith, Virgie Eliza Chisholm, George Langford, Glenn Thornton, Richard Henry) was born on 11 May 1978 in Modesto, Stanislaus, California, USA.

He had the following children:

    521 M i. **Ayden James Griffith** was born on 3 Feb 2004 in Modesto, Stanislaus, California.

394.   Aimee Lynne Griffith (David Clark Griffith, Milton Clark Griffith, Virgie Eliza Chisholm, George Langford, Glenn Thornton, Richard Henry) was born on 23 Feb 1972 in Modesto, Stanislaus, California, USA.

Aimee married **Daniel Bullis** on 26 Oct 2003 in Las Vegas, Nevada, USA.

They had the following children:

    522 F i. **Rielly Morgan Bullis** was born on 12 Nov 2005 in Modesto, Stanislaus, California.

395.   Joshua David Griffith (David Clark Griffith, Milton Clark Griffith, Virgie Eliza Chisholm, George Langford, Glenn Thornton, Richard Henry) was born on 20 Jan 1979 in Modesto, Stanislaus, California, USA.

Joshua married Lacy Alee Reg on 2 Sep 2001 in Modesto, Stanislaus, California, USA.

They had the following children:

> 523 M i. **Carter Angelo Griffith** was born on 30 Mar 2006 in Modesto, Stanislaus, California.

417.   Jacob Mueller (Rene Inez Chisholm, Ronald Lee, Stanford Dalton, George Langford, Glenn Thornton, Richard Henry) was born on 27 Nov 1989 in Dubuque, Idaho, USA.

Jacob had the following children:

> 524 F i. **Kayla Rene Mueller** was born in Aug 2005.

418.   Jessica Mueller (Rene Inez Chisholm, Ronald Lee, Stanford Dalton, George Langford, Glenn Thornton, Richard Henry) was born on 15 Jun in Dubuque, Idaho.

She had the following children:

> 525 F   i.   **A Alayah Mueller** was born on 3 Sep 2006.

434.   Mary Ann Smith (Adrian Randall Smith, Adrian Aaron Smith, Addie Bell Chisholm, Daniel Fore, Glenn Thornton, Richard Henry) was born on 14 Sep 1963 in Idaho Falls, Idaho.

Mary married Greg Leber

They had the following children:

> 526 F   i.   **Madaline Leber** was born on 17 Nov.

435.   Mary Lou Smith (Adrian Randall Smith, Adrian Aaron Smith, Addie Bell Chisholm, Daniel Fore, Glenn Thornton, Richard Henry) was born on 13 Feb 1966 in Idaho Falls, Idaho.

Mary married Cliff Coppinger .

They had the following children:

> 527 M i.   **Jordan Coppinger** was born on 21 May.
>
> 528 M ii. **Nickolas Coppinger** was born on 9 Mar.

437.   Angella Gail Nylander (Bonnie Luann Smith, Adrian Aaron Smith, Addie Bell Chisholm, Daniel Fore, Glenn Thornton, Richard Henry) was born on 12 Aug 1977 in Boise, Idaho, USA.

Angella is the daughter David Nylander had before he married Bonnie Luann. After David was killed and Bonnie Luann married again to Michael Rowland, he adopted her.

Angella married Chad Tiffany

They had the following children:

> 529 F i.   **Makenzie Menlane Tiffany** was born on 22 May 1997 in New Mexico, USA.
>
> 530 F ii. **Kaylee Lehlani Tiffany** was born on 14 Dec 2006.

441.   Brandi L West (John Larry West, Melissa Ellen Smith, Addie Bell Chisholm, Daniel Fore, Glenn Thornton, Richard Henry) was born on 14 Nov 1983 in Lewiston, Idaho, USA.

Brandi married Jonathan Thrall on 5 May 2000.

They had the following children:

> 531 F i.   **Madalynn E Thrall** was born on 21 Nov 2001 in Lewiston, Idaho, USA.
>
> 532 M ii. **Alexander W Thrall** was born on 22 Jan 2006 in Fort Lewis, Washington, USA.

TC

CHAPTER EIGHT

EIGHTH Generation

I made many good friends and met many a family member during my search, that made everything worth it.
Zenna Chisholm Snowden

445. **Jessie Robin Lynn Farnham** (Jerry Lee Farnham, Joyce M Evans, Oscar Tedford Evans, Jennie Chisholm, George Langford, Glenn Thornton, Richard Henry) was born on 23 Apr 1966.

Jessie married William Charles Shepherd .

They had the following children:

    533 F   i.   **Robin Louise Marie Shepherd** was born on 11 Jul 1986.

    534 F   ii.   **Eleanor Ruth Ann Shepherd** was born on 17 Dec 1987.

 +535 M   iii.   **Charles Lee Shepherd** was born on 21 Feb 1989.

    536 M   iv.   **Jerry Steven Shepherd** was born on 6 Sep 1990.

447. **Diann Marie Farnham** (Earl Wayne Farnham, Joyce M Evans, Oscar Tedford Evans, Jennie Chisholm, George Langford, Glenn Thornton, Richard Henry) was born on 19 Nov 1968 in San Diego, San Diego, California, USA.

Diann married Jeff Bielcik

They had the following children:

    537 M   i.   **Ryan Bielcik** was born on 12 Dec 2000.

    538 F   ii.   **Hanna Bielcik** was born on 9 Aug 2003.

---

449.   **Jeffery Keith Farnham** (Jack p Farnham, Joyce M Evans, Oscar Tedford Evans, Jennie Chisholm, George Langford, Glenn Thornton, Richard Henry) was born on 3 May 1971.

Jeffery married (1) Mariella Finaldi daughter of Pasquale Finaldi and Carmela DeLuca. Mariella was born on 18 May 1971.

They had the following children:

    539 M   i.   **Keith Jordon Farnham** was born on 26 Oct 1993.

Jeffery married (2) Kimberly Denise Sims on 2 Feb 2002. Kimberly was born on 22 Jan 1968.

They had the following children:

    540 M   ii.   **Jade Nichol Farnham** was born on 9 Mar 2003.

---

453.   **Kevin Lee Farnham** (Timothy Farnham, Joyce M Evans, Oscar Tedford Evans, Jennie Chisholm, George Langford, Glenn Thornton, Richard Henry) was born on 31 Mar 1972 in Riverside, California, USA.

Kevin married (1) Shelly Lynn Sharp daughter of Dale C Sharp and Robin Jeanine Norris. Shelly was born on 2 Feb 1972 in Edwards, California, USA.

They had the following children:

    541 M   i.   **Kameron Dale Farnham** was born on 27 Dec 1991.

Kevin married (2) Christin Monza daughter of Vincent John Monza on 12 Jul 1997 in Riverside, Riverside, California, USA. Christin was born on 5 Aug 1970.

They had the following children:

542 F   ii.   **Morgan Chrislyn Farnham** was born on 3 May 1999.

543 F   iii.   **Brooke Justine Farnham** was born on 17 Jan 2002.

464.   Lislie Martin (Betty Lorene Hedgecock, Blanche Lucille Traylor, Bessie Loraine Chisholm, Martin Gaines, George Langford, Glenn Thornton, Richard Henry) was born on 7 Jul 1979.

She had the following children:

544 M   i.   **Cameron** .

465.   Juanita Hedgecock (Kathy Lynn Hedgecock, Blanche Lucille Traylor, Bessie Loraine Chisholm, Martin Gaines, George Langford, Glenn Thornton, Richard Henry).

She had the following children:

545 F   i.   **Lindsey Hedgecock**

471.   Ashley Rose Rondeau (Karen Upton, Johnnie Louise Traylor, Bessie Loraine Chisholm, Martin Gaines, George Langford, Glenn Thornton, Richard Henry) was born in Jul.

She had the following children:

546 M   i.   **Bowen Rondeau**

547 F   ii.   **Alxa Stanley Rondeau**

548 F   iii.   **Angelinia Cieneros Rondeau**

HC

CHAPTER NINE

NINTH *Generation*

I visited the graveyard, and walked where they walked. There's still so much to learn.

Zenna Chisholm Snowden

535.   **Charles Lee Shepherd**   (Jessie Robin Lynn Farnham, Jerry Lee Farnham, Joyce M Evans, Oscar Tedford Evans, Jennie Chisholm, George Langford, Glenn Thornton, Richard Henry) was born on 21 Feb 1989.

Charles married Kemberly Hall

They had the following children:

    549 F   i.   **Heather Marie Shepherd** was born in Dec 2004.

EPILOGUE

RH Chisholm Land Grant

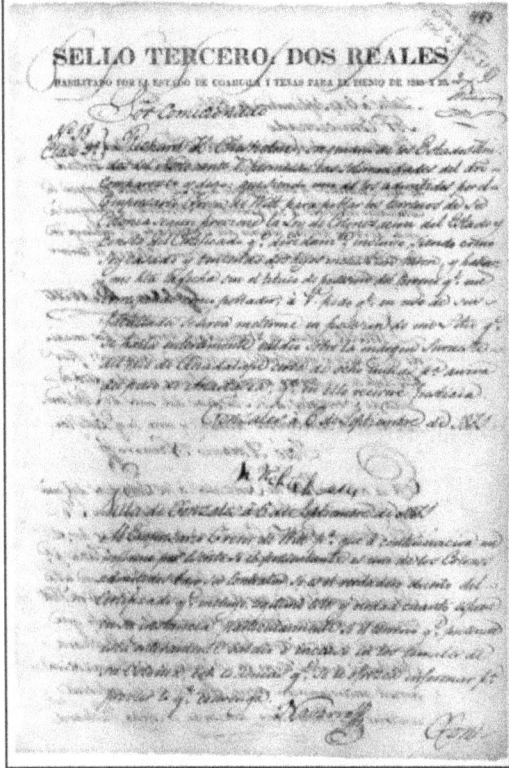

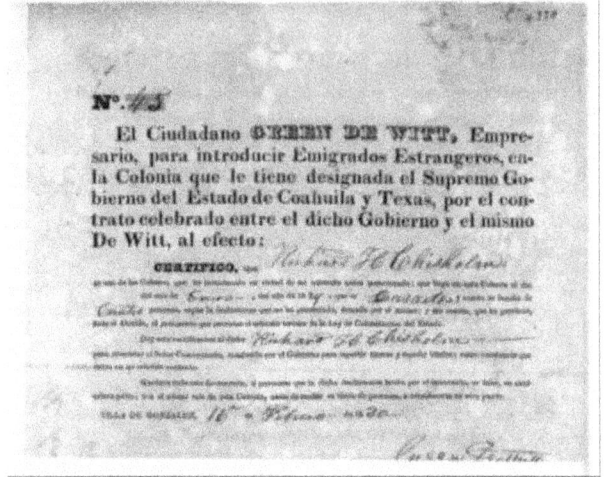

Town of Clinton, TX then and now

Clinton, TX map transparency 1850, over Google map 2017

Left Arrow: Chisholm Creek, Right Arrow: Chisholm ferry and rd to Clinton, Bottom Arrow: Public Square

Finding Hope in the New Year
A short story by Dana S. Chisholm

The New Year. The season of fresh starts. And this year, Jennie Chisholm had chosen her word for the year: Hope. Her faith and hope was really all she had left. If she was going to survive at all, she could only rely on her faith and search for hope, some relief, that the new year might be better.

Last year she had chosen a word for the New Year 1868 of "Peace." Looking back, it was anything but. So many times she had told her kids, "Ya know, the Isrealites didn't know God would part the Red Sea the next morning! But, they started each day with hope and expectation that God was gonna do something big in their dire straights – and He did!"

Jennie Chisholm (b. 1838) thought the year 1867 had been particularly difficult. Yes, the War Between the States had ended, but now the once great independent Texas was nothing more than an occupied Territory of the Union, and the strain was showing in the little town of Clinton, TX that her father-in-law had founded decades before. Her in-laws, RH and Hardina Taylor Chisholm, were first in the area as part of the DeWitt Colony. Jennie married their son Glenn Thornton when he was 21 years old and she was a young lady of fourteen in 1852. Her parents had died when she was very little back in Mississippi, where her brothers and sisters remained. Thornton was the love of her life and his parents were the parents she never had. Jennie fell in love with the whole family right away – cousins on both sides of the Guadelupe River, the Taylors and Chisholm - and married Thornton on Chisholm Ranch, where he had been born. It was a large event with the whole extended family and friends who built the little community at Clinton. Jennie loved Thornton's whole big family and community – exactly what she had longed for and missed in her young life.

When his parents died in 1855, just a few short years later, she was heartbroken at the loss of parents all over again. Because she had lost her parents and family so young, Jennie matured faster than most. And at the loss of her in-laws, she was seventeen and the woman of the house on the Chisholm Ranch in Clinton. She and Thornton had his brother Bradford (20yrs) and little brother Richard Henry Jr. to care for. Richard Jr. was only five years old when his paretns died, and Jennie understood her role in his life immediately. She was surprised that she was actually thankful for the experiences God had given her so she could uniquely love on Richard Jr. She would know the fears of forgetting lost parents and the longing to be able to keep traditions alive without them – and even start new ones without guilt of not being able to share them with those lost. Jennie and little Richard Jr. shared an immediate and special bond.

The Chisholm Ranch house was always open to strangers. Jennie used to say, "make yourself at home! If you don't feel at home, ya ought to!" They had a long kitchen table with benches on both sides to sit many guests. There home was full of love and many shared in letters to friends that the home was always welcoming, and no one ever left hungry. Thornton and Jennie often teased each other for who would "bring home more strays" – whether it be an animal or weary traveler, all were welcome and cared for.

Jennie and Thornton added to their happy home starting in 1856 with their eldest, George Langford. His Uncle Rich Jr. being only six years old, was more of a brother to George than an uncle. Thornton's little sister, Maryann, was only four years younger than Jennie, and she felt she had a little sister and best friend in Maryann. Maryann had married John Kelso in August 1857, and they started their family with little Winchester Kelso in 1858. Jennie enjoyed having the whole family over to the Chisholm Ranch, eating and singing around the organ while the boys played fiddle and guitar. She and Thornton wanted a big family, and set about it with intention to fill the ranch home on the edge of Clinton, stretching back to Chisholm Creek.

They had Thornton's brother, Rich Jr. "R.J." (1850), and then their children: George (1856), Cora (1859), Samuel (1860), Jessie (1861), Annie (1864), and Daniel Fore "Jim" (1866). The War Between the States had divided the family, as Thornton and his brother, Bradford, were called upon to fight. Jennie was home as a solo-parent with the five younger kids, and her sister-in-law and best friend, Maryann, and her four kids by that time. After the War, the Union soldiers occupied the town of Clinton, TX and the community felt "punished" more than anything, but grateful to have their husbands home and in one piece.

The War had ravaged the local businesses, and the family was struggling financially as Jennie was reflecting and choosing her word for the New Year 1866. He chose "Pioneering"as a reflection of the parents lost, her in-laws who fought for Texas Independence, then Statehood, founded the town and a ferry and cattle ranch. Thornton knew he had to do something and was planning to start out on a cattle drive north in the Spring, just as soon as their next child was born. So, Jennie thought "Pioneering" for 1866 was appropriate as they now needed to lead the way into a fresh start, and follow Hebrews as Christ was the Pioneer and Perfector of faith. Jennie thought pioneering was more creative than "Faith" for the year. It wasn't *just* faith in their lives, it was the first, unknown, jumping off into the abyss kind of faith that was needed.

True to his word, her love, Thornton, waited for little "Jim" to be born at the end of March, and then set out with a team of men driving 1800 head of cattle north on April 1, 1866. Jennie was unsure if she would ever see Thornton again, but at least he got to kiss his new son. She clung to the pioneering faith, the One that set out before them. For seven months and ten days, Jennie counted until the men returned, having sold the cattle that survived at market in St. Joseph, MO and they did indeed lose a man on the journey. She thanked God it was not Thornton, but grieved with the family who lost a loved one in order to feed the families back home. She was a strong woman of great compassion, and had solo-parented and took care of the Ranch while Thornton was gone, and was so thankful to have everyone home again.

Her husband had made it home in time for the holidays, Jennie's very favorite time of year. Jennie had hoped he would be back, but knew it would be a special blessing if he actually did. Every Christmas, the traditions Jennie kept alive for young Richard Jr. were having the whole family over for Christmas Eve dinner, then everyone would go over to the Court House for a community-wide Clinton Christmas Eve Service. Then the kids would get to open one present on Christmas Eve when they got back from church – usually pajamas Jennie had made from the mercantile fabric Thronton had traded for. Then Christmas morning, the family would gather to read the account of the birth of Jesus out of Luke, Thornton would lead them in prayer, and the kids would open the rest of their gifts. Jennie was so thrilled that Thornton had made it back for all their traditions.

While he was gone, his brother Bradford had married a girl from New York, Harriet, in October 1866. She was a year younger than Jennie, and fit right in the large family. Although born a city-girl from the East, Harriet definitely fit the pioneering spirit for that year. Thornton and Jennie were pleased with this new love, and a little surprised Bradford had even waited that long after coming home from war…and married a Yankee on top of it! – they liked to tease. The family kept growing and Jennie could see how God had provided a Pioneering Faith for the year. The coming year would be Jennie and Thronton's fifteenth wedding anniversary – the Crystal anniversary. Jennie had her eye on some new glasses she was hoping Thornton would get for her for entertaining at the Ranch. So, for the New Year of 1867 Jennie chose the word "Love" and there was to be plenty of it.

Bradford and his new bride got a little place of their own built on the Chisholm Ranch, and Maryann had another baby, Rhoda Kelso, named after her husband's mother. But, as much as the family was growing and the Chisholm Ranch was a welcome refuge for friends, family, and strangers, tensions were still high in town.

Union Troops and more and more divisive people continued to move into the area – sometimes stoking old wounds even her father-in-law had incurred years before. It seemed as if some were looking for ways and reasons to settle old scores among the new and changing political climate. Some of the men in town were jockeying for position, trying to make a buck and leverage control over the community. Jennie didn't like what was happening to the small close-knit community. Not at all. So, a year ago on the eve of New Year's Day 1868, she had chosen "Peace."

Now, as 1869 was upon her, she wondered how she could have been so wrong with Peace the previous year. 1866 Pioneering Faith, 1867 Love, and 1868 Peace.

Thornton and Jennie were so looking forward to a new baby in 1868. Jennie was pregnant again, and feeling pretty good with this one. Thornton didn't have any big cattle drives planned, a couple of short trips into Mexico for goods, but nothing out of the ordinary. Richard Jr. "R.J". was turning 18 this year, although he had been a little "man" out roping cattle since he was eight, it was still a big year. And their oldest, George was turning 12 years old. How the time does fly!

Peace was shattered in March, but not in town where Jennie had been praying against. No, this snuck up on her and knocked the wind right out of the young wife and mother. She thought she was strong, but nothing could prepare her for this. Jennie was going about her normal day, feeling very pregnant and heavy, but caring for the kids, planning for the evening meal, hoping Thornton would be home soon from his latest freighting trip. Instead, the friends who had gone with him came to the Chisholm Ranch. Thornton was not with them.

Jennie tried to collect herself and listen as best she could as the friends who had gone with him shared the details. Just like their days on the trail, Thornton was always first in if there was a dangerous river to be crossed. He never ate before all the others had eaten first. He took the shifts of other men when they became too tired during the night. And on this trip, they were trying to move freight up a steep hill and the team was having trouble. Thornton was riding the wheel horse, named Ned, and the trace broke and Thornton was thrown in front of the wagon wheel and it ran over him. It was four o'clock in the afternoon when he was injured, but the men sat him there in the road – unable to speak and in great pain – he finally died about two o'clock in the morning. The guys used the side-boards of his wagon to build a casket and buried him there between four Oak Trees in Burnet County, Texas.

Jennie was too stunned to ask questions. She thanked the men and hustled them out of the home. She was not herself. Her husband was too young for this! He was only 37 years old! Jennie was only thirty! How could she raise the children by herself? How could she have this baby by herself? If love were waves that washed over you, she was surely sinking in grief. She had to pull herself together and go break the news to Maryann, Bradford, and young Rich Jr. that their brother was dead.

Jennie didn't feel right not burying Thornton in the Clinton Cemetary or even on the Chisholm Ranch where he was born, where all their kids were born, her heart and home. But, what was done, was done and she had too much to think about to figure out how to have him moved. Jennie just needed to survive each day.

The months dragged on and Effie Lucille Chisholm was born later that year. As Christmas and the holidays neared, Jennie was going through the motions. She was not looking forward to the first Christmas without Thornton. No traditions or keep traditions? Jennie just couldn't think clear. Richard Jr was helpful, and he kept Goerge out of trouble for the most part, out working on the ranch and in town. Jennie had solo-parented before, but this was different. It was permanent. Thornton wasn't coming back. Her anchor, her future, had been ripped from her, but there was little time to think about the pain. George was 12yrs, Cora 9, Samuel 8, Jessie 7, Annie, 4, Jim 2, and baby Effie. Maryann helped as much as she could, but she had five of her own by this time. Braford and Harriet had not had any kids yet, and were a great comfort and support to Jennie.

Jennie's heart was so empty, and she felt in a fog all the time without Thornton. She had chosen to focus on peace, and having the entire extended family over for Thanksgiving had brought her a bit of cheer, having music in the house was a great comfort. Thornton would have loved that. He was such a great dad, had waited for Jim to be born before heading out, and now everytime Jennie held little Effie, she was reminded that Thornton never got to see his beautiful daughter. Jennie pressed on and prepared to have the entire family over to the Chisholm Ranch for Christmas Eve dinner and then head over to the Courthouse for midnight Christmas service to welcome the King of Peace on His birthday celebration.

There was no church building in Clinton, just yet. Right now the congregations shared the Courthouse on the Public Square for a meeting space. Jennie actually liked that, because each year on Christmas Eve the whole town got together as one big congregation, no division, nothing separate, and she had a bit of peace…in years past. This year, she was just busy cooking and preparing and sent Richard Jr. into town to make sure his cousin made it over to the house before dinner. The Taylor cousins lived across the Guadelupe River, and had to come over the Chisholm Ferry, into Clinton and over to the Chisholm Ranch. Jennie got word that cousin Buck stopped in town for a drink on his way over, but some of the Union sell-outs were also in town looking to stir trouble. Jennie sent Rich Jr. to get Buck and avoid any more trouble this year. Jennie just didn't think she could handle any more greif.

Jennie was balancing the baby on one hip, chatting with Maryann and Harriet, and the women were just getting the food on the table when one of the young boys in town came running up the road to the Chisholm Ranch, "Mrs. Chisholm! Mrs. Chisholm! Come quick! Richard has been shot!"

Jennie handed off the baby, told the girls to stay there, and ran down the street to the Public Square and Court House. There in the street was Richard Jr – only 18 years old – and their cousin Buck Taylor – both shot in the back. Dead. They were both dead by the time Jennie reached him, and she could only hold her boy and cry. All the tears stored up since March. All the tears she thought she could not contain. She lay in the street holding him and cried. She couldn't even remember how she and young Richard Jr. got back to the Chisholm Ranch. She assumed their friends in town had collected them up and gotten them out of the street for fear for her life, as well.

Back at the Chisholm Ranch, Bradford and Maryann had already gathered to say goodbye to another brother. And Bradford had friends stand guard at the edge of the ranch all night in case the shooters decided to hunt down the rest of the family. How could they do this on Christmas Eve, of all times? Jennie thought. What kind of evil is unleashed in men such as these. There was no joint Christmas Eve Service for the family this year. Instead, the families made it back to the Taylor Ranch and Chisholm Ranch and grieved.

Maryann and John, and Bradford and Harriet stayed up all night consoling each other, and remained on alert. There was no more trouble that night. Bradford and John saw to that. But, the kids did not know what to do. Little Jim and Effie were far too young to understand what was going on. But, George knew what to do. Christmas morning he brought the family Bible to his mom, and read from Luke the account of Jesus' birth. Jennie smiled for the first time in months, and thought the small smile might be the last one she would be able to muster up for many more months to come. But, she was so proud of young George – that he would think to bring her the Bible, keep tradition, even in this most dark hour. Of course, she knew, that is exactly when they all needed it most.

And so, this New Year's ending 1868 with no peace in circumstances, but peace in the Word. She chose Hope. What was left, but Hope?

Jennie could not have known what was just around the corner for her, the kids, and the whole family: that the killings on Christmas Eve would touch off the longest and bloodiest Texas Fued, that Clinton would remain the County Seat only a short time longer, that she would be a single mom for eleven years before marrying her next best friend, that she would experience more heartbreak when she lost little Samuel before his tenth birthday, and her best friend and sister-in-law. But, she could choose love, faith, and joy each and every day- so much so that the grandkids and great-grandkids would remember her for her faith, and that her home was always welcoming and open, with much song and laughter, and God's grace.

Jennie chose for the coming year, Hope.

And then she lived it.

For Nathan A. Chisholm (1995)

(Grandpa's heritage - Dana Suzanne, Boyd Langford, Stanford Dalton, George Langford, Glenn Thornton & Jennie, Richard Henry & Hardina Taylor Chisholm)

(Grandma's heritage - Dana Suzanne, Anita Jean, Miles Richard & Mary Imogene Ewing)

Artrip, Louise (1949) *Memoirs of Daniel Fore (Jim) Chisholm and the Chisholm Trail.*

Chisholm, Fannie G. (1966) *The Four State Chisholm Trail,* San Antonio, TX

Parsons, Chuck (2013) *The Sutton-Taylor Feud: The Deadliest Blood Feud in Texas,* University of North Texas Press

Taylor Stark, Linda (1999) *Josiah Taylor (1754-1838) : his ancestors and descendants : the history of our branch of the Taylor family from 1630-1999*

https://www.facebook.com/notes/chisholm-family-foundation/finding-hope-in-the-new-year/1768313339905544/

ABOUT THE AUTHOR

ZENNA CHISHOLM SNOWDEN
WICKENBURG, ARIZONA

SEP 15, 1921 – FEB 6, 2014

Zenna was a kind soul that will be sorely missed. I enjoyed her **spunkiness** *and her willingness to try new things. Watching her research her genealogy tree was great while she was learning how to do it on a computer. How awesome was that? Pretty awesome in my book. I am sure her family will have many fun memories to share of the time they all spent together. A true* **pioneer family***.*
Jean
February 10, 2014 | Peoria, AZ

https://www.legacy.com/obituaries/name/zenna-snowden-

Zenna was a beautiful woman! She carried herself as a woman who knew she was beautiful and important in the lives of her loved ones. She was judicious in her generosity, taking time and consideration over the many purchases she made for others. She spoke her mind. Her mind was just and fair. She loved and trusted God with all that she had. She was careful to speak to each of us about her assessments of the surgery risk. I appreciate her low key method in telling us good bye. I loved Zenna as a sister in the faith, but she also was born the same month and year as my own mother! I think she was a unconscious mother figure to me.
Mrs. B J Bannister
February 15, 2014 | Congress, AZ

Zenna cared for those of us in her church, and she was loved in return. While we will deeply feel the loss of her participation, we praise God for her commitment to Him and for the memories we will cherish as we look for the day when the Lord will return and bring life to all those who trust in Him.
Stephen Gibson
February 13, 2014 | Phoenix, AZ

Zenna was a great lady, talented and compassionate and with a healthy sense of humor. Her openness and and optimism was contagious. She exemplified the qualities that characterized her generation as **heroic.**
Carl and Shirkey Johnoff
February 11, 2014 | Congress, AZ

I have known Zenna all of my life. She was caring, generous with her abundant knowledge and skill, and oh so talented in everything she set out to do. She always had a **twinkle** *in her eye and* **quick wit.** *What a role model she will continue to be for me!*
Linda Brewster
February 11, 2014 | Peoria, AZ

Zenna was a very close friend. I appreciated the wisdom of her years coupled with the sympathy and courtesy acquired from a long life. She will be missed as much as she was enjoyed.
Cathy Titgen
February 12, 2014 | Wickenburg, AZ

I remember her coming to Selma California to visit our family(dena cline-pollard) and we always getting so excited for her coming. She went to watch one of my brothers basketball games and was the biggest fan in there. She was like a teenager in high school hooping and hollaring. She was a great loving, caring and excited about life person. She is missed by so many.
Nikki Pollard (George Langford (I think), jess Chisholm, dorothy Chisholm- Cline, dena cline-pollard, Ellen Baxley*(pollard) Richard Henry Chisholm)*

We have only gotten to know Zenna over the last 2 years, and yet were intrigued by her from the very start. So many stories she had to share with us! We soon learned that she loved God, was not afraid of adventure, was an excellent seamstress, and was no nonsense wrapped in a loving spirit. Her commitment and love for her Saviour was inspiring. We many times talked of answered prayers as she would take our prayer requests for our prayer chain. Oh Zenna we look forward to time in eternity when we all can be together by the grace of God.
Our hearts go out to Zenna'a sisters and other family members as we know you will miss her!
Don and Diane Droze
February 12, 2014

INDEX

D

Y

www.ingramcontent.com/pod-product-compliance
Lightning Source LLC
Chambersburg PA
CBHW081510040426
42447CB00013B/3180